The
Collected
Poems of
Paul
Blackburn

Persea Lamplighter Titles
Essential Texts in Poetry and Poetics

M. L. Rosenthal, General Editor

*The Collected Poems of Paul Blackburn*
edited by Edith Jarolim

*A Guide to the Cantos of Ezra Pound*
William Cookson

*Maximum Security Ward and Other Poems*
Ramon Guthrie
edited by Sally M. Gall

# The Collected Poems of Paul Blackburn

edited, with
an introduction, by
**Edith Jarolim**

Persea Books • New York

© 1955, 1960, 1961, 1966, 1966, 1967, 1968, 1969, 1970, 1971, 1972, 1975, 1978, 1980, 1983, 1985 by Joan Blackburn

Introduction and annotations © 1985 by Edith Jarolim

Foreword © 1985 by M. L. Rosenthal

Persea Books
225 Lafayette Street
New York, N.Y. 10012

Library of Congress Cataloging in Publication Data

Blackburn, Paul.
   The collected poems of Paul Blackburn.

   Bibliography: p.
   Includes index.
   I. Jarolim, Edith.   II. Title.
PS3552.A342A17      1985          811'.54          85-9309
ISBN 0-89255-086-4

The publication of this book was made possible in part by grants from the National Endowment for the Arts and the New York State Council on the Arts.

Photographic copies of "A Very Great Treasure" and "McClure Poem" were provided by the Mandeville Department of Special Collections at the University Library, University of California at La Jolla.

Designed by Peter St. John Ginna
Set in Electra by Keystrokes, Lenox, Massachusetts

Printed in the United States of America by
BookCrafters, Chelsea, Michigan

First Printing

*For Carlos*

# Foreword

Here at last, owing to Edith Jarolim's fine labors, we have the poems of America's most gently passionate genius brought together in one book. She has summoned them from the fugitive volumes of ghost-presses, from lost magazines that appeared for just one issue, and from the masses of typescripts and journal entries that had to be reassembled and collated. Paul Blackburn, dead of cancer (at 44) these dozen years and more, returns in full voice. The general reader can come to know him now as only his fellow-poets, and a loving few others, did while he was alive.

He was one of our true poets, more or less obscured by his own reticence and the notice given to more fashionable writers. I don't think we ever had a more "natural" poet than Blackburn. His mother, the poet Frances Frost, encouraged his companionship in her world, and he absorbed the melodies of past poets just as the most talented young composers do those of their forerunners. Growing up in New York City, he became streetwise; he picked up the city's rich composite lingo on the sidewalks and in the jobs he held and quietly mixed its tones and rhythms into the body of his writing.

He also acquired the learning he needed, in universities but also through his own travel and studies, following Ezra Pound's lead in translating the great Provençal poets but actually outstripping the master at his own game. Here he was ahead of most of his poet-friends, the contemporaries and younger figures to whose work he paid so much encouraging attention. He had a lovely and unusually rigorous sense of form, and knew how to learn from the past without being stifled by it. Blackburn is close to William Carlos Williams, close to Ramon Guthrie, in his spontaneous-seeming poems with their depths of emotion and complexity and restrained knowledge. But he is a special variant of the cosmopolitan New Yorker who yet is unmistakably of the people. The range of feeling is wide, humanly inconsistent: now boisterous, now wry or bitter, now sweatily coping with near-poverty or absurdly elated or softly miserable over crooked love and marriage gone wrong, or sinking into a landscape or seascape in sensuous reverie as far from the sounds of the Big Apple as Malaga is from any BMT station. And on the other hand, he can make a gaudy pageant, with nearly cabalistic overtones, of the movements of a mechanical crane at work in New York.

Blackburn's art is the real thing, intimately close to us, speaking for the sensibility we share but rarely objectify. Yet the poetry is much more than a series of personal confidences. Start with its simplicities of lively expression; it will soon carry you into the kind of awareness we all seek, vibrant, subtler than its immediacy might at first seem to allow, and never chic, never pretentious.

*M. L. R.*

# Contents

# Introduction

Was it Paul Blackburn's modesty? The prevailing winds of poetic fashion? The reasons are more complicated and less important than the fact: until now the work of one of our most talented poets has been largely unavailable. Early Blackburn volumes were slim and published in very limited editions (*The Dissolving Fabric*, 1955; *Brooklyn-Manhattan Transit*, 1960; *The Nets*, 1961). By the time two larger, more widely distributed collections of middle-period work appeared (*The Cities*, 1967, and *In . On . Or About the Premises*, 1968), the first books were out of print. *Early Selected Y Mas* recovered those volumes in 1972, and three years later *Halfway Down the Coast* and *The Journals* made available a substantial portion of the late poems—but by this time the collections of the middle years were no longer in print. Furthermore, over one-third of Blackburn's published poetry appeared only in magazines and anthologies, many of them ephemeral and obscure.

This collection brings together, in the order in which they were written, the original poems published during Blackburn's lifetime (November 24, 1926–September 13, 1971) and those in clear preparation for book publication at the time of his death.[1] What does this gathering and arrangement reveal? At first glance—or heft—it becomes clear that he was a prolific poet, especially considering that he died at the age of 44. But then it's common lore that he had a great facility with language, "one of the best ears in poetry," and "perfect pitch." More surprising is the cumulative evidence here of his *achieved* naturalness, of the erudition and artifice that underlie even the most casual-seeming later poems. Blackburn made only rare—and usually misleadingly informal—statements about his poetic practice, but in a 1958 letter to Gregory Corso he summed it up neatly. "It seems to bug you," he wrote, "that I set down 'real' experiences . . . but in ordered form, strictly controlled. My own life is somewhat disorderly, and when not, is on the point of becoming so, almost always. I order my life in my work."

Certainly Blackburn's life was intricately connected with poetry from very early on. Poetry took his mother, Frances Frost, from the family home in St. Albans, Vermont, when Paul was four and his younger sister, Jean, three. Frost (no relation to Robert) was selected for the Yale Series of Younger Poets in 1929; she separated from her husband William Blackburn the next year. He went to California and she went to the big city—first Burlington, then New York—to try to earn a living as a writer, leaving the children in St. Albans with her strict and elderly parents. Only rarely, and not until much later, did Blackburn write about his unhappy childhood; the bitterness of such a poem as "My Sainted" may be explained by the beatings he would get daily from his grandmother.

After age 14, when his mother brought him to New York City to live with her on Horatio Street, his contact with poetry was more direct and on the whole more salutary. She encouraged him to write and gave him a wide variety of poetry to read, although her own verse was fairly conventional. (Her private life was much less so. She and her lover, Paul's "Aunt" Carr, struggled to earn even enough money to keep themselves in—admittedly prodigious—supplies of scotch.)

Blackburn's formal education in poetry at New York University was interrupted the year it began: hoping to be sent overseas, he joined the Army in 1945. An armistice was declared within days of his enlistment and he was sent to Staten Island instead. After two years in the service, working mostly as a lab technician, he went back to NYU where he studied with M. L. Rosenthal and was briefly poetry editor of the school literary magazine, *The Apprentice*. It was at NYU that he began reading the poetry of Ezra Pound.

When Blackburn transferred to the University of Wisconsin in 1949, he started corresponding with Pound, occasionally hitchiking to St. Elizabeth's to visit him. Pound was soon responsible for Blackburn's first publication in a major literary journal: he encouraged James Laughlin to print the work of the unknown poet in *New Directions* in 1951. Blackburn also attributed what became a lifelong involvement with Provençal poetry to an initial frustration over not understanding the snatches of it he came across in *The Cantos*. Pound encouraged him in this direction—or rather he didn't *dis*courage him. Pound's wife, Dorothy Shakespear, told Blackburn he was the only one who expressed an interest in the subject that Pound didn't vigorously warn away.[2]

And it was to Pound that Blackburn owed his first—and last—affiliation with a literary school, for better and for worse. In 1949 Pound prompted the voluminous correspondence between Blackburn and "a chicken farmer in New Hampshire," Robert Creeley. Creeley in turn put Blackburn in touch with Charles Olson, Jonathan Williams, Joel Oppenheimer, and other members of the group later dubbed the "Black Mountain Poets." Creeley also introduced him, via the mails, to Cid Corman, whose historic literary magazine *Origin* was the first to publish regularly a good deal of Blackburn's work in the early 1950s.

Blackburn always opposed the division of poets into schools and did not like the role of Black Mountain poet into which he was cast by Donald Allen's anthology *The New American Poetry* (1960). He embraced all types of poetry, citing the value of "all work, if you work 'em right" to Robert Creeley in 1961, apropos another so-called poetic movement. His association with the Black Mountain group was in fact a tenuous one. He never attended Black Mountain College or taught there, and his affiliation with the *Black Mountain Review*, established in 1953 to raise money for the financially floundering experimental college, was short-lived. He was contributing editor and New York distributor of the first two issues only, and then a quarrel with editor Creeley caused him to sever his connection with the journal.

But if Blackburn disliked the label, and if the styles of the poets with whom he is generally linked are often dissimilar (for example, Blackburn uses a longer, more varied line than Creeley and is less directly allusive, more consistently musical than Olson), all these writers did share aesthetic concerns. They were, as Blackburn later put it, "all working at speech rhythms, composition by field. . . . By 1951 Olson had tied a lot of it together in that 'Projective Verse' essay. So we even had a lot of principles to keep in our heads." Blackburn, whose typing skills had been polished in the Army, took naturally to Olson's concept of the typewriter as a means of notating the oral performance of a poem, on the analogy of a musical score. More than anyone else associated with the Black Mountain aesthetic, he refined the use of punctuation, line breaks, and text alignments that characterize the practice.

During the years of his most extended contact with the *Origin / Black Mountain* writers, 1950–54, Blackburn was living in New York and working in various print shops. The first thirty-six poems in the present collection, representing—with the exception of the earlier opening poem—these four years and the preceding one at the University of Wisconsin, bear clear traces of Blackburn's literary education. His Provençal studies show up in such poem titles as "Alba" and "Cantar de Noit," in the characters of unkind ladies who don't give signs and birds who offer sympathy, in the casting of the poet as singer and half-crazed purveyor of truth. Other literary traditions are on parade as well: we find shepherds and Greek gods, a sensitive young voyager-poet who makes a trip to the underworld—represented, à la Hart Crane, by the New York subway system—etc.

Perhaps inadvertently, Blackburn created an accurate self-portrait in his young painter of "The Innocents Who Fall like Apples." Like the artist's picture, some of his early work is stylized and relies overmuch on convention, but, as the poem puts it, "this dabbler speaks truth also." In "The Innocents" Blackburn had already begun to undercut the poetic devices on which he continued to rely. The opening lines of the poem irreverently address the prophet of their exotic Eastern setting: "Mohamet, old navigator, your flying coffin suspended between heaven and earth." And the conventions he chose early on—the trope of the unkind lady, the romantic linking of love and death—naturally held more than literary interest for him. Over the years he developed them, built a set of personal associations around them—in short, made them his own.

Other signs of the mature poet are discernible in the early pieces. An impulse toward formal control and a simultaneous drive toward relinquishing it are played out thematically in such complementary poems as "The Search" and "What the Tide Gave." The first sees the poet seeking a defining, totemic image for his art; the second uses sea imagery to project an ambivalence about loss of control ( = loss of identity = death), which Blackburn continually associates with love. The recurrent "limits," "lines," and "definitions" that begin to turn up in the vocabulary of the poems are at once desirable and restrictive, as the repeated image of gull flight mixes admiration for its grace with a simultaneous antipathy for its predatory nature. The as-yet unnamed gull of "The Birds" and the literary "ur-gull" of "The Lanner" are the first of many surrogates for a poet who is a master of form and works continually to do away with it.

In the poems written around 1953–54, we especially recognize the subjects and techniques with which Blackburn became associated:

> On the farm it never mattered;
> behind the barn, in any grass, against
> any convenient tree,
> > the woodshed in winter, in a corner
> if it came to that.
>
> But in a city of eight million,      one
> stands on the defensive.

> ("The Assistance")

Later on Blackburn is not so coy about the scatological "it" in the first line, but riddling opening sentences or cryptic titles remain his rhetorical trademarks. So too he later perfects the wit of the final two lines of this passage—the visual pun of separating "one" from the "city of eight million"; the verbal play of "stands on the defensive" on the psychic and physical posture of the speaker; the mock-heroic tone.

But alongside the jazzy, street-wise voice of "The Assistance" and, to an even greater degree, "The Continuity," we hear sonorous intonations of a (rather precocious) sage in such pieces as "The Dissolving Fabric." And in fact it is the quieter rhythms of the early imagistic lyrics—"Friends," "The Sunlit Room," and "The Quest"—that predominate in the next group of poems, written during the three-and-a-half years Blackburn spent in Europe:

> The one-half moon is over the mountain
> and the star is over the sea.

> The star will go down
> into the sea.
> The moon will also go down.

> ("The Gift and the Ending")

When, in the spring of 1954, Blackburn was awarded a Fulbright Fellowship to study Provençal language and literature, he and his new wife Winifred Grey left almost immediately for Europe. They spent several months in Majorca, Spain, until Blackburn was assigned to Toulouse in southern France. His increasing dislike of that city (see, especially, "Sirventes") didn't prevent him from staying on there for another year as Fulbright "lecteur Américain." He simply escaped as often as possible, usually to nearby Spain, where he spent most of his post-Fulbright time in Europe (1956–57) as well. He grew increasingly, romantically, to admire Spain, its people and especially its language and literature. It was during this time that he bought a copy of Federico García-Lorca's *Obras Completas* and acquired his lifelong habit of translating from it.[3] And at the end of Blackburn's stay in Europe, a friend who knew of his interest in Spanish-language literature introduced him to the work of a little-known Argentinian writer living in Paris. Although he didn't manage to meet Julio Cortázar then, he eventually became his close friend, U. S. literary agent, and sometime translator.

A few of the poems in this European group recount Blackburn's diverse travels. Most of them show him already arrived, sitting and watching—

> Today makes 20 days
> that some ants follow the same route
> across 2 of these steps
> never varying from the line.

> ("Canción de las Hormigas")

or walking the streets and listening—

> *Que buen*
> *números me quedan!*

> *Mañana*
> luck is
> always for tomorrow
> or tonight, when
> the lottery is drawn

> ("The Lottery")

The literary traditions of Europe naturally enter into these poems, but far less obtrusively than they did in the earlier work. Mostly Blackburn focuses on the living history of the continent, the everyday activities that continue to be performed as they have been for centuries. Poems such as "Atardecer" and "The Misunderstanding" evoke a timeless, almost mythical Europe. The sacerdotal aura they bestow on secular routines anticipates that of the series of "ritual" poems Blackburn began on his return to the States. As for the "official" rituals, the Christian festivals witnessed in "Ramas, Divendres, Diumenga" and "Verbena," Blackburn emphasizes their sensual, celebratory character, their closeness to pagan nature-worship sources.

So he religiously counts the number of days a group of ants walk across some steps, and confers significance on configurations of people sitting "five and six" and "seven and eight" to a bench ("Plaza Real with Palmtrees"). But just as he mocks the rhetoric of easy solutions in his numerous "how to" titles ("How to Get Through Reality," "How to Live with One Another Somehow"), he often steps back in these poems from a Noah-like propensity for grouping and tallying: "Café at Night" is a mock-heroic account of the poet's venturing to break the dominant color-pattern of food in a local restaurant and "Song for a Cool Departure" finds him wondering "where to put" the "2 cypresses, 3 elms" of his poem.

If self-irony sometimes undercuts aspects of his, the poet's, vocation, the value of that vocation is never in doubt in these European poems. It is often expressed in terms of an aesthetic pragmatism Blackburn shares with the other New England-bred members of the Black Mountain group—the notion that poetry must be utilitarian, be functional, be work:[4]

> The principle, the demarcation
> of my fascination
> is use
>
> ("City Museum, Split")

Also characteristic is his democratic notion that "poet" is just one among many potentially meaningful occupations: the balloon seller of "Plaza Real," the eponymous "The Captain" and "The First Mate" are afforded equally respectful attention. What one does is ultimately less important than how one does it; the "easy, confident step" of the driver in "The Busride" of 1957 is a precursor of "the organized waddle" of the waiter Blackburn elegizes in "The Touch" ten years later. With the Elizabethans as much as with Ernest Hemingway, Blackburn shares the notion that style—not as surface attribute, but as "coherence" or outward manifestation of inward clarity and intactness—is all-important.

The Blackburns returned to New York in late 1957, ostensibly just to recoup finances, but things didn't work out quite according to plan. The marriage soon broke up and Blackburn had a good deal of trouble finding a job. In 1958 and early 1959 he supported himself by doing publisher's reader reports and occasional translations; for the rest of 1959 through 1962 he worked as an in-house editor for Funk & Wagnall's New International Year Book.

This was a time of turmoil, but not all of the turmoil was negative. There were new loves for Blackburn—most important, Sara Golden, whom he married in 1963—and a new literary scene. Blackburn had returned to New York at a time when the beginnings of the Beat poets' influence had awakened an interest in local poetry readings. His own interest in oral tradition made natural the active role he soon took on New York's Lower East Side. For one thing, his enthusiasm for the troubadours led to his arranging and taking part in a number of programs offering translations of medieval European poems, along with the original Provençal or middle English lyrics, to jazz accompaniment.

Readings at the Deux Megots Coffeehouse and, later, Le Metro Café provided the main outlet for Blackburn's interest in contemporary poetry. The Wednesday night guest program he hosted at Le Metro in the early 1960s was known for its quality and eclecticism, having as participant readers key members of the (so designated) Beat, New York, Deep Image, and Black Mountain poetry schools. Blackburn also helped with the poetry and drama series at the Judson Church (among other things, he played Doc Watson in Joel Oppenheimer's production there of "Billy the Kid"), and he was poetry editor of both the *Judson Review* and *The Nation* in 1962.

The poems Blackburn wrote in the five between-marriage years, 1958–63, are among his best known and most successful. The time spent in Europe had confirmed his sense of vocation; this confidence combined with a continuing youthfulness to produce work at once energetic and highly crafted. A number of these poems retain a timeless, European feeling—some, in the beginning, are still set in Europe—but Blackburn soon returned to transcribing the sights and sounds of American life. In baseball and space travel he found new rituals to observe; by the end of the period he was reporting increasingly on the rites of American politics.

And in late 1957, with "The Yawn," Blackburn inaugurated the subgenre (so to speak) with which he is most often associated: the subway poem. Such pieces as "Clickety-Clack" show him at his most deceptively simple:

> I took
> a coney island of the mind
>     to the coney
>     island of the flesh
>         the brighton local
>     riding
>     past church avenue, beverly, cortelyou, past

          avenues h & j
king's highway, neck road, sheepshead bay,
brighton, all the way to stillwell
avenue
          that hotbed of assignation
          clickety-clack

We take a joy ride of the senses as we follow the poet through Brooklyn, listening to him read poetry aloud and watching him unsuccessfully attempt to engage the affections of a not-so-amused female passenger. Blackburn skillfully duplicates the lurching rhythms of the train, and anyone familiar with what is now New York City's "D" line might observe that he eliminates those stations that don't fit into his rhythmic scheme. But the poem also has a wide outside frame of reference, a broad range of literary allusion. A tribute to Lawrence Ferlinghetti, its typography and rhythms evoke the San Francisco poet's *A Coney Island of the Mind* as well as the subway's movement. "Clickety-Clack" also offers echoes of Edward Fitzgerald's "Rubbaiyat" ("Let's fling that old garment of repentance, baby"), lines from Yeats' "Under Ben Bulben" ("Cast a cold eye/on life, on death . . .") and less direct evocations of numerous other poems and poetic traditions.

One of the standard comic devices of "Clickety-Clack"—and indeed too many of Blackburn's other poems—the characterization of woman as (often prudishly unwilling) sex object, is no longer the unquestioned source of amusement it was when Blackburn wrote these pieces. For Blackburn, the type of bravado expressed through this device may be seen not only as a product of its times, but also as the flip side of a fear of women and love expressed much more powerfully, if still obliquely, in "The Purse-Seine":

     the sea
     lies in its own black anonymity and we here on this bed
     enact the tides, the swells, your hips rising toward me,
                    waves break over the shoals, the
     sea bird hits the mast in the dark and falls
     with a cry to the deck and flutters off  .    Panic spreads, the
                    night is long, no
              one sleeps, the net
     is tight
     we are caught or not, the tom sliding down ponderous
                    shall we make it?
              The purse closes.

Earlier in the poem Blackburn warns, "Never look a gull in the eye." He follows his own advice: the vatic tone of "The Purse-Seine" and, to an even greater degree, the group of poems based on the Celtic tree alphabet, as elaborated in Robert Graves' *The White Goddess* (see, for example, "Venus,

the Lark...," "The Vine the Willow Lurch to and Fro," and "Bk. of Num-
bers"), lends the distance and authority of myth to painful personal events.
Nor does Blackburn's alternate lighter, colloquial voice tend to address love
directly, even when the experience recounted is a positive one. Such pieces
as "Remains of an Afternoon," "Ciao," and "Love Song" are inclined to "study
the artifacts," as Blackburn puts it in "Good Morning, Love!"—to examine
carefully the traces or *after*-effects of physical love.

Often cryptic, Blackburn's long, autobiographical "The Selection of
Heaven" is nevertheless one of the exceptions to his general practice of avoiding
the gull's stare. Its first sixteen sections, written in the early months of 1963,
concern the deaths of Blackburn's paternal grandparents; the death of
Blackburn's second marriage is the subject of the final section, appended in
the summer of 1967. The years encompassed by this poem were in some
ways Blackburn's most active and productive ones. He was enjoying a new
degree of success as a poet: two major collections, *The Cities* and *In . On .
Or About the Premises*, were slated for publication, and poems were being
accepted by an unprecedented number of anthologies and journals (including,
to Blackburn's bemusement, *Poetry* and *The New Yorker*). Large and interesting
translation projects were offered him: the Spanish medieval epic *Poem of the
Cid* for Studymasters in 1966 and Julio Cortázar's *Blow Up and Other Stories*
for Pantheon in 1967. And for the first time he was getting teaching positions:
he was poet-in-residence at New York's City College from 1966 to 1967 and
ran poetry workshops at the Aspen Writer's Conference in the summers of
1965, 1966, and 1967.

Nor did Blackburn's activities on the New York poetry scene let up.
From 1964 to 1965 he ran a show on radio station WBAI of interviews with
and readings by poets. (It was terminated a few weeks before the completion
of its contract because of the—even more than usually—"strong" language
of one of his participating friends, LeRoi Jones.) It was Blackburn's idea to
move the readings at Le Metro Café to St. Mark's Church-in-the-Bowery,
and he was instrumental in establishing what officially became (and still
continues as) the Poetry Project there in 1966. He was an indefatigable attender
of all types of poetry readings, and he carried his large, double-reel tape
recorder with him wherever he went; his tape collection, now at the University
of California, San Diego, is probably the best oral history of the New York
poetry scene from the late 1950s up until 1970. And through all this Blackburn
continued, with increased demand for his services, to do what he had done
since the early 1950s: serve as a kind of unofficial one-man reception commit-
tee for poets coming into the city. He helped them get readings, gave them
advice about publication, gave them practical assistance in such matters as
finding jobs and places to stay. These activities—which also included such
less successful schemes as trying to get poetry placed in juke boxes across the
country—attest to Blackburn's commitment to making a reality his belief in
a genuine community of poets.

The poems written during this period provide a graph of American life on the left in the 1960s. The pieces Blackburn wrote against the Vietnam War focus particularly on the way in which the government originated and maintained the war through deliberate distortions of language. There are satirical reports on sports events and the space program: "Laurel," for example, probes the economic superstructures of horseracing and "Newsclips 2." takes a literal look at the men inside the space suits. We get news of the music scene in the wonderful jazz variations inspired by "Listening to Sonny Rollins at the Five-Spot," and of the poetry world in "Torch Ballad for John Spicer: d. 8/17/65."

But into these songs of active engagement with world events and with the art scene there increasingly enters a counter-strain of bitterness and despair. Images of helplessness, passivity, and death begin to proliferate. Love, friendship, the meaningfulness of the past—all eventually come into doubt. Even faith in the constructive powers of poetry, literally and metaphorically demonstrated in the impressive edifice of "The Watchers" in 1963, is eroded. Less than three years later Blackburn says, in one of his "Sixteen Sloppy Haiku" dedicated to writer Robert Reardon:

> Love is not enuf
> Friendship is not enuf
> Not even art
> is / Life is too much

A body of work which had always stressed the importance of alertness and attention now shows a strong drive toward eliminating, or at least diminishing, consciousness.

"What do you do about love?" Blackburn's friend Joel Oppenheimer asks him in "The Answer." Blackburn had already replied earlier in "Two Songs for the Opp": "Stay drunk. . . / then you'll never have to know /if the girl loves you or no." The advice about this particular consciousness-reducing method is often followed in poems populated by men who sit in bars together, sometimes talking about baseball, often not talking at all. In one of the best of these pieces, based on an Andy Capp cartoon strip, Blackburn elaborates on the character's misguided effort to explain his presence at a wake:

> He t'ought it were a weddin but
> it was a funeral . So?
> what is the question . or,
> who is a friend of the groom ?

> ("Night Cappy")

The drive toward relinquishing consciousness is likely the impetus as well for the group of dream poems written from 1963–67. Earlier, Blackburn had incorporated dream sequences into his work—see, for example, "Park Poem"—but now for the first time entire poems are based on dream transcriptions. "At the Well," the most successful of them, expresses the dreamer's desire to rid himself of civilization's discontents. At one point he longs to join the group of mute tribesman who come to him "at the edge of the desert" and with them

> terrify the towns, the villages
> disappear among bazaars, sell our
> camels, pierce our ears

Such atavistic impulses, ultimately rejected at the end of "At the Well," resurface in the first significant group of poems to retreat into the past, both that of Blackburn's childhood ("Concomitants," "Hesper Adest") and a rather romanticized version of America's past ("The Old Days," "Ritual XIII: The Shot"). The child's vulnerability in the first group throws light on the man's *machismo* in the second. Experimentation with "found" poetry ("Ya Lift a Cold One") and purely associative verse ("The Pain") are other progeny of this period of decontrol.

Not all of these mid-1960s poems are successful. Some are needlessly cryptic; others, fatalistic or simply morose. But some pieces derive a strong evocative power from their lack of clear external referents:

> KEEP no names that give us not
> our death
> . . .
> O swift current, O buffalo .

> ("Baggs")

The desire for death, described as "that softness we rut toward," is made more palatable here by its projection unto unfamiliar, mythic terrain. Then, too, if this non-sober lurch toward the past is responsible for such darkly comic poems as "The Assassination of President McKinley"—which might boast, among its other attributes, being the only poem in the language to contain the phrase "schluk-schluk"—we have reason to be grateful.

Whatever the cause—the dissolution of his second marriage, the imminence of return to scenes of a retrospectively happier past, or the shipboard romance with his third wife-to-be, Joan Miller—almost immediately after embarking for Europe on a Guggenheim Fellowship in September 1967, Blackburn experienced a psychic or spiritual renewal, made incarnate in a poetic form he soon came to designate "journals." The pieces written in this form are generally longer and more discursive than his earlier work; they tend to be divided into discrete, if related, sections, and to cover a relatively wide time-range—days, or even weeks. Chronicles of everyday life—and the public, reportorial sense of Blackburn's chosen term should be kept in mind—the journals came increasingly to use a wide variety of structures, including prose, to capture its textures. Final evidence of Blackburn's continual struggle, often with himself, to extend the boundaries of what could be considered poetry's fit subject and form, the journals offer bits and pieces of his own sights and insights as examples.

The journals and other poems of this period selectively detail the final four years of Blackburn's life. After his 1967–68 year in Europe, with a brief interim return to the U.S. South for a Woodrow Wilson Fellowship reading and teaching tour of black universities, Blackburn spent two years back in New York City teaching in City College's pre-baccalaureate SEEK program, at Mannes School for Music, and at the New School for Social Research. In these years he translated Pablo Picasso's long, surrealistic poem *Hunk of Skin* (City Lights, 1968) and Julio Cortázar's *Cronopios and Famas* (Pantheon, 1969). In addition to his continued local poetry activities—to cite just one, he helped set up the reading series at Dr. Generosity's coffeehouse—he began accepting increasingly frequent invitations to give out-of-town readings. The birth of a son, Carlos, to Joan Blackburn in 1969 changed the family's census status but not their way of life. Within weeks of Carlos's birth the three took an extended cross-country trip in the Gaucelm Faidit Uzerchemobile, the VW van Blackburn bought in Europe and named after the portliest of the troubadours.

What had promised to be a relatively quiet year of teaching at the State University of New York, Cortland, turned active in a new and terrible way within months of the family's move upstate. In December 1970 Blackburn was diagnosed as having cancer of the esophagous. A series of radiation treatments proved ineffective against (and perhaps accelerated) the disease, but at least, as the poetry shows, neither they nor the cancer seriously curtailed Blackburn's routines until the very end. Journals written little more than a month before his death in Cortland on September 13, 1971 record Blackburn's still-acute observations of the events at the National Poetry Festival in Allendale, Michigan.

In typically paradoxical fashion, however, there is a retrospective cast to poems written long before Blackburn learned of his illness. In the 1967 European journals, Blackburn the seasoned traveler alludes with some irony to the poems Blackburn the neophyte poet had written some ten years earlier in Europe. The fourth section of "The Glorious Morning" quotes lines from the 1957 "La Vieille Belle" describing the same rainy reception by the same city at the same time of year: "September, O Christ, Paris . tout à fait normal." Now, however, he notes in words he would not have used in the much more romantic earlier poem, that the Place Dauphine-en-L'Isle is "all fucked up by construction." Setting the original 1956 "Plaza Real with Palmtrees" against his 1968 "Second Take" of the Spanish square, the terms of the change are clarified: the first poem is like a Greek vase, figures poised, potential but frozen, while the second is more akin to a contemporary painterly canvas, full of movement and boldly displaying the artist's brushstrokes.

By the last year of his life Blackburn was using the journals form exclusively, but before then, and particularly during the year in Europe, he was still writing what he liked wryly to distinguish as "poems." A number of these poems, later slated by him for the posthumously published *Halfway Down the Coast*, show an intense preoccupation with death that predates by almost three years any conscious knowledge of illness, and that differs, in its bitterness and ferocity, from the resigned fatalism of the mid-1960s poems. In spite of what must be seen here as an exacerbation of Blackburn's usual association of death and love, he seems concomitantly to have arrived at the metaphorical middle ground of the collection's title poem. At least the possibilities of reciprocity and nurturing, expressed only jokingly in the poem's final punning line—"And love? What is that many-faceted mother?"—are taken up seriously in some of the later domestic journals. "Journal April 19: The Southern Tier," for example, asserts the value of setting aside destructive memories of past relationships in order to make way for new ones.

When they do come in, in the last 30 or so poems, Blackburn's reactions to his illness are much like his reactions to other bad news: wry, ironic, bitter, for the most part resigned. He also treats the subject with characteristic delicacy—not lightness, but deftness and subtlety. Apropos of waiting for death, in "Journal 26 . VI . 71 The News," Blackburn writes that it is "NOTHING I CAN'T STAND"—only to admit in the next line "I don't believe that, either." His penchant for the self-ironic and mock-heroic underplays the genuine strength that lies precisely in his ability to resist being heroic. These final poems attest to Blackburn's rare gift for precision without reductionism, his talent for resisting all definitive solutions save musical ones in his poetry.

The same intellectual openness and flexibility may have been responsible too for Blackburn's avoidance throughout his life of any strict adherence to a single belief system. Neither purely rationalistic nor rigorous in his spiritual views, Blackburn used transcendent or religious symbology—often out of the Catholicism of his youth, but also from Greek mythology, Celtic goddess-cults, alchemical lore, and Buddhism—to suit particular poetic purposes. His last poems continue to play with the possibilities. At one moment he employs liturgical Christian language in describing himself as

> a doomed man planting tomatoes
> backyard of a house he lives in
> belongs to somebody else . kneeling
> on the earth
> his hands move earth

("Journal: June 1971    110 in the Shade")

and in the next he dismisses the entire system, asserting acidly in "Untitled (We cannot agree)" that "There are no resurrections planned."

If any controlling idea can be gleaned from this collection of Blackburn's work, it might well be the one he expressed mid-career in "Pre-Lenten Gestures":

> Every organic thing, o philosophers, man
> plant or animal, containing as seed the flower
> its own destruction, its own rebirth

Such a belief would account for both the fatalism of the poetry and the potentiality for significance Blackburn saw, and made others see, in the most mundane things. At its best, the work offers a feeling like Blake's "Everything is holy."

Perhaps the only change in Blackburn's eschatological views at the end is the result of the perceived loneliness and "otherness" of death. Many of the last poems wishfully project familiar, anthropocentric afterlives. In "Journal : 26 . V . 71 The News" Blackburn asks a friend, "Will I talk to you then, fill / yr / ears with words"—only to retreat bravely in the next line, "Let / each man's words be his own." In the next-to-final sequence, heaven is humorously imagined as a kind of ideal poetry festival, with Blackburn still in charge of smoothing the proceedings. These visions of death are entirely in keeping with the final representations of his life. The last journals find Blackburn reading poetry, attending poetry readings and festivals, directing nearly all his farewells toward poet friends.

Clearly Blackburn did not so much allow his life to enter his poetry as—to an unusual degree—allow poetry to enter his life. It was not only the astounding amount of time he spent involved with poetry and poets, but also the quality of attention he consistently gave everyday occurrences. Early on, in "The Routine," he transformed a bleak winter interior into a spring garden by leaving an onion to sprout in his kitchen cabinet; to the end he retained his gift for seeing ordinary things anew. In the second-to-last journal he reappraises the formerly disparaged hollyhocks of his youth: "Those delicate blooms. The awkward stems. The hairy leaves." Although his ear was also unfailing, it would be difficult to refute his perception of his impending death as, most of all, an obscuring of sight. "Journal Nov/Dec . 1970," the poem in which Blackburn obliquely announces his illness, opens: "The darkness wins here." But finally it doesn't, at least not for long. Not here, in these poems.

Edith Jarolim
New York, 1985

# Notes

[1] Although the vagaries of publishers necessarily played some role, the 523 poems comprising this volume (out of a total of approximately 1250, including juvenalia and scribbled and abandoned drafts) are essentially those Blackburn wished to have published. If he liked a poem he would keep submitting it until it got into print, sometimes many years after he wrote it. The present volume is arranged chronologically by date of composition rather than book-by-book because there was sufficient overlap within the collections to necessitate either repeating poems or deciding from which collection a poem or several poems should be eliminated. More important, a presentation based on dates of publication would perpetuate an already distorted view of Blackburn's creative development. He began writing in the middle 1940s, but not until some twenty years later did he have regular access to publication. The title index to this volume provides a listing of the earlier collections in which the poems were printed.

[2] Almost from the start there developed a symbiosis between Blackburn's poetry and his translations from the Provençal. He brought to the troubadours the rhythms and idioms of American speech; they gave him much of his knowledge of lyrical tone and poetic form. *Proensa*, a small collection of Blackburn's Provençal translations, was published by Robert Creeley's Majorca-based Divers Press in 1953. A larger anthology was accepted by Macmillan Co. in 1958, but Blackburn was never able to complete it to his satisfaction, and Macmillan finally abandoned the project in 1961. The excellent translations of troubadour verse on which Blackburn worked for nearly twenty years were not published as a group until after his death (*Proensa*, ed. George Economou, Univ. of California, 1978).

[3] Some of Blackburn's Lorca translations were published in *Origin*, *New Directions*, and *Evergreen Review* during these years. *Blackburn / Lorca*, a collection of these and later translations, was published posthumously (Momo's Press, 1979).

[4] Look, for example, at the rhetoric of Olson's 1951 "Projective Verse" essay: "[Poetry] is a matter of, at *all* points (even, I should say, of our management of daily reality as of the daily work) get on with it . . . the whole business, keep it moving as fast as you can, citizen. And if you also set up as a poet, USE USE USE the process at all points. . . ."

# Note on the Texts

The texts and the titles used in this volume are those of Blackburn's last revised versions. Except in those cases when readings were clearly erroneous and unintentional, no changes in punctuation, alignment, or spelling have been made. Only poem titles were consistently styled.

The two dates in brackets following the poems are the date of composition and the date of publication, respectively. If an accurate date of composition is given in the poem itself, only the date of publication is provided.

The
Collected
Poems of
Paul
Blackburn

## WALK AFTER RAIN

The after-flow of water in the gutters,
the slow wind that mutters,
the drenched night, the soaking shadowed grass,
the cars that pass
need be a part:
but only touch
the summer-swollen heart.

[1945?/1948]


## SOUTH WIND ON MY RIGHT CHEEK

After seven months of discomfort
I shall return with my words to the city
where my thoughts live between the rivers,
thoughts blown like yesterday's newspapers
scud morning pavements.


If she will play with me with her
        blouse off,
we will rewrite Lawrence between us,
cleave to clarity of statement
        and doubtless
hold classic methods of communication
able, recherché, edifying.

1

And all day long, with the sun streaming
through the venetian blinds
    while she works
or combs her short hair to a dark shining
    mask in back,
or reads in a book
or bends to a meal
or dries her face on the towel bending
  toward the mirror,
I shall lie on her couch and study
the sun on the wall and the curve
    of her back as she rises
stretches.


                  Whatever she does,
however she moves, lithe body catching
    lines of sunlight,
we will spin long tales from the warm air,
and in the evening
without lights
    we shall be a tangle of shadows.

                            [1948?/1950]


## THE INNOCENTS WHO FALL LIKE APPLES


Mohamet, old navigator, your flying coffin
    suspended between earth and heaven,
start with a projection : 30-North, 75-East
should center this locale. Lahore at 2 o'clock,
    mountains on three sides of the town :
beyond the mountains horizon curves blue to white,
Russia, China; the jungle at our back
a greendark far tangle where rains steam. But here
    no rain will fall for months.
At noon the orange rocks on this dry hillside
keep hot shadows beneath them; and here
the horse and runner where the arid wind
    barely stirs the sand.

Though Akbar awaits, no howeverdevoted runner
intends to hurry, though North and West,
far from horizon are huge, wooden
    tables on which
English, Portuguese, Dutch, dice,
heavy blue veins standing out across their hands,
caduceus to the crafty forefinger, for
    turquoise with black veins,
strange woods, balas-rubies, myrrh,
embroidered works of slender hands,
their palms flashing gold in the sunlight,
    their goats stirring dust by the temple.

The old minister on the balcony, the painting
    held at arm's length :
    "Good, yes, Shūkere Khudá.
But there are no winds in that region.
Know not artifice of brush and paint
    but I know winds.
(Peach trees shed bright blossoms in the water.)
But tassels are blowing from the saddle cloth,
and the tail on that beast flies
    out, though not quite straight.
They're supposed to be running. The runner's hand
    holds his cap
    clamped to his head
and his legs are in movement. Doubtless Akbar thinks
his runners race the horses over hot
    desert to the walled city.
    Flattery then,
for neither this pale boy nor his blue
charger casts a shadow and the picture
    is flooded in sunlight.

"But this dabbler speaks truth also : that red flash
on the saddle cloth is a cloak the boy's gotten rid of;
and this choice of ornament on both horse and man,
         tiny, perfect circles, gives away
a real condition, both perspire.
And that horse isn't running. No horse I've ever
seen could run, his legs balking, rearing
         for the plunge. Agh,
far the days when my back was straight,
eye keen and knees close-clinging,
those long days of the antelope hunts,
clear air of the plains southward,
         can nearly smell it and feel
         the animal's warmth jogging under me.
My bones ache with remembering.
But the wind in my peach trees, my wind, sire . . ."


He leans the painting against the balustrade,
and turns a dim eye east through evening
to the blue mountains, considers a walk in
his garden's coolness, where his
         daughter and the young artist
              sit by the fountain each
                   watching the other's
reflection in the pool soften, waver.
And peach trees shed bright
         blossoms in the water. Tomorrow
he will present the picture.

[1949/1950]

## CANTAR DE NOIT

This bird speaks to me from the night,
From chilled autumn dark;
There is plaint in the song he makes
In his midnight field.
He remembers a sun-shaft smile
And soft air,
As I remember in my heart and
With my flesh
A smile that made the sundrench
Seem less bright,


Made my soul more lucid than
Any sunlimned world.
And on my back, awake in a
Single bed,
This room without light, hearing
A bird speak
My flesh to me, I, groping
For the light switch,
Must climb out, struggle into
A robe, making
Two late singers mourning
A lost time.

[1949/1951]


## TWO GREEKS

The straight-backed shepherd

hand warped to the crook

beard greasy and wild as

the fleece of his animals

stands on the mountainside his back to the herd :

short cloak flaps in the wind

Below,

      the temple in sunlight at Philagei :

      the black specks are goats grazing

      among worn rocks

      there is a child guarding them :

two cypresses throw ragged shadows across

      the wind-smooth pillars

      and ruined declination of hewn stone


         *


In the evening I hum sad songs and twist

thread in my hands

you do not comprehend

      Here, my breast

      tawny as a round fruit

      it is a firm fish swimming

        and sings to you

My thoughts

are flowers in your dark hair

      your proud adornments

But you do not say any kind word to me

      nor bow your head

under their delicate insinuations

              [1949/1952]

## THE BIRDS

I want them to come here
I want to see them here
 at this round boulder.
                    White spots against the sky, each
                         there, a swollen white spike on each
of the line of rotten piles that reach
                    out from shore.
Others skim the sea, strange
cries, wings flapping
                    I want to see them here
                    I want them to come here.
                    I swim my mind, swim it
in the moving water of all my world
                    in moving clouds
                         in sun.

                    And I was young
and neck began to wobble clear, but feet
          were rooted in this beach, for I
feared the dark march to the sun again; and each
stiff inner motion moved me into song
                    instead of into living :
but now I know what thing is worth the having
and fear the imperfection in my singing; but now
can lie here and swim my mind in it
                    and still know when to leave
                    touch bottom to darkness where
I no longer fear to ask much of the gods.
          It has taken me a long time to realise
I want them to come here
I want to see them here.

                                   [1949/1951]

**SPRING**

My branch cut from the tree I
spin towards ground
and the rain paints her human image on the earth
the amputation proving both costly and painful

Yet the rain
yet I spring with it

But we may not sin here, neither any repenting
and tho I spring with it
    I
        am ashamed of the naked impulse
        and ashamed of not sinning anyway

[1950/1951]


**SUMMER**

Girl child,
standing toward the field's edge
      —change, school's out
        time, a word before bed—
I hear your clear gayety lifted,
face up toward some
neighboring foliage in the windless sun

"I didn't hear you EIther, treetop!"

[1950/1953]

## ALBA

Small clouds fill the edge of sky at dawn,
thin strips of cirrus riding window-height;
force eyes half-open to give the day good morning.
I lie here, not daring a move from bed
fearing to wake a love who sleeps
her blondeness close : her face, a mask of peace,
will shatter on the light to make my coffee
which I shall drink before the sky is red.


In mind, the walk to subway thru the city dawn :
before the clattered descent, eyes measure height
of greystone buttressed, washed in sun of morning.
And all the while, body supine in bed
grows tense above a love that never sleeps
but changes like the light and knows no peace.
Eyes measure the swift descent and shatter. Coffee
a theory poised above the street.   And red


the mask of dawn mounts the hardening height
of a metal-stripped morning where no one can love or sleep
or measure peace. But blonde or dark or red,
I'll have my coffee before I move from bed.


CODA : (a soft mocking voice from beneath the covers)

> "Shagreened:   that cudden's nerve astounds.
> Pot:   friend pot, are these not grounds?"

[1950/1951]

# THE ODYSSEY

Heavy rains were predicted for the early hours
but there was low white fog for the trip;
but the raincoat I carried, folds, fits in the pocket,
and was no encumbrance.
                                White sleep over the bay
thick near the waves, over which
ice-cakes floated, following the ground-swell:
overhead saw the small white clouds gathering
                                and four stars,
clear beyond the fog (bong) to where
                                (bong)
cumulus convene.
But was so heavy at deck-level, the
buoy light marking the channel barely
seen through the (bong) but heard spilling
its slow double-tongued (bong) through
                                the thick night
over the slow wash of ship's-wake its
                                articulation.

                                And on the island
waiting in the pier for the next boat,
a tall guard with a squint rubbed
a stubble of beard and helped me spend
                                my coffee time—spoke of death:
"Influenza uzso quick
"nineteen 18, nineteen 19
"rite here on this eyelund (S.I.)
"rite afterth' war, ef'n *any*one
"in yer famly gottit
"yu hadta go out'n dig the grave yerself."
                                and thinking on the end of life
                                spoke of the new pension plan
"Retire in '55, put in
"t'ree dollarsa week."

The persistence of the theme in conversation,
casually, easily, faced. Death.
I could see it in him
how he carried it in
his long skinny chest.
Put dignity on him, that,
his knowing he carried it.
Blind Tiresias foretelling the manner thereof
"uzso quick"

Back in Manhattan, they'd changed the subways on me
and it cost me a dime to find out.
Two Seventh Avenue Locals through, twenty minutes apart,
woke the attendant in the change booth, to hear:
"Lex's outside now, go up and across the street.
"No more Lex trains routed through this side of the station."

And that year they tore down the el
between Chatham Sq. and the Battery.
And I saw a drunk that spring standing
on Fulton St. staring downtown
at the waist-high stumps of el-posts
cursing Impelliteri
with tears in his eyes.

                      Between Bowling Green and the Battery
                                a shuttle of two cars:
                    "Is this a local?"
                    and the conductor,
                    "This ain't no local, this ain't  n u t h i n !
                              a shu⊬ul!"

                    The stubby stairway at Bowling Green:
I smoked a cigarette leaning over the turnstile
                      seeing trees
and an edge of park, and a lit building.
One side of the wide shallow stairway
had peeled its white tile sepulchral facing, leaving
stained black rock bare
      in the dark air
against the dawn dark.
      Behind the black buildings speckled with electric lights,
schist, rock of the island, on which the island sits, the basis
the stuff itself, black against black air, as
the island from the sea must rise, black upon black. It will
                      be morning where I surface,
                      dawn in an hour. The clock
                            behind me
like the sound of dripping water in a cave, tock
tlock.. tluck.. tluck, slow (bong) slow cold tune
the stuff itself (bong) dripping from the bay
                      a death/
                            The train
came with its great rushing of wind.

And then I descended into the tunnel
and the express was strewn with grey faces
drowned males dripping from the bay
swish, swish in the eye-socket
and that dead boy slept in the corner
seaweed fell over his eyes and
the man of fifty
           in his hands
his head
a taut throbbing drum.
He relaxed once, so shaky
he seized hold again, bent
his neck arching tight. It
           was morning where I surfaced.
Orion, unpropitious to sailors, how
shall we cross your wintry seas?
With what rites shall we enter the mountain cave
in the change of year?
Shall we drain the mixing bowl *a pascor*, the sweet time? And Death?

        "One enters the cave with torches.
        "Bring new shoots to the altars.
                The apple
        "buys the life
        "and this is the island of apples."

                [1950/1956]


## YOU ASK ME WHY

Say that Spring is a momentary answer,
say that I have planted it for you
and that certain green things offer
tender bloody shoots in a sunny corner.


Pan stretches his shaggy limbs at ease
tootles his flute and the music is simply
shrill excitement along your arteries. Say
you no longer move to the wall but can

stand smiling at me over your cup of coffee
with strong brown limbs parted and glowing
beside a young plant—
                    Enough to stop there


except to say that I am made a god :
and being god
I say this Spring is yours
I planted it for you
and come to terms with death each time I look
and see how you know it and how you lower your head.

                                        [1950/1952]


## THE EYE OF THE STORM


Struck by the wind, the taut guitar of rain

moves panicked on my window, phrase and chord.

Speee-k to mee of love

        W I N D   R A I N ,     speak!

Lord, how my head cruises, wind!

no matter she has not come to me wet thru
that I might warm her and do for and to, but
speak of her wind, speak of love where
        she is all music stilled
and rich
and dark as a spring night.


        Till light comes
I sit here pretending to
warm myself with coffee, furious :
cake half-eaten, the bed turned down,
the dishes washed, I lower my head
hearing the long rain wash the city
hearing the wind bellow the streets
delirious with wetness, myself, gone
serious with storm, molten with fright—

Over
her somewhere sleeping head the storm
        swings whose
eye is in this room,
and in tomorrow's sun no dissonant
splinter of night's tune    but she
smiling, will take my guitar from off the wall
and name a song she likes while I
complain, happy and warm as any singer in Spain.

[1951/1952]


## TELLING YES FROM NO IN A
## TELLING EYES FROM NOSE IN A DELICATE SITUATION
## TELLING AYES FROM NOES IN AN ETC.

            this mouth is not so tired, no
            it buds its flower to me, tho
            it was betrayed not long ago


            by someone else : its tongue is slow
            trusting mainly I do not know
            what it thinks it does not show :
            that, altho it softly flow


and merge with mine and kiss a glow
into the open, speaks not that low
inevitably to   m e . So.


            no matter. Go.
            and in these eyes
            now heavy-lidded, tears will grow
            as if this were one also
            with her other white first tries.

[1951/1955]

## COMMITTEE

My two cats sit toward me resting,
one on the desk and one on the bookcase beside it:
half-open eyes like yellow flowers

move at intervals from
my face to the door and back, asking
when my girl will open it, for she has missed the hour.

When the key turns in the lock
they will be at the entrance before me

rubbing her ankles.

Until that time I shall imitate their curious patience

and rest here with half-closed eyes

and hear the clock and my breathing.

[1951/1955]

## THE RETURN

He had sought

sour badlands and walked
desert hills covered with flat stones,
year of the red-necked buzzard flying,

fox' bark:
muddy coloured snakes, lizards sunned
stretched under clear air on rock,

fled as he approached.

And the long-forgotten came upon him in that place
and thrills of love shook him in the dark;
but the desert wind that had touched his face

now grated a lesson like rattle of death
                        and the animals watched.

Thus the footmarks turned
and thru the burnt land he marched,
slowly, mountains came nearer,
foot-tracks thru the hills, then
                roads: dust rising, an
occasional horseman
gazing from behind his eyes at the traveler.
                        As yet, no words.

At the turn of a hillside he saw a crowd
of steep roofs, flat roofs, stone spires, bridges,
towers, and from
the net of shaded streets, the unceasing
              hum rose to him
and his love defined itself as need
                      to add himself.

He knew beforehand the brutal look in their faces
their coarse words, their clanging loud-mouthed crafts
            and his heart kept off:
but thru low windows the long tables at evening
                  and the children
wriggling excitedly on old knees.

        The feast day and bells
        tuned minds to joy:
fiddles reeled thin thru streets
                dancing, dancing,

folk ran from their doorways laughing,
women shouted window to window, the town
blurred under his eyes
and his love pinched
and staggered his ankles down thru the warm dust
                    to speech
                    casting at dice to buy his loss.

[1951/1952]


## DEATH AND THE SUMMER WOMAN


Curious reason in the choice of words:
        "Summer" I said, after my second thought,
        "Summer is all your flower. Much

harder or softer than you are
one could say Spring" and yes,
                    the green arched
aching intensity you wear
fringes that season, but Summer
            is your sea-green innocence;
                    is the brown easy
slope of back and shoulders moving into surf,
how you lower your head when I try to look at you,
a hot sunny innocence, yet sea-green coolness

and your eyes know us;
your open palms, the sweated tracings
show the door stands open.

But the trap of will
will trip it snap shut like brass
the slightest touch,
haul you hooked inside and kill the season, Death
smiling cool at you the whispered

"no"

[1951/1951]


## THE COCKTAIL PARTY


Alone with the sandwiches I watch the movement
her mouth makes:   can't hear words or music:
lifting, I find her eyes again, watchful
amid her speech, of me, never looking
to whom she talks, avoiding. I
look at a canvas, and back to that steady glance
that falls
wherever I walk, looks where I look, and back,
as though I were alone in the room with her
and poor, or mad.


Not much to look at. Finish a drink
and to hear a friend's familiar voice
I dial a number on the telephone.
She will ask me, later, who it was,
and I shall have to choose.


Public safety. She will never level:
alone, will refuse to meet my eyes,
dare not answer any of my questions:
composed in every feature, will advise
I find myself a pale love, or glorious future.

[1951/1956]

## WHAT THE TIDE GAVE

Oiled bodies tangent hand on hand
imprint the sand, feed golden flesh with sun:
three days are one long dreaming on this shelf of land
where the kelp lies black, inescapable, and the tides run
back to the black deep center of the world.


Nightly the river of hair she spills
pounds all the lean and lift and touch and rise
until he rides that pitch of wave : they wheel and
together plunge, following their tides under
the crest of sea surge, surfacing at last
lost in the dark trough, darkened, hearing
surf sound close : are cast
up on the calmed bed at daybreak's move.


Long swells dragging the shoals dissolve
tumbling to foam in the shallows.


Mouths undone and slack, the tangent hands
                    hold without needing
the morning's sea-wind in clear, upturned fingers,
                    and the tides run back
to the black unlocked deep center of the world.

[1951/1953]

## THE LANNER

Delicately ravaged,
scared
afraid to lean into it;
tongue
swollen in my mouth, the
tune
caught in the throat.
Words,
the words, damn them
thrash in the ear
bash in the ear,
will, by no means,
move.

       Nothing,
       nothing remembered singly
       but all
       here
       stumbling about singing
       altogether too loud
       and way off key.
       Afraid
to sit back and let the song ride clear,
afraid it won't ride and won't ride clear.
This purpose dares not shape an imperfect bell.

But fumbling seizes purpose by the nape, and
together they roll and stagger toward the tune,
liquored up and blind to sleep it off,
dreaming Segovia, Lorca and Daniel.
       And at 5 A.M.?

Dawn

falters from the horizon of the sea,
hesitates behind the skylight, filters
through
and I
rise straight up from the cot
rising from that metrical inferno, feel
the first notes break, sit down again, start
a low cadence riding articulate
in the grey light
and know that

again

the lanner is my bird.

One day she will move
straight up from the hand, and diving
prove herself my huntress, seize
the word, the line, the stanza, all
I hawk for ever:
another day
the bag hangs empty from my shoulder
because of this coward.
But the days when she is forward
when she is all there is of boldness,
I am glad she is my huntress,
and the lanner is my bird!

[1952/1955]

A SONG

Of sea and the taking of breath
and to match the impress of it, the
giving of breath :
of mercy, the true quality of,
and the rhythm of certain movements I
sing, lady

How heavy and soft
your flesh at morning
when we wake together
O lady, how heavy and soft
your eyes when I reach for you
the

line of your back
half circumscribes our summer
centers love, that
tall    sweet    mast to your vessel
and we enact
how underneath the pleasure piers the seas
move

[1952/1962]

# FOR MERCURY, PATRON OF THIEVES : A LAUREL

The hour before dawn
fog came in . Stayed all day .
Ragged thin filter of sun, a lover's
        touch on bared skin .
        Dock smell, oil, machinery
        smell of sea,
        pulse of city in thigh-vein,
sea-pulse distends the delicate vein in the temple,
throbbing above eyes still caked with night . The head
        sways
        bends in amphibious light
on the dangerous shoulders of the day.


        At dawn
        all places equal :
Athens, Paris, Brighton Beach and Arizona.
        The trap.
        The bear
dies in the trap : Mercury too a thief,
the cat's walk lives . The difference
        is feet


Feet !  The cool air brushes an arm and
feet spring the walk, respond to the swaying head.
The sensitive pavement reacts, receives
holds the off-weight tread, holds and releases
wings to the god's foot man's foot, sends
an alternating current of love and sense
        between man and street.


Pay down the price of cigarettes, receive the pack, grasp
in the living hand, the cellophaned firmness . Dammit
        *enjoy* your smoke.
The sidewalks of spring
love us as we love them, no better, caress the feet
the way the feet press them . And sun, fog-
filtered, touches like lover   lovers' arms
who thieve each other   naked   tall   and warm.

[1953/1953]

## THE FUNERAL

Returning from the funeral
    I saw her and liked her. The air
was very quiet
        near spring.

For a week I had opportunity to flirt;
and the last three days of the second week,
fortunate enough to share certain
        spaces with her.

                    [1953/1955]


## THE SEARCH

I have been looking for this animal for three days now
          and four nights
          not finding him.
Probing into the corners of my mind to find him,
glancing at store windows and into the faces of women.

    Sometimes I think it is a bird
        but then again not.
    Once I was sure it was a lizard
facing my left trouser-leg at a pet-shop window,
        crouched
with his tongue darting out in primeval coldness.
But I found myself looking again the following day.

So neither very-hot blooded nor cold blooded,
        those early creations.
It is small, it has four legs and fur.

I saw it, almost, under the dark brows
of a Puerto Rican child in the street.
                A garment worker.
        Her belly was small and round
                and it was growing.
But she saw I looked and the thing changed in her eyes
                and it was a woman.
I have a woman. That's not what I look for now.


                My cat gave me a clue.
He was lying on his back, his feet in the air
                asleep.   The thing was
        the mixture of attitude in his face,
the sublime trust and disdain, careless, sure.


        Turned out it was a hamster.
You find them in cages with treadmills, which
                seems to me a symbol.
        This from a magazine someplace
                with a set of pictures.
        Mine was not in a treadmill. He
lay on a ledge in the sun in the window
        of a shoe-repair shop on Sixth Avenue,
his legs stretched out behind him, sideways,
for he lay on one side in the sun
washing his face with one paw like a cat
                ignoring the traffic.


        And having found him out
I didn't know what to make of him, except that
he was a small fat rodent and looked careless,
that he was a mammal and sure.

                                [1953/1954]

## AFTER DINNER

The small cats disoblige to pose; she
lays pad and conte crayon on the ledge.


Lilt of conversation.    Then.


" H E Y !    Those are my art materials!"
The pointed living gesture turns to flight. The cats


work under cover of our conversation.


Nor is reading simple : a second one
presses affectionately against his sweater
                    effectively decomposing
                    the page suddenly
                    in mid-sentence.


                A third arrives to reinforce the fun.


Half-pleased to find it in his lap
"Jeezus Christ, another!"    and she,
"Leave my goddamned conte crayon alone!"


                The first resumes
eyeing the bookcase, a more ambitious scheme.


            They have the situation well in hand.

[1953/1955]

# FRIENDS

Perhaps it is right
that you shall not be there. Perhaps
good friends should remain apart.

the sea beats on the rocks
or that proximity

But there are friends, also close in space.

[1953/1955]

# THE CONTINUITY

The bricklayer tells the busdriver
and I have nothing to do but listen:

Th' holdup at the liquor-store, d'ja hear?
a detective
watch't    'm for ten minutes
He took it anyway
Got away down Broadway        Yeah?
Yeah.

And me:

the one on the Circle?
Yeah.
Yeah?    I was in there early tonight.

The continuity.
A dollar forty-
two that I spent on a bottle of wine
is now in a man's pocket going down Broadway.

Thus far the transmission is oral.

Then a cornerboy borrows my pencil
to keep track of his sale of newspapers.

[1953/1954]


## THE MIRROR


The lazy dragon of steam issues
                    from manhole cover.    Tires hiss
The wet streets of my city speak to me


this rain
now almost stopped


                    or say :
even with winter rain here, youth is back
to walk on these reflections
but now the neon images shimmering
                    across cement are
more solid than glass or building block or stone
or
my image?

[1953/1954]


## THE SUDDEN FEAR


The marble blocks guarding the gates to the park are monsters
wobbling, crushing in as we try to get in
                    past them

They are not always that way. Sometimes
a summer day, we stroll thru happy, not heeding them, into
a glistening day

        green grass   warm smells   all


        But not tonite, not
now, at the beginning of winter     (how

                  white they are
                  how cold)
now, seen at side-glance from   the seat of a bus going
              past and away from them

                              [1953/1954]


## THE ASSISTANCE


On the farm it never mattered;
behind the barn, in any grass, against
any convenient tree,
            the woodshed in winter, in a corner
if it came to that.


But in a city of eight million,    one
stands on the defensive.
            In the West 59th St. parking lot
it has long since sunk into the cinders.


But in the shallow doorway of
a shop on Third Avenue, between
            the dark and the streetlight,
it was the trail of the likewise drinking-man who preceded me
            that gave me courage.

                              [1953/1954]

## THE SUNLIT ROOM

Here

we find our private temporary limit
the depths we swim to and then
spring the gap
                    ourselves
what has been possible
for us strangely
from the beginning

[1953/1955]


## THE DISSOLVING FABRIC

He who has own wound
cannot speak of it.
Nor is there any geography which
takes cognizance of it.

To know and then to heal
that is the rule.
But discipline is not sufficient
despite our speculations.

And there is no one, not the god
who understood it.
And the fact is that she withdrew it,
the fact is that she owned it.

She possessed her own life, and took it.

[1954/1954]

# HOW TO LIVE WITH ONE ANOTHER SOMEHOW

              Last September, a letter :
22 cloudless days gone
with swimming,
           now it sccms to be fall
and the birds gathering on the front lawn.
Julia has a severe ear infection
fought with penicillin, and so forth,
otherwise a most beautiful Indian Summer.
           and HOW on earth can I face another
           summer "at home"
           (i.e., with my mother)
how on earth be able to keep face with
close living, to share, with the others?
Except for the one you married and your children,
           how
can anyone live with ANYone else
for more than a weekend, I wonder,
I'd better.

and we have matchstick panels hanging
before our windows since yesterday
One looks through both ways, but
they shed golden light.

Now, in January, more 'news'
she is facing no more prospects

('except for the one you married and your children'
reduced to the face in the glass, to see
the violation

when she owned her own life and took it
   (gold light, close living


when she owned her own life and took it.


   Thanks for your letter: and please send the two books, and
thanks, no libretti . . .

[1954/1959]


## THE EVASION


The light that enters
not a definition


Against the light
your polite uncertainty keeps asking questions which
can be answered obliquely:
your innocence demands, almost, no definition,
edges us to those areas where no
syntax or other act can be direct


The other is a warm-hearted fool
and very likeable


Against your murmuring silence he puts
a graceful chatter,
disgracefully entertaining, entertains
his hangover, takes
what is his due, the stranger's gift
black bread and chowder, our hot spiced liquors
But you


eat and drink in silence . No one knows
what ghost you feed
Against his clumsy warmth you lay

     (the light fading behind you

a distant politesse, an ambiguity
which does not answer our hospitality
                    tho it is you we greet .

                                        [1954/1966]


Here is a marriage!

            Here is a marriage!

            Here is cake and a knife to divide it

                              two hands on the knife
                              like petals enfolding each other
                              folded onto the wood of the handle where
                              is imbedded the blade
                    a flower
here is a flower
                    and above it, air
                    and the sun's fires above it
and under it earth
and under that water
and under that rock
and under that
fire
                    Here is a marriage!

                    Here is a marriage!

                                        [1954/1955]



**THE MESSAGE**


The man who writes a letter to the TIMES
or sends a telegram to Washington
                    shows courage
                              makes
a solitary gesture in the face of

            (there is a confusion of values and
                    the markets are shifting

The man who stands outside a Ninth Avenue bar
continuing his altercation with
whomever it was
alone :


'Ah, ye'll hev reason to remember Moike!'

                or whatever he should have said;
eyes staring down the now-imagined enemy
dully,
is likewise meaningless, is
                the face of decay.
                A dream.


    These counters are assessable. But
what does she mean?
this handsome young woman, her
boyfriend on her arm,
who talks to the wind for the present,
when she narrows her eyes looking on me
in passing, and pays
no attention to what she is saying?


    Even then,
is this dream any different?
Is the dream of the future, of more valor
or value, than, to anyone, or me,
the dream of five minutes ago
                or seven centuries?

                                    [1954/1955]



**THE QUEST**


No image

is decisive argument

                and it cuts me loose

                        altogether

to feel, the roots set down
stubbornly
into rock, even
strained by this.

[1954/1955]


CABRAS


To sing the democratic man today
or the marxist man, for that,
is no proposition.
So I sing goats.

Hardly anymore the issue, to
move to the line, take up the quarrel against it. Each
man is forced back some by the damned noise, will
hold any line against it, his own.

What else can be intelligent or warm—
no communal man at all.
Some little human conspiracy in letters
or the possible handshake,
but such accidents of fate or inner nature
are certainly occasional—yet

all of us eat and shit and walk or ride.
But goats, asses, pigs, sheep enjoy
equal rights,
make their droppings and stink, each
according to his natural inclination.

Burros came up the hill today with flagstones,
left their dung on the steps, were patient,
walked very carefully, without resentment.

Sheep die silently, pleading with their soft eyes,
pigs scream under the knife, and for a long while.

The goats in the next field, however, are hobbled,
being otherwise difficult to catch,
    they are so quick and stubborn
and full of fun.

[1954/1955]


## LIMITS

there is a line some
where outside,
but very close
just over your right ear,
if you
lie on your left side, for instance,
a line
down under which the senses reduce
their scope, drowse, slip
into sleep,
the line moving closer and closer, even in sleep, until
it floats
dead center of one

[1954/1955]

## THE LINE

It had nearly entered my body
my only awareness the warmth
by which it was sinking, slowly, into me, that
being-included of body heat,
the steadiness of the source next to me.

When she had left, softly, tho doubtless under
the pressure of some urgency,
part of the warmth remained there
on the abandoned sheet, which
lessening of that power and my awareness of it
increased my own in such wise that
                              on the return
my warmth was greater than hers,

and the line moved again,
into undefined spaces,
near the roof,
the scope of senses and man extended to
such degree as was called for.

[1954/1955]

## THE FRIENDSHIP

Now we can wonder
how that star that

sat there
so high, so
high on the peak of the mountain

                    (follow, the seasons follow

now appears
in a cleft between hills
further down, further down

And the light appears dimmer
at least it has more red in it

Now, too, we can wonder
that the truck moving through
the town below
casts more light

(can, besides, make noises
being in that sense humanistic
i.e., a human contraption

tho
the shadows close in behind it

Starlight casts no shadows
Better not play with stars
Better the shadow dissolving,
better the human contraction

So the light appears dimmer,
so there is more red in it,
so it does not sit so high, so
cool on the peak of the mountain

It takes a man to drive the truck.
The shadows close in behind him.
And the seasons follow.

[1954/1960]


**VENUS**


This star, see,

she comes up and leaves

a track in the sea.

Whatcha gonna do, swim

down that track or

drown in the sea?

[1954/1955]

## THE GIFT AND THE ENDING

The one-half moon is over the mountain
and the star is over the sea.
         The star will go down
            into the sea.
The moon will also go down.

And the cat sits on the rock
chewing the bacon rind I have given him.

He took it from my wife's hand,
still, she may not touch him.

Later he will clean his face,
lick himself in much contentment.

         The moon will also go down.

                  [1954/1955]


## A PERMANENCE

The bear
does not go down into the sea.
He is also called the Chariot.
         There are not many things eternal.

He takes the fates of men in his paws,
strews them all over the horizon.

Seven stars swinging forever.

He strews them all over the horizon.

He is there

even in the day, when we do not see him.

He does not ever go down

never, into the sea.

[1954/1955]


## THE RETURN


That this would be his homecoming,
an almost ghostly visit.
The door and halls were familiar
against which he got his life.
His supernal wife was now superable,
                his friends strange to him.
Only his children were living   .   His life.


Walking through familiar rooms
attended by an empty chatter,
                        attended by no gracious fingers
                        attended by no graceful silence.


                        The courtyard that had known him
                        knew him again, his feet on its stones.
                        The street knew him, his   feet
                                in its dust.


But no voice answered.
The voices of children
had nothing to do with his question.
The voices of children, though living,
nagged and were separate from him.


Now he has rented a room with adjacent kitchen
                where he may work in the silence
                        and make his own pot of coffee
                                and answer his own questions

without the strangeness of familiar things
without the nagging life of children's voices.

His oldest boy tells us about it:

"It is like living in two places at once."

And he thinks it is very odd to want

to live in two places at once  .

[1954/1955]


## WNW

Rosy-fingered dawn
with her saffron cloak
spreads it over the world, and all that
but on this coast we see only sunsets.

One would have to swim a mile out into it,
the same sea,
or go in a boat
to see Himself rising over the headlands
or out of the ocean stream;
the mountains rise up from the sea-bord,
the angle of this coast.

[1954/1955]


## THE STORM

The field below dark green, solid and
dark, filling us
with a sense of the ominous.

At the horizon, a line of cumulus
with black along its belly.

       "See? There is light on the slopes!
       It is only one cloud
       darkening those fields."

"I know it is only one cloud.
But it is ominous.
Did you look at those on the horizon?"

"I looked at the horizon.

It might blow over."
       "Yes
       it might blow over."

                  [1954/1955]


**NERVE**

There are no true images anymore?
      or my own are garrulous?

      Say I had 5 lines,
I could write the tune of the church bell
from St. Sernin
as it strikes 2
I whistle the *entremeses* when alone .

I could write the sound of the train whistle
      as it heads south
      My head . this ear

will hear it always searing the winter rain, or
the 2 cats on the roof outside, the same,
singing their insults and songs . No
                2 .
                        are ever the same .


It is the fie-
                nal sow-
und
where voi—ce & claws cut
                A I R
                        I could not dare .

                                [1955/1964]


## BAÑALBUFAR, A BRAZIER, RELATIVITY, CLOUD FORMATIONS & THE KINDNESS & RELENTLESSNESS OF TIME, ALL SEEN THROUGH A WINDOW WHILE KEEPING THE FEET WARM AT THE SAME TIME AS

End of February
beginning of Lent.   How prevent
the clouds from moving now.   Where
                sunlight falls...


        The walls
keep the wind out, but the house
                cold, cold
Feet under the fold
        of the tablecover
edge toward the brazier under-
neath.   Old house.
Warmer outside, where is
        sun
                when sun is.

Sheaves of love and talk
wave at the attention.
More hot coals are added.   Loud
thanks.
Focus on direction.   Analyze.
Keep the eyes
peeled
are changing now, clouds


Southwind:
and lines of clouds walk across the mountains, straight
across the sea;   the land, the mountains at angle.
Between the cloudbanks
sun falls.
Lemon trees
outside the window under sun
making a sweet quadrangle:
parallel lines of sun straight,
trees bent
under the double weight,
wind
fruit.
How prevent
the clouds from moving, now that sun . . . . Sunlight on


pear blossom, apple blossom, the red wall,
roofs' tile, red and yellow, yellow!
lemons under sun.
The mountain   now in one
shadow, huge;
the colors in old wood, the door, sun,
dark green of pines, dark blue of rock, more

cloud, the

wing of a cloud

passes.

Alas!

*Alles, ala,* the wing, everything

goes.


No.

Always is always all ways.

No, not so.

My love says to me, —Not so.

I am humble under this wind

but stupid, and hopeful even.


"Come

into this cold room.

The smell of wildflowers is

in every corner.

The mind

is filled with flower smell and sun

even when sun is not."

[1955/1959]


**THE HOUR**


Noon-and-a-half :

waiting to eat

we have sat on the stone bench in the sun for an hour

ignoring the time

except for the time of our bodies, our

hunger . We

sit here fixed,

driven back on ourselves,

     listening,

caught in the blue silence of this wind,

  hungering for that too

     after northern winter


listening to the warm gnawing in the stomach,

  the warm wind

through the blossoms blowing .

        [1955/1966]


## THE MARGIN

Late morning on this island: cocks

enchanted with the sun

compete across the mountains,

blossoms here already in February!


Excitedly, we sit here talking

nonsense in this sunlight.

The lemon tree is heavy,

these giddy roosters also crow at noon

just to hear each other.

A few good things are left on earth

and they are not manufactured.

[1955/1960]

**RUE DU TAUR**

*for Jean Séguy*

THE MIRACLE HAS happened .

Here, after long winter, to see

this man

looking at his town,

walking thru the air of it,

tho the sun is still pale on the walls

but thru the air of spring

looking at the sun on the walls


smelling it

head high .

Not a glance at the window of the bookstore

which has taken   5   minutes of his attention

each time he has passed it

all winter .

*Toulouse, March 1955*

[1964]

## THE IDIOT

I do not stammer
but speak slowly
when I speak.

Having often nothing to say,
I say nothing.
Having often nothing to say
sometimes I talk too much.

But there are no rules :
and sometimes I am in
without great division between
intention and end.

But however I can be shrewd
I am hardly ever practical
and the matter rests unconcluded.

[1955/1960]

## VERBENA

You can have it by being in it
you can have it by dancing and drinking
you can have it by being jostled by crowds
        or standing in the street yelling
        or standing and listening quietly :
        but in words it is not possible
to have it.

        There were

                fires in all the streets!
        at every intersection, bonfires,
        noise all night in the streets
                in the parks
        carnivals
                & fireworks.

Dancing all the next afternoon
in the Plaza de San Jaime,
the bodies weaving like wheat
a whole plaza-full of movement :
and when the music rises, comes
     down harder on the beat at
the end of the *coblas*, a whole sea
leaping circling saulting bodies, the
     waves of the sea.

     Go ahead, lieutenant, photograph it.

          In the Junta del Puerto
          2 streets blocked off for dancing.
Not the delicate & precise steps of the *sardanas*
     in the Plaza, the ordered circles,
     circles within circles, here
the individual abandon of couples
the individual shyness of couples
  and the music from loudspeakers
  and boys walking off to the beach with their girls.
          Fiesta.
          Potato chips and *churros*.


          Impossible, impossible,
the life's too near the skin—now look,
  in the Junta del Puerto, fires.
They drink beer from the glass *porones*,
2 streets blocked off by dancers, the music
audible from the shore, surf juxtaposing.
          Bars
               open all nite,
          fires throughout the city.
The clack of the watchman's stick,
the formal and delicate dancing.


          In the calle de los Marineros
          a small girl in a white dress
          a small boy with a firecracker.

BARCELONA
23-24 de junio
1955

               [1967]

## PLAZA REAL WITH PALMTREES

At seven in the summer evenings

they crowd the small stone benches

back to back

five and six to a bench;

young mothers

old men

workers on their way home stopping

off, their faces

poised in the tiredness and blankness

recouping

taking the evening coolness

five and six to a bench.

Children too young to walk,

on the knees of their mothers

                make

seven and eight to a bench.


           The older ones play immies

             or chase each other

               or pigeons.

Sun catches the roofs, one side

of the arcade;

the whole of the plaza in shadow between

seven and eight of an evening.


The man with balloons

rises above it almost

his face deflated & quiet

blank

emptied of the city

as the city is emptied of air.

The strings wrapped to his hand

go up and do not move.

He stands at the edge of the square

not calling or watching at all.

The cart

with candy has food for the pigeons . . .


A lull,

a lull in the moving,

a bay in the sea of this city

into which drift

five and six to a bench

seven and eight to a bench

> Now
>
> the air moves the palmtrees,
>
> faces.
>
> All of it gentle

Barcelona . 27 . VI . 55

[1961]


## EL CAMINO VERDE

> The green road lies this way.
> I take the road of sand.

One way the sun burns hottest, no relief, the other
sun   (the same)   is filtered thru
> leaves that cast obscene
> > beautiful patterns
> on roads and walls . And

> > the wind blows all day.
Hot . sirocco, a chain
of hot wind rattles across
high over the mountains
rushes down from the peaks to the sea
laving men's bodies in the fields between
> > Days when
the serpent of wind plucks and twists the harp of the sun.

In the green road, pale
gray-green of olives, olive-wood twisted
under the burning wind, the wet
heat of an armpit,   but in the mouth

this other road. And the dry heat of the mouth is the pitiful
possibility
of finding a flower in the dust.      Sanity . See
there, the white
wing of a gull over blindness of water,
the blank black wing of a hawk over stretches of forest . Wish
to hold the mind clear in the dark honey of evening light, think
of a spring
in an orchard
in flower
the soft sun amid ruins, down there
the serpent
hidden among sweet-smelling herbs, down there
a small palm offers its leaves to the wind .
On the mountain, olive,
o, live wood,
its flawless curve hangs from the slope.


Hot . sirocco . covers everything
and everyone, all day, it blows all day as if
this were choice, as if
the earth were anything else but
what it is, a hell.   But
blind, bland, blend the flesh.
Mix the naked foot with the sand that caresses it, mix
with the rock that tears it,   enter
the hot world.

Cave of the winds .

What cave?   the

reaches of Africa

where an actual

measure

exists.

[1955/1961]


## MESTROVIĆ AND THE TREES

The wood.

You never get past the wood.


The man's feet are sunk in it.

It climbs up the back of the legs to the silent crotch.

The woman's feet are free of it,

cut clean, although

it floats about the back of both their heads,

heavy rough clouds of wood in opposite corners brooding.

Rough.

No polish of sand, the mark of the chisel,

unfinished.


Yes we are.

Our father and mother.

So these trees stand there, our

image, the god's image, stand there

naked.

And the world becomes visible.

The beginnings of things are shown.

[1955/1972]


## CITY MUSEUM, SPLIT

The national costumes were simple or complex
colorful, I suppose.
Such artifacts as bed-warmers, fanning shovels
jewelry & spindles, Okay.
the practical or delicate. The adorning

I liked only the weapons
& the musical instruments.
The principle, the demarcation
of my fascination
is use.

Creation/Death

The intentness
sunk in either process.

[1955/1965]

**THE LETTER**

> The legs being uneven
> the chair opposite wobbles by itself .

Clear air of Adriatic morning
On the bridge the captain reads it out:

|          | 49 hrs. | 14 min. | 42 sec. |
| -------- | ------- | ------- | ------- |

sextant error                02 min.     0 sec.

49  –  12  –  32,   he reads,
49  –  02  –  00

> second correction . The
horizon a perfect circle .
Ship the moving center of the circle .

> The sun is the stick, an
> absolute time .

|                    |           |
| ------------------ | --------- |
| Lat.               | 41° 34′ N |
| Long.              | 16° 58′ E |
| Declination of sun | 24° 09′   |

Say I know where you are
Now you know where I am
Time on Board (not Greenwich)
9 hrs. 24 min. 52 sec.
the 3rd of August, 1955.

> Your son and daughter-in-law send you herewith
> greetings
> and that we thought of you,
> this, your day .

And there were dolphins this morning
early, tho I did not see them
and was reading .
Freddie told me about them .

           The barometer is rising .
           The sea is anyway fair
           *and* incredibly blue
           damned incredibly blue.

Horizon is a circle
and the ship its center
All sea-rings have centers, as we know,
and all worlds are one
        in appearance :
the rest a geometrical projection of
what otherwise might be proved a hell, but is
in fact an Eden, where no tree grows
and land is beyond imagining, my mother.
          The blue
          the blue .
      This is all my news.

     Both of us are well and send our love

     All things contain themselves and pass away

      By this hand, the third day
      of August . '55,
      from the ARSIA
      in a timeless sea .

                [1965]

## THE CAPTAIN

In port, laughing & drinking
    *jocundus jovialis*
      yesterday.


    Today, horizon
holding the ship lightly
    is a girdle.
     His eyes
    are its eyes
light with residence where
    he has it all
      all of it.


        The law is the sun and stars

        The wheels turn at his bidding

        In his hand

        the voyage. And he knows it


Indifferent as the sea he walks above
his will with or against it, as
winds decide, or what god prevails.
His walk upon the bridge is its
      own ease and slope.
The movements are simple, watchful.
    No hunter / a sailor
his need for no man's love, not today.


        Economy
is one occupation of the undiluted mind.

                  [1955/1962]

## THE FIRST MATE

20 hours to midnight
        the mate's watch.

    He takes it clear of the net,
naming all the islands in the dark.
And when the islands slip behind us
        he names stars.


    Two changes of course :
he plots the third and draws, one side of the log
        painfully, a sketch of the ship :
            4 holds,
        the weight in each hold.
            Painful exactitude.
The Captain's will, the source of his extension.
        Inside his stubby body
                        He writhes against it.
                        But his love of number
                        is arabic, and tender.


His core is a brutal resentment
        already balanced.
Softness in his movement, not command,
        hardly to be commanded,
        mastered still, but
                        although he waits
                        and hates, the
balance is laughter and love


even if the laughter is mocking
even if the loving is brutal.
                        But he waits


and when the cat prowls the deck
        thin and alone,
it is he who bends to it, in a
        tenderness of recognition,
                        how
        he himself moves.

                        August 1955
                        The *Arsia*, Split-Piombino

                        [1962]

## NIGHT SONG FOR TWO MYSTICS

That man,
this man, never
            satisfied
is almost enough.
The sense, the half-sense of his
of any man's in-
            corruptible loneliness
incorrigible and terrified,
            should be enough
to cave society in
his need and ours.

What's melancholy is the most abstract.
Yet skip it back
seven centuries,
that same centrifugal leaves a sediment
whose taste is sweet

'when the light from the beloved's room comes

            t o   i l l u m i n a t e

the chamber of the lover, then
all the shadows are thrown back,
then he is filled and surfilled
with his peculiar pleasures,
the heavy thoughts, the languors.
And the lover will throw all the furniture out of the room,
everything,
that it may contain his beloved'   That he may.

            And Llull is taught what red is
'and what new vestments he shall put on,
            what his arms are for
            and what they shall embrace,
and how to lower his head to give the kiss'
            which is good training for a lover.
            But the beloved remains forever
far enough removed
and in a high place
as to be easily seen from a distance.
Which pride is unforgivable.

So you see where we stand, where you stood, Yeats?
And must it always lead to gods?
The man's shadow dissolves in shadows.
Most men go down to obliteration
with the homeliest of remembrances.

       (pride, avarice, lust, anger
       gluttony, envy & sloth

       What are the positive virtues
which come between a man and his world,
estrange his friends, seduce his wife,
emasculate his god and general manager in charge of
blow his earth up?

       (down, sailor,
       blow the man

    c o i l e d  d o w n  t h e r e

in the dark pools of the mind , their time

they wait the violent lunatic wind
           at the star's dimming.


Dust, Yeats, all dust,
tho Llull remain a lover.

                     [1955/1958]


## HOW TO GET THROUGH REALITY


The long low hills humped back against the night
filled with stars
Grey bursting nite-sprays of olive, miles of orchard
near the track

                    Andromeda !

          Orion !

The Car !


grey blossoms of olive trees
         the long hills

Those who work us, with         stones

who create us from our stone, who live

       among    stones    here

       the rest pass through

Our beauty under glass is your reality, unreachable

       sliding our gift to you


            Darkness

      pass through


Beauty is the daily renewal in the eyes of


Bursting sprays of olive

   the long hills

and behind them, stars


      Stones,

          staowns!


One could kick the glass out, no?

        No.

     Pass through.

                [1955/1961]

                    where sleep goes
                        over from


                        to where the light rises, comes
                    up


        terrace above terrace


                    rank upon rank
                                small

                                    rise


                                            greens
                                The grays &



                                of olive trees
    higher even than the almonds, the twists
                                        terraces
                    the village, & higher, more


            terraces


    THE SEA


    STRUCTURAL /

                                        [1955?/1961]

## RAMAS, DIVENDRES, DIUMENGA

Before the cathedral, the plaza
is a forest
                    tall fronds
The trunks are people in bright clothing
the plaza in bright sunlight
the yellow palm leaves waving

        young forest on a brilliant breeze
        in the bright air of heaven.

                    At no signal
            the trees face the church
        and stamp with the butt of the fronds
                        muffled sounds
                but in unison.    Aediles
        demanding for the whole people,    a benison
                        which is given.

Afterwards,
the children carry them mostly,
slowly through the streets of the city,
walking home from the mass.

"Mine is taller'n yours!"

—*El mío es mas alto qu'el tuyo!*

—*No es verdad!  Mira!  Mira!*


Whipped to competition, the palms wave unconcernedly

in the bright air

in the shadows.


Pigeons walk in the sunlight.

The people feed them.


o   o   o


Death day by the sea without crosses.   The beach

stretches its cold sands under

a dirty sky full of scud.   The wind

chill.

No trees, nothing to break it.

All the tears have fallen already into the sea.

Even the sourness of salt on the air is galling,

the surf   dull and lifeless   but continuing.


Clouds darken on the horizon at three o'clock.

The wind picks up.


o   o   o   o   o

The ark of the tabernacles

is drawn up by two white bullocks

with olive-branch tied to their horns.


They stand white and imperturbable

among the fireworks.

Barcelona . Sète . Firenze
Holy Week . 1956

[1959]

## LOVE IN THE SOUTH   OR   THE MOVIES


Beauty is a promise of happiness
which is why we take pleasure in it
why we ache when we cannot possess it


What we have of it is on account
the ache
the pleasure

Once we possess it, it
comes as near to us as at noon
feeling the heat alone rising,
a man's shadow comes,

so close that we do not see it. What's


the good of a *mystique* like that?   Yet
' How miserable I am! ' and
' How beautiful the world is! '
are   2   cries
that arise from the same place

[1956/1958]

## SONG FOR A COOL DEPARTURE

When the track rises
the wires sink to the fields

Trees absorb them in and blot them out
black running
pencil-lines against the fields' green

Shrubbery close to the track goes by so
fast it hurts the eyes

Rain has quit
We have arrived
at Salut or Castelnaudary


A woman laughs harshly in the corridor
The soldiers on either side sleep beautifully
peacefully, one with his mouth open, the
other has his closed
The world is certainly diverse!
Wires begin again to
fall and rise
Small fruit trees stand in quadrangles
in a field otherwise planted
The brook tries to escape notice and where
shall I put 2
cypresses,
3 elms?


Old woman in the corner
wrestles her rented pillows and cannot sleep
One finally arranges itself
under her right arm, the other
entirely out of control, she clutches
on her lap, the comfortable weight,
her rented buffers against a hard world
and stares direct in front of her and cannot sleep


My wife holds her face up for a kiss
Brow puckered and tired, she also cannot quite
sleep,
worrying about a pair of sunglasses we
left at someone's house yesterday
in the round of farewells.

Having left that town
we have left nothing behind.

The world is surely diverse enough
and if the information is sound, one
could ride forever and never fall off
     let others sleep—
I am so wide-awake I want to sing, while
the wheels turn, the windows clatter, the door
     jogs, the wires
rise and change and fall
and the green grass grows all round, all round
and the green grass grows all round.........

[1956/1957]


## FINGERS, FEET, & KNEES  OR FOLKDANCING :
## A VERY INFORMAL STUDY


Banquet downstairs, on the phono-

graph, *cante jondo* . The

guitar breaks upon almost-speech

     flows up-


     hill . stops

pounces on a chord

pulses . break-

breaks out . starts

a melody again


And the children dance in the courtyard to each other

Sound of heels on pavement, hands clap-clap, one

     girl

howls words so marvelously elongated, broke-inflected

they're incomprehensible

The next record is a *sardanas*
The kids dance that one too
The hard excited tap – clap
is replaced by pad . shuffle, LEAP
the melody they hum, the dance they
dance with one another

> (Furthermore,
> whatever it is about scrubbing floors
> makes Spanish maids sing while doing it, I
> personally, am grateful . . . )

> > (Barcelona,
> > 1955

> > [1956/1962]

## MYTH, NO MYTH

The head of Eurystheus singing

or Orpheus's, equally detached

and floating down to the sea

and then across it singing

> singing!

is a very attractive image

today,    to a poet,

who often sings his sweetest

detached from the facts of his life

and to no one.

> [1956/1960]

## THE PROBLEM

My wife broke a dollar-tube of perfume


The arab

who owns the perfume shop insisted

    it was good luck


           Sure it was .

To break any vessel is, if we know

the appropriate formula to make it sacrifice

and know a god

to dedicate it to .

                [1956/1960]


## SIGNALS I. : TANGER, AUGUST 1956

1.      Even in Algeciras
        that cesspool :


when the wind came up suddenly
               on a hot afternoon,
a half-dozen people on that corner
scrambled
       to pick up
           gently
the empty cones of the ice-cream vendor
the gust had scattered   .

2.

Tonite,

after   10   minutes watching

and listening to early roosters

a dog joining in from the street

                a lonesome ass

screaming from the market

for company

or food

            one

                        burst toward the Spanish coast

                        It was orange

[1956/1959]


## SONG OF THE WIRES

            Wires in the countryside are never still :
            between each pole they rise, dreaming upward
            till each pole breaks their dream
            and snaps them rudely back again to earth.
                        Rise and fall.
                        Rise, snap down and rise dreaming
            against the early sky   patterns of wires
            change their spatial relationships
            parallel shifting lines streaming
            crossing down the sky contract and open


Riding french trains

even italian trains,

you notice the wires beside the track

                rise and fall.

            In Spain

            if things are dull

you talk with people in the compartment.


            If the landscape is anything

            you cannot take your eyes off it.

Here are    3    mules threshing wheat
by running around in a circle
                            dragging a sledge


There are    7    men asleep
under the tree at a station
                            where we do not stop


There are adelfas blooming
wherever there is water,
following the lines of water
                            their fall of red


There is the head of a goat
showing above the embankment;
in his eye a devil
                            or some god

                    There is always something
to touch or feel or smell or see or people, you


never notice the wires.

[1956/1960]


## ALAMÉDA


          Monday morning early
          Sunday evening late


A tram goes by, outbound
taking the late drinkers
the restless moviegoers
or the blossoms of girls with their escorts
home
          sleep


The conductor on the final run
standing there in his slippers
                    facing the track

The ladies sit at café tables in twos
An old man sits
    reading at a table alone

    the new day's news
letting his beer get warm
letting the sky be enough

                    Winter 1956-57
                    Málaga

          [September 1956/1960]


## THE NEEDLE

    Two blocks away
        night traffic goes whipping through
the avenue,
the fast motors.

It's not as tho one could see it
It's not as tho nothing were good

Even above the rooftops stars are mixed with cloud
        only the brightest come through:
the absolute bureaucracy of size and closeness
        which coefficient is power.

    But the cat
crosses the tiled roof at this hour
        in the dark night
        in the moon.

                Málaga, Sept. 1956

                    [1960]

## MOSCA

A fly

sits &

scrubs his front feet,

then rubs his back feet together

cleaning them, then

washes his wings and his eye    .    Why

do people call flies dirty?


It looks like a pleasant process .


Self-absorbed & self-contained,

directed, especially in flight,

certainly curious and active—

W h y   i s   b u z z i n g   c o n s i d e r e d   i d l e ?

[1956/1963]


## SUERTE

You shall not always sit in sunlight watching

weeds grow out of the drainpipes

or burros and shadows of burros

come up the street bringing sand

the first one of the line with a

bell

always.

    With a bell.

    Grace is set

        a term of less than a year.

Another bell sounds the hours of your sun

    limits

        sounding below human voices,

counts the hours of weeds, rain, darkness, all

    with a bell.

The first one with a bell always.

                        [1956/1957]


## THE OPEN ROAD

Housewives walk in the street
carrying two milk pitchers
pouring what passion is given
them, from one into the other

        The wall is black from old fires.
        But the sky is blue, isn't it?

The crab gropes the sea bottom .
slow six-legs, two front ones alert .
on shore two dogs in the sand sing
to a moon that drips water or blood.

And the wall is black from old fires.
But sky is blue, isn't it?


Hands and heads scatter the lawn :
there a foot, here a whitened bone.
And tho he carry a scythe
Death is a figure of fun.


Wall's black from old fires .
isn't the sky blue, isn't it?


The joglar carries a sack
and a stick to beat off the dogs.
But the dog tears a hole in his pants
and one white buttock sticks out.

The sky IS blue, isn't it?
Yes.   But the fires, this wall.

[1956/1959]


## PAISÁJE

*for Lorca*

The mule walks on the sand
the man sits on the mule
The man's head sits on his shoulders
    In his head
        his eyes
           look out

Five men are hauling a net
Gulls stroll at the surf's edge
       the boats
       on the sea
He looks between his mule's ears
at driftwood
at the birds
at sunglare
on the sea
off where day comes up

The mule leaves tracks on the sand
The man sits on the mule
His thoughts enter the air
His hands rest on his thighs
*His eyes*
       *leave tracks on the wind*

                        [1956/1960]


**WHEE!**


A goat lies in the grass beside

     a dry irrigation ditch


     Sun-glitter on sea
The boats drift in with the tide


Grazing cattle shy away

their long horns down & waving

In the hills the earth is red

What a day!


Along the road, a gypsy

raises her water gourd

in a fine

gesture to the passing bus


*"QUIERES?"*

*"PROVECHE!"*

Nov 1956
Málaga-Algeciras

[1960]


## THE LOTTERY


*Que buen*
*números me quedan!*


*Mañana*
luck is
always for tomorrow
or tonight, when
the lottery is drawn


The horse-drawn carriage rattles
and clatters down the street
The horse's bells jingle
on the embroidered harness
The driver sits alert and wears
a hat
That is part of it


No one pays attention
The man will pay the driver

The cobbles will stay in the street
      but luck is felt
in the small dark stores, the doorways
as the sound of bells and hoofs
on cobbles


Travelers are good luck
here
they cry   *"maleta! maleta!"*
and run and touch the suitcase
      for luck

" Nail
those long shadows to my cross ! "
darkened doorways in sun-glare
a hammer
        Silence of black skirts
        unbelted
In the shadowed eyes
an ultimate patience
Death lives among the people
      as Life does

Luck never
Luck is for people in carriages
      for voyagers

*Que buen números me quedan*


      *para*  H O Y !
   *último par* '  H O Y !

[1956/1958]

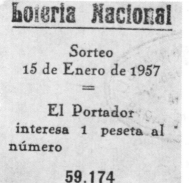

## MÁLAGA

Warm autumn night, light
   cloud, a few stars
Two young men run down the street
The sound of heels is normal
   like fiesta   almost

Pushcart on the corner
stopped roasting chestnuts early
    tonight   no one buying
Street conversations lasted
till long after midnight   Something
   going forever gone and again
      renewed

       Even the quiet man next door
       came home drunk and whistling

Sound of bicycle bells
& starting motor bikes
intermittent

    Finally
      the neighborhood
flickers and goes out   The
street lamp on the corner is
sentinel over the darkness

I have drunk my white wine and worked
I have lasted it out into silence

Smoke a cigarette on the balcony
Fine.    Light cloud, a few stars,
        and the silence
World wheels its night and is warm
        and empty
Everything in this underworld is asleep
        or broken
A great white dog of silence lounges
   alone there in the street
   ranges curb to final curb
                lies down under the street lamp
     attentive
     silent

                Then a motor bike starts up
                and a bicycle bell rings

                      [1956/1960]


## LIGHT

White flare of stone in the sun
Day's begun    The sea
flickers the light back pleasantly


Last flare of red on white wall
Sun fall    into the sea
Night thickens gradually

Day's done       Stars come out

My thought       drifts like the sea

No grip between it and my act

I lose my luck too quickly


Cold      flare on the sea

Moon has come over the hill

Still no act by which I can

say there's been a man

in the house all day


Star on sea leaves a track

Act is something one does if

one thinks of it       And the cliff

falls away up       back of me

as the sea flashes up in the night

to touch and darken my sea

[1956/1958]


## INSTRUCTIONS TO A NEW TENANT

Two small cats were their PHARMAKOI,
they objected to the smell in the house.

Now they go. We are rid of them.
What have we as purification?

Convention's a pit, a noose.
Let us return to tradition
to rid us of further contagion.

      The winnowing fan's out of date.
      One can still find incense and
            a censer.

Go to a church and borrow them—
say to the holy father you've
a friend whose house is polluted
and who wants to be rid of it.

      Evil is actual
        physical
      and contagious
        as luck is

I do not blame you for staying clear yourself,
tho a gesture of defiance
might have dispersed it—

        that time is gone.
        Now you keep it for us.

      Before you move in, purge it.
      Use an Arabian incense.
      Rid us all of the ἄγος

      And if he comes to the door
      beat him with leeks and branches
        seven times.

That is an old Athenian trick
to keep the city from harm.

[1956/1965]


## CAFÉ AT NIGHT


White snow of paper sugar
wrappers on the floor
next the counter.
2   men stand over their wine
                    (white)


The men are white
The wine is white
                    Two
women come in, they order hot


milk . Everything is still white
                    (white)


Finally someone orders a cake
                    I pluck
        courage up
        and order
                    black
                    coffee
                            (black)

Málaga, Winter 1956-57

[1961]


## AFFINITIES II.


                Why do gulls like
                to sit in the sea
                only when there are waves, when there
                            is ground swell?

> And never will
> when it is smooth?
> Must be they take pleasure from
> the motion of wave
> as I do,
> the lift and ride and rise, the swing
> down the trough, climbing
> effortlessly
> the next crest.


Best to sit in the sun afterward, tho,
on rock,
watching the rollers break, spill-
slide up the beach,
letting spray fall back its jet
upon wet rocks, brown legs, the next
against the sun.
We never learn
to distrust such motion, Carroll.


I recall your long legs
tumbling in such a sea
at Bañalbufar that summer,
white
body reddening
taking its first day's sun
with brown face set on top with already
thinning hair.
Caring, steadily caring, for ideas alone
had not kept you from trying to rise
to your feet, smiling against such a sea,
the surf cracking you back to a sitting
posture against the stone
beach, the sea sliding around you
no god to help you, only your stalk-
white, reddening legs
could lift you timed in the face of it.
No god there that afternoon, Carroll,
only our powers, not yours, our demons
sea  .  sun  .  wind-squall
among us found a balance.
It was your own.

This winter sun
streams across my legs and chest, flashes
across the crashing surf-line.
A fisherman comes down with a heavy line and
drags it out its length along the beach,
heaving
each portion out
into the surf
until it's a snake part in, part out of water.
He washes, not too carefully
the oil slick off it . Long rope
it takes him a long time . He finishes finally
and sticking to rock
avoiding the sand he
hauls it again to the top of the sea-
wall and coils his rope
to dry in the sun,
slows his coiling to talk to a friend
gives the line a last turn
the work done.


When will we learn
so naturally to
quit, when what we have to do
is done?
Or that the print of rough stone,
rock
set deep in the flesh of the palm,
my own or yours,
see what we will in reading it, patterned
palms . pyramids . cuneiform
tablets, a cross, some
small starched waves or winging gulls, the shell,
the flower
we see or think we see . there
no matter
we trust and fear
this movement, that god,
will disappear
inside this quarter-hour?

Málaga, Winter 1956-57

[1963]

**SIRVENTES**

*Un sirventes ai fach*
*Contra'l ciutat de Tolosa*
*On m'avia pretz ostalatge*
*D'un sen salvatge e famosa*
*Del mons...*

PB / 1956

I have made a sirventes against the city of Toulouse
           and it cost me plenty garlic :
and if I have a brother, say, or a cousin, or a 2nd cousin,
I'll tell him to stay out too.
           As for me, Henri,

           I'd rather be in España
           pegging pernod thru a pajita
           or yagrelling a luk
           jedamput en Jugoslavije,
           jowels wide & yowels not
           permitted to emerge——
           or even
           in emergency
           slopping slivovitsa thru
           the brlog in the luk.
           I mean I'm not particular,
           but to be
           in the Midi

           now that rain is here,
           to be sitting in Toulouse
              for another year,
           the slop tapping in the court
           to stop typing just at ten
            and the wet-rot setting in
           and the price is always plus,
             I mean, please,
                must I?

Whole damn year teaching
trifles to these trout with trousers
tramping thru the damp
with gout up to my gut
taking all the guff, sweet
                jesus crypt,
                god of the he
brews, she blows, it bawls, & Boses
(by doze is stuffed)
by the balls of the livid saviour, lead be
back hindu eegypt-la-aad
before I'b canned for indisciblidnary reasons.


                O god.
                The hallowed halls
                the ivy covered walls
                the fishwife calls
                & the rain falls

                Bastal!


Jove, god of tourists, the whores in Barcelona are beautiful,
you would understand.
Weren't there Europa and Io? and Aegina, twin sister of Thebe
both daughters of Asopus?
and Maia and Antiope and
Niobe of the Thebans.
Eagle, ant, bull, beaver, flame, otter, how *not?*
Remember Leda?
I swan, you never felt old.
Your shower of rain at least was a shower of gold.
A gentle white bull with dewlaps.
The bulls in Barcelona are beautiful, Jove,
need no persuasion, are themselves as brave.


My old Guillem, who once stole this town,
thinking your wife's name enuf reason to . . .

St. Julian, patron of travellers, *mi des mercey* !

Who else invoke? Who else to save
a damned poet impaled by a *betterave?*
Mercury! Post of Heaven, you old thief, deliver me
from this ravel-streeted, louse-ridden, down-river-
gutter-sniping, rent-gouging, hard-hearted,
complacent provincial town,
where they have forgotten all that made this country the
belly of courage, the body of beauty, the hands of heresy,
the legs of the individual spirit, the heart of song!


That mad Vidal would spit on it,
that I as his maddened double
do —— too
changed, too changed, o
deranged master of song,
master of the viol and the lute
master of those sounds,
I join you in public madness,
in the street I piss
on French politesse
that has wracked all passion from the sound of speech.
A leech that sucks the blood is less a lesion. Speech!
this imposed imposing imported courtliness,    that
the more you hear it the more it's meaningless
& without feeling.


The peel is off the grape
and there's not much left
and what is left is soured
if clean :
if I go off my beam, some
small vengeance would be sweet,
something definite and neat,
say total destruction.


Jove, father, cast your bolts
& down these bourgeois dolts !


Raise a wave, a glaive of light, Poseidon,
inundate this fish-bait !

Hermes, keep my song
from the dull rhythms of rain.


Apollo, hurl your darts,
cleanse these abysmal farts
out from this dripping cave
in the name of Love.

[1957/1959]


**AFFINITIES I.**


Montalban, N° 3, piso 2°
             is not exactly a pension
but a lady who rents rooms
             occasionally.

             And this big room has a small sink
             with a tap where
             no water has ever run:
                         and a drain
             in which one sets a cork.
             And on the brass plate is written

                 VERDAGUER        BARCELONA

that half-mad priest and poet
who listed all the peaks
in the catalunyan Pyrenees,
and here you are on a sink-drain.
Has it come to this, Jacint?


     Also,
there are two balconies looking out
over the roofs of the city
             to the mountains.
And the lady, when she was younger,
             lived in Granada
and remembers that García Lorca
always wore broad-brimmed Córdoban hats
          and a black string-tie, and was
              *un chico simpático.*

         So
it is not very strange
that the words are always there
when one looks out of the window
over the roofs of the city


     "and to see clouds and mountains
     in the motionless distances
     the heart twists in itself"


                    "y al mirar nubes y montes
                    en las yertas lejanías
                    se quiebra su corazón
                    de azúcar y yerbaluisa"


                              [1957/1967]



**SPRING THING**


                    Tomorrow Ramas
                    & the moon will
                    come to full
Tonite at 9:25
she had just come over the mountain . a few
light clouds pass quickly over her
the shadow along the bottom
                    brilliant
                    between  2   planets
                    one
                    golden,
                    one red


The stone steps down to town washed
                    in her light, the
ribbon of road curving out far below, white
                    white .
A red cat darts by on the steps,   light
          cloud over the sea, sea
          patched with shadows
          & sewn with a glitter of moon


At the last minute
I will not pass back of the church
where there is a cross in stone,
tho it is not tonite that the moon is full

Meaning
to avoid it by the middle stair
I fart all the way down the steps, absent
mindedly
& find myself directly in front of it . I
have forgotten how the town is built
under the pale brightness of moon . Two

women come by in black veils
both hands held palm upward
carrying rosaries, probably

                 I see that their hands are empty.   The
                 moon does not reach into this street
                 I offer goodnite
                 & take two back
                 & hurry on

Both trucks have arrived
One can tell by the empty baskets piled by the wall
means the cigarettes have come in, the first in a week
one is jubilant to have calculated the hour . The
       men in the café
which is grocery and tobacco-store both, sit
         and smoke over their coñacs
         and show no undue emotion .
I give one goodnite and get twenty

       Climbing again
              more slowly
          enjoying the smoke, the
            moon is everywhere;
     over a terrace of fruit trees first
     then over the pines higher up, then
     over houses on the first transversal
As I turn the last terrace to the house, she sits
over a great cactus clump
light clouds, a few stars
           A yellow cat darts by on the steps

In the kitchen my wife
has left me a small fire
The power plant has gone off for the night
      I have some candles to write by
      I forget what the argument was
              about . still

goofy with moonlight I
pick up pen and write

S L U T  O F  A  P O E T
        and
F O O L  and
flower-crowned, season-driven, white samovar of corruption
            from which sweetness
                & also


            f u c k      h e r !

I forget what the argument was about . Carefully
I feed the coals some dried sticks, blaze warms my hands & feet
the
bamboo blowpipe is yellow . the hot coals are red


And outside
the moon sits over the cactus clump

In an hour the day will be Ramas
and the moon full .

                the inversion .

                                    [1957/1965]


THE MISUNDERSTANDING


Morning sun clear on the mountain
            milky to seaward;
light cloud on the sea,
        where the boats ride, a *niebla*.
        Sun burning it off.
Light breeze from seaward.


From the far boats it looks as if
the cloud were over the island;
the blue mountains look milky.
        Sun burning it off

*l u m i n i s   c l a r i t a s*

The day will resolve as crystal.
Light refracted through drops of perspiration
on a man's forehead
as he lifts his head from work
to speak.

[1957/1961]


## THE BUSRIDE

The   26   kilometers

between the city and this village

used to take an hour-and-a-half.


The new driver

a young man

from Estallenchs

makes the same trip in an hour.

The old man's been

relegated down to ticket-taker.


1   hour

Neither rain nor fog nor low-lying cloud on those mountains etc.


1   hour

But the new man crosses himself

like any woman before starting,

a big cross,

wide    slow    and sure.

And despite the breakneck weight

of his big foot on the accelerator

his passengers ride

confident and relaxed.

[1957/1969]


## FISHERMAN

The moon-bitch lies in the morning sky
over the tower face-down
and asleep.
Light wind comes off the sea and cools my behind
as I come up the mountain with fish,
while her bronze lover
blinds me from the opposite sky, her
fat, red-faced daddy-boy
watching her sleep in the dawn.


Performing a daily task
this climbing up, I
am caught in the poles of the world
entangled as if I were fish
and they held my nets between them.
My feet are slow on the steps.

Last night I dreamed that the moon
            stood on either side of me
and the sun lay cracked and broken
                   under the world
like an old axle-wheel.  But there he is
            beaming like a fat idiot
while that pale bitch sleeps on one arm
face down.

This evening, climbing these steps,
he will sit in the opposite sky and warm my can
            which is more to my liking.
Flesh mends and grows firm in the sun.
That other was a malignant dream only
    and a strange heaven.

[1957/1959]

## CANCIÓN DE LAS HORMIGAS

Today makes   20   days

that some ants follow the same route

        across   2   of these steps

       never varying from the line.

Always this same line of ants

across the same   2   steps .

They may even be the same ants,

tho this would make a difference :

if the line budged one centimeter

        it would make a difference.

And I do not know what the job is

or when it will be finished.

[1957/1958]

L'écrivain est alors celui qui écrit pour pouvoir mourir, et il est celui qui tient son pouvoir d'écrire d'une relation anticipée avec la mort.

Le secret doit être brisé.
L'obscur doit entrer dans
le jour et se faire jour.
Ce qui ne peut pas se dire
doit pourtant s'entendre

## ANSWER TO TWO INSCRIPTIONS

*Quidquid latet apparebit.*
Tout ce qui est caché
c'est cela qui doit appa-
râitre, et non pas dans

But the poet is he who writes

l'anxiété d'une conscience
coupable, mais dans l'in-
souciance d'une bouche
heureuse.

to be able to move .

He has his power to make
winds blow or sun come out
from his anticipated reality, his
                    relation with movement.


Death guilt and anxiety
have nothing to do with it.
And if they are the movers
the bell isn't ringing right.

             Hear wind .  See sun
             Stop there if you can


OKay, the secrets of the light
and of the dark
should be laid out clearly and
delineated . What's
hidden in the heart laid open
with a laughing mouth and
       open,   OPEN!

             Stop there
             if you can

THE OBSCURE SHOULD ENTER THE DAYLIGHT
AND CREATE LIGHT
THERE   .   But

stop there
if you can

[1957/1960]

## HOW TO SUBLET AN APARTMENT TO FRIENDS

' Que los cobre '   me han dicho

But the earth is so full
the night so full of stars
neither time, thought, nor inclination, Miranda.

But the words burned a second time, consumed
                        the manuscript

' —such people in it '

        Friends may forsake me
                        sonnyboy,
but a flight of small green birds
from the irrigation-sluice where they were bathing
in the morning freshness,
bursts at my left hand
                        as one sound
into the wild blue yonder of a
                        fig tree

which I don't care a
whether there are or not
grey skies
this fine cool morning,
    I know your worth, sonnyboy.

[1957/1964]


## AT THE CROSSROAD

   Close
  but far

strayed into the half-cultivated country
    of meditation
woven into it wholly
enlaced in the rare herbs of silence

another,
a lost stranger, our friend
asleep, perhaps nearly dead

Nite-stir of silence
Water runs beyond summer its gutters
    Rustle of wind, light
    Moonlight over it all

In the next field
the May ass screaming
drunk on the new hay

[1957/1958]

## DEPTH PERCEPTIONS

Man's hand touches the strings of his guitar
and the melody that emerges hammers
delicately
into this mound of night

> Oblong of brightness stands
> isolated in the mountain in
> a flat blackness
> without distances
> Someone has left a door open
> where there is no house

Truck labors up mountain
Crickets          night bird

>          Birdsong
> knifes the night open
> 'Mound of night
> Tree of stars'
> Guitar hammers       will
lay all of it wide open—
fruit of tree and flower of tree
     burst with the seed
          of song!

>          Wrong.
The *guardia* turns up his radio and
it flattens, blares flat this rounded


>     world of night

                                        [1957/1960]



## ATARDECER

The waves come in from the north

>               but softly

after   2   days of storm.
The wind comes in from the west

>               but gently

cross-hatching the pattern

Further out

strips and circles

where the wind makes it otherwise

South to north in the strips

Dead

calm in the circles

Magic circles

that no wind

touches


Woman comes up the hill

but slowly

after    12    hours of work

after    2    hours of *camino* :

rising before the light

returning at sundown

She is over    60    years old, she don't

stop to admire the sunset

Bandana is tight on the forehead

Her stick is slow on the steps

[1957/1961]


"Things are different when you come           **LA**
across them again; they seem to have
increased power to enter one's soul           **VIEILLE**
more sadly, deeper still, more soft-
ly than before, melting into that             **BELLE**
sort of death that is gently accum-
ulating inside one, day by day, un-
derhandedly, each day making you
defend yourself a little less than
the day before."
                —Louis-Ferdinand Céline—

✳✳✳✳✳✳✳✳✳✳✳✳✳✳✳✳✳✳✳✳✳✳✳✳✳✳✳✳✳✳✳✳✳✳✳✳✳✳✳✳✳✳✳✳✳✳✳✳✳✳✳✳✳✳✳✳✳✳✳✳✳✳

After many times,
and never having liked the town,
Paris is softer this time.

The 1st reservation indecently cancelled on us,
a fight with the *concierges* in a second hotel,
   we are now peacefully settled
   in the Place Dauphine en l'Isle,
   *au plein con de Paris.*

The sex of Paris.
40 trees in this square
opposite the very white Palais
  de Justice
   *que n'existe pas.* But

soft . . . but then,
we have seen it softer when it was an indifference.
    One can
understand the aura of a woman—without contact, not
    falling in love
but now? September? Rain? o christ, Paris

     *tout à fait normal.*

Window left open all afternoon
and a dozen leaves drifted in
*feuilles des marroniers*
   *dans cette place 40.*
How the wind lifts them up!
   Indifferent. Wet leaves.


   Our string of peppers hangs by the window.
   The owner has a southern accent. Good
   coffee in the tabac
   on the corner,
   with buttered bread for the mornings.


      In passage
   Paris is softer this time
   —or we are, for once,
   altho *la misère existe*
   altho *elle est partout*
   for once it is Rome, New York, Athens, Madrid, and
   like them, unique, herself, not *just* capital. The


     one man I know who loved her
      is gone

*Et puis, maintenant,*
*c'est déjà l'automne...*

*on a des choses,*
*on a tellement des choses . Et maintenant,*
       *la Paris,*
       *cette vielle belle,*
*c'est à nous.*

*Les feuilles mortes* drift in at the window.

*C'est à nous,*

*c'est à nous.*

[1957/1967]


## THE ENCOUNTER

Staggering down the road at midnite
home from the bar, the

mexican Bandit stood facing me, about
to improve his standard of living

Two
fingers handled the moustache gently,
the other hand fingered the pistol. My asshole

dropped out/
and crawled all the way back to El Paso

[1957/1960]

# THE YAWN

The black-haired girl

with the big

     brown

          eyes

on the Queens train coming

       in to work, so

opens her mouth so beautifully

     wide

          in a ya-aawn, that

two stops after she has left the train

I have only to think of her   and I

             o-oh-aaaww-hm

           wow !

[1957-8/1958]


# DEATH WATCH : VIEILLE D'HIVER

Intravenous is a lousy replacement
for a plate of baked ham and potatoes.


With the mercury below 0
you check the thermometer each time you leave the house
and report the new figure back
as tho it were vital statistic.
It is hard to know what is best.

So the man lies there in that white bed,
       groaning sometimes,
breathing loudly against his hour, restless
against his inaction, tossing
unconscious, but that is no rest.

      Luckily, the perfection
      of the unbroken shapes of the world
      under the new snowfall
      after the mercury rose,
      gives us no hope at all
      luckily for us.

          [1958/1961]

## EL DÍA VIENE COMO UNA PROMESA DE CALOR

      White clean sun in this dry street
      from the white walls of white houses

Light of a half-cool morning with that dull
edge of heat
threatening us
with noon
        Our own hot swelter    But

for this one hour the sun cuts without
      glare, cleanly

Hoofs falter on the cobbles, goats
distracted by a tuft of grass between the low cobbles
quickened by the whirr of a switch in a boy's hand
on the inclined slope clatter    A shout

              The blue
of a slim    shimmering    boat-sustaining
                  sea
          Its slack sails

Close our eyes under these leaves
Breathe sweetly as tho we were wind
   moving these leaves
        black
beauty of such heat behind the eyes
      The leaves
      move by themselves


   and cease


Each one his own hand
the cooled wine in the glass
touch lips of glass in the shadow


O C Y C L A D E S !

       OKay .
       Say another summer never come,
       this would be enuf to die within .
       a season where we wear our only skin
       and beauty is what we daily are
          in the presence of

            [1958/1963]


## LOVE SONG


Beauty is a promise of happiness
wa-hoo.
And happiness is a big, fat-assed
stuffed bird
that cannot, in its ideal state, move
off its fat


i.e., I am not Ariel,
I am Caliban,
and sometimes it is very ugly.

            [1958/1961]

## PROTEST MEETING

Because the host displayed a decidedly cool
    and unaffectionate attitude
        to his negro mistress
           however importunate
    another young woman, apparently
to demonstrate her disapproval, squatted and
        peed on his floor;
which however, only indicated the rather
        too complacent latitude
    awarded her by her own husband in
        place of love

[1958?/1959]


## EVENTIDE

white arms

beside the Shalimar

my ass

two breasts

four legs


other entries

[1958/1958]

**SIGNALS III.**

Spring, being what it is this year,

    and it has been cold up to now

    and the heat later will be, my

    god, how shall we stand it?

but after that storm Sunday, we

have acquired several slug-

    gish flies.    I

am very tender with them.

                     [1958/1958]


**GOOD MORNING, LOVE!**

Rise at 7:15

study the

artifacts

    (2 books
    1 photo
    1 gouache sketch
    2 unclean socks

perform the neces-

sary ablutions

    hands
    face, feet
    crotch

even answer the door

with good grace, even

if it's the light-and-gas man

announcing himself as " E D I S O N !

Readjer meter, mister?"

For Chrissake yes

    read my meter

    Nothing can alter the euphoria

The blister is still on one finger

    There just are

some mornings worth getting up

& making a cup

of coffee,

      that's all

                    [1958/1958]

## INVITATION STANDING

BRING a leaf to me

just a leaf just a

spring leaf, an

april leaf

just

    come

Blue sky

never mind

Spring rain

never mind

Reach up and

take a leaf and

    come

just come

               [1958/1966]


## HOMAGE TO THE SPIRIT


T H E   M O O N   is my beloved
and I am Hercules
        holding it all

circle .   circle .   circle

Here, plant trees
in the proper
        (time
circle


There are   (there will be)   figs,
pomegranates, vines, the
        milk & the
honey—he said
& we shall come to judge the quick
      & the dead .   or

"move on the face of the waters"
that's for sure—
he said,
who is your comforter

[1958/1960]


## BK. OF NUMBERS

My heart is 3 . 7 . 9

3 orifices
7 mountains
9 seas

You
build these 3. 7. 9.   down into me

into 1

and dance and swell in my mind
and dance and swell. . . .

[1958/1961]


## COUPLETS

To be a spot-headed cat on a forked tree
is to be inversely what my baby is to me

I know the names of the stars from north to south
a gifted hunter with a warm song in the mouth

A february rabbit is what I hunt in may
A word in this book is closer than the sea

Women are vowels     I hear the crashing wave
" I am the queen and hope of every hive "

it could kill you

[1958/1961]


## VENUS, THE LARK FLIES SINGING UP
## BLUE SMOKE   BLUE GULL   THE
## YEAR HAS COME FULL CIRCLE


SUMMER had 5 . leafy center of the year

Winter was the three-headed bitch of Death
      Queen of the hive
      tomb of every hope

Clear is the color of wind, but it
      turns mad in March like any hare
      brained poet or golden thing
      13 snipe on the sand beach
      Wind blows off the cold sea
      racing wild over foaming water

Death is twice on the ear-finger
      Tree of Ross on the eve of the winter solstice
      Here is the king's coffin and his cradle
      The wheel
      of existence has come full circle

The fire-garnet of Judah, terrible crystal
    Saturday's child is a lonesome gull
    crying over quiet waters
    where the fish do not come
    An alder-whistle will call the wind

Elder December's tree, also for hanging
    and the power of witches
    Its flowers are best at midsummer
    at which time also, Death is . Maera . Deino
    The 13th month begins one day
    after my birth
    Rook cries for the year that dies
    Blood red
    are the ragged leaves of the elder

Autumn goddess of rut and combat
    the stags' horns' clash sounds on the wind

The oak door looks forward and backward, outward and inward
    St. John is the day of our burning
    Verbena is the odor of our burning . sweet
    smell of scorched flesh . holocausts
    in all the streets . fires
    at all the crossroads . Death
    at midsummer, making
    magic at the top of hills
    surrounding the city
    Burned stumps of trees in the shovel .   The king
    is dead! Long live the king!
    burnt

Gayety? O yes, drink the unmixed wine and rejoice, but
    rejoice in the blue haze on the hills
    Blue is the smoke of burning weeds
    Blue the skies before November rain
    The swan is mute
    The year comes down

                    [1958/1961]


## THE VINE . THE WILLOW
## LURCH TO AND FRO


FATE and I distribute, am
    the hill of poetry unabashed by men

I (yew) establish what must still be said
    as we did where
    the eaglet's maw proving insatiable
    stakes were driven through our bodies
    trying to keep us separate
    separate, even dead

But we slip through, escape, consumed by fire
    We are the wise salmon swift among the pools

Hawthorn, guardian of boundaries
    you are fair among flowers
    In this next month, o goddess,
    clothes are torn, hung on the thorn trees
    temples to be swept, the images scrubbed
    and the black night-crow brings terror to our eyes
    when they are closed

Aspen next, to shield our heads and our repose
  the whistling swans of autumn, red
  the color of bracken, the fox

Floods cover the meadow . on the rocks rain falls
  The boat on the sea, loath to return
  Quickbeam, its red berries for the mouths of gods

Pitdan stones, fourteen of them, all
  of yellow chrysolite , set there in the helm

White poplar leaves trembling on the wind
  2 tin leaves hang from each ear
  and a poplar wreath for the hair

The moon owns us finally with wicker baskets, seats for chairs
  I'll wear a sprig of willow in my hat for charm
  tree that loves water best . and while I drown
  16 hawks scream from the cliffs
  The meadows are fine-coloured in this month
  the thrush sings
  the bright new leaves are here

BENIGNISSIMA, SOLI TIBI CORDIS DEVOTIONEM QUOTIDIANAM FACIO .

[1958/1961]

## ABRI : COTE D'AMOUR

I am an unquiet bird
My head falls forward with fatigue at evening

wings folded
several successes several failures, yes
it's been a long loveless day

If I'd hunted the stones to the south

   (the stone outside us is beauty
I might have done better
Well
tomorrow,
no matter, tomorrow . . .
   (and the stone within us is love
     both

stones will bust the beak
or break the foot or the wing,
there is no other way to live

I suppose we are all Orpheus if we would

   No, I'm not
dozing and dreaming of home.
   I am home.

                                   [1958/1962]

## MARRIED MAN

YOUR LOVE like any cage

   I say, has bars

that break my head, my pride, my balls

besides all which is wet but not

   hot somehow.

Well.

There is moisture I am thinking of, a rain

      which is not gold

cometh not from the father,

silver rain of the moon, a softness

I trust in,

as well as an implacability

feminine and effulgent.

I think about this when I am alone

      or

"it is so goddamned dry on these rocks"

                           [1958/1961]


## THE LIMITATION

The driver

has a wheel between his hands

& every rose

rose, as the road goes


The trees

standing, & each time

he sounds his horn at each

curve sees

rounding the bend

just to where his eye can touch

a world end

[1958/1962]


## THIS COULDN'T HAPPEN AGAIN

the heavy pressure

of the presence of your body in the room

moving

O love,

is the end of my

imaginings

this late afternoon

feeling again at this window

the sensation of weight received

in that displacement

the small waves

lapping against me

constantly

[1958/1965]

## REMAINS OF AN AFTERNOON

Flick of perfume, slight, and faintly bitter
on my wrist, where her hand had rested

Two wrist-bones and the soft thud of veins
printed on the hard flesh of her palm

The drinks
finished but untasted

[1958/1965]


## CIAO

I'm sorry

life was tranquil (sort of)

then


'when you but lifted the glove of one white hand'


etcetera

[1958/1966]

# THE FRANKLIN AVENUE LINE

at Park Place

or Dean Street

  across

decaying open platforms with their whitened wood

       wash

waves of weathered greenness down the line

waves of somewhere unimaginable blossoms blowing

a late spring to tired faces     in this half-

  forgotten  slow  half-empty train

passing in the rain   in slow dreams of pleasure

       toward the spur's end where

vaguely   in-

decisively     train and rain

come at the same

time

  to a measured

     stop

[1958/1960]


# BROOKLYN NARCISSUS

Straight rye whiskey, 100 proof
you need a better friend?
Yes.    Myself.

The lights
the lights
the lonely     lovely     fucking     lights
and the bridge on a rainy Tuesday night
Blue/green double-stars     the line
that is the drive and on the dark alive
gleaming river
Xmas trees of tugs scream and struggle

       Midnite

Drops on the train window wobble . stream
          My trouble
              is
it is her fate to never learn to make
          anything grow
       be born or stay
Harbor beginnings and that other gleam . The train
is full of long/way/home and holding lovers whose
     flesh I would exchange for mine
     The rain, R.F.,


     sweeps the river as the bridges sweep
     Nemesis is thumping down the line
     But I have premises to keep
     & local stops before I sleep
     & local stops before I sleep

             The cree-
             ping train
             joggles
             rocks across
             I hear
the waves below lap against the piles, a pier
             from which ships go
             to Mexico

a sign which reads

PACE O MIO DIO

    oil
        "The flowers died when you went away"

Manhattan Bridge
a bridge between
we state, one life and the next, we state
is better so
is no
        backwater, flows
                        between us is
our span our bridge our
naked eyes
open here
see
bridging whatever impossibility. . .PACE!


PACE O MIO DIO

        oil

                                "The flowers died. . ."
                                Of course they did


Not that I was a green thing in the house

                I was once.
                No matter.


The clatter of cars over the span, the track
                        the spur
the rusty dead/pan ends of space
        of grease


We enter the tunnel.


The dirty window gives me back my face

                                                [1958/1960]

# CLICKETY-CLACK

*(for Lawrence Ferlinghetti)*

I took
a coney island of the mind
to the coney
island of the flesh
the brighton local
riding
past church avenue, beverly, cortelyou, past
avenues h & j
king's highway, neck road, sheepshead bay,
brighton, all the way to stillwell
avenue
that hotbed of assignation
clickety-clack


I had started reading when I got on
and somewhere down past newkirk reached
number   29   and read aloud
The crowd
in the train
looked startled at first but settled down
to enjoy the bit
even if they did think I
was insane or something
and when I reached the line : " the cock
of flesh at last cries out and has his glory
moment God "
some girl sitting opposite me with golden hair
fresh from the bottle began to stare dis-
approvingly and wiggle as tho she had ants
somewhere where it counted
And sorry to say
5   lines later the poem finished   and I
started to laugh like hell   Aware
of the dirty look I was getting I
stared back at her thighs imagining
what she had inside those toreador pants besides
her bathing suit and, well
we both got off at stillwell

Watching her high backside sway and swish down that
street of tattoo artists, franks   12   inches long, past
         the wax museum and a soft-drink
         stand with its white inside,
I stepped beside her and said: " Let's
fling that old garment of repentance, baby ! "
        smitten, I
hadn't noticed her   2   brothers were behind me

        clickety-clack

        Horseman, pass by

                        [1958/1960]


## CLARKSON AVENUE RAMBLE


——Sarah!   Saaraah!   Hoo-hoo!.... Saaaraah!.... Hooo-hoo!


        les gens sont jaloux
        ils nous prendraient notre mort
        notre mort à nous . . .


The bum sits on the curb
        scanning faces, feeling
        in anticipation
the smoke of the first panned cigarette enter
his sturdy beggar's lungs used to all kinds of weather.
Another sleeps drunk in a doorway, hand wrapped around
        an empty pint of muscatel.   Escape?
        Sure, hell why not?
Mrs. Wiggs and her Cabbage Patch
        that's crap
who could support themselves on cabbages?
What was she really selling?
        I want to know.

              Night   now
              Sound
of automobile in the street :
taxi driver going to Parkside
              to get a cup of coffee
Jack fell down and broke his crown
              and jill, jill,
what was she really selling?
   People are jealous, jill, still
coffee, cabbages, poems or pints of wine
we are all beggars when it comes to love.
              *Il faut se soutenir*      you
              gotta live somehow . Why


              are there not bordellos
on elevated platforms with their wood washed by sea-air
              island-changed with waves of Brooklyn
              green turned white, the smell of blowing
              blossoms down the line, the light
blush of a late spring to tired train faces that only sit
              and stare, bright
gay ladies with beds in curtained cubicles to make
              men of these gray faces for a moment,
              to sit on a hot rock for a bit
              why not?

But

              Saa-raah!      Hoooo-hoo!

                                          [1958/1960]

# THE ONCE-OVER

The tanned blond
                in the green print sack
in the center of the subway car
                                standing
tho there are seats
                has had it from
1 teen-age hood
1 lesbian
1 envious housewife
4 men over fifty
(& myself),   in short
                the contents of this half of the car


                Our notations are :
long legs, long waist, high breasts (no bra), long
neck, the model slump
                the handbag drape & how the skirt
cuts in under a very handsome
                                set of cheeks
'stirring dull roots with spring rain'   sayeth the preacher


        Only a stolid young man
with a blue business suit and the New York Times
does not know he is being assaulted


So.
She has us and we her
all the way to downtown Brooklyn
Over the tunnel and through the bridge
                to DeKalb Avenue we go
all very chummy


She stares at the number over the door
                and gives no sign
Yet the sign is on her

                                        [1958/1960]

## LOVE SONG

Upon returning home tonite

and it is a home

now

surely,

being the animal I am

when I had undressed, I

wrapped my hand around my

balls, and their now-limp appendage.

And afterward

smelled my hand.


It was you.

As your perfume is still on my undershirt

so this perfume also.

[1958/1967]


## ( VALUES )
### COLD SOON

It is a

goddamn

fucking

shame

to let a woman

(woman!)

built as you are

(built)

go


and this some bright november day when wind whips dis-

carded    (so many)    afternoon    (birds)

newspapers    (about us

swirl of

gulls)    above

the subway gratings

[1958/1967]


## WINTER SOLSTICE

At twenty-of-four in the afternoon

a handful of sunlight


caresses

not wholly

the lower half of a gouache
I had hung in a new position on the east wall.

Unexpectedly—
blue, blue-grey and two yellows are so


separated out and redefined with light
filtered thru an imperfect pane of glass


the painting


takes its life in a new way.
Tho it change from that, tho it become
all other quiet aspects of sea,
can never again be the same.



A sparrow

flies from the edge of wall

at the roof,

and lights, huddled
in the crotch of a young branch held into

clouds and sun,
some blue.
Simplicity moves in this sudden dream
where I am that bird and that forked young branch is you.


( Poems will not do :
it is a kind of minuteness of application of whatever blessed
things the goddess has put in our hands . We sharpen them
and march to do single battle, but
we cannot plunge these so-handsome

knives

into our lives

and not get cut. )

[1958/1959]

## MORNING SONG

Warm bed is a winter morning.   Brilliant

sunlight beyond the window sills extends

its fingers inward

beckoning.


They stay wrapped in each other, touching lengths.

Simplicity is the quiet image of their arteries,

           that tangle.   Five

clouds sail east, an

airplane's line of flight is westward

catching its wings in the cloud, attraction of parallels.

Another, and all images meet in that angle

and balance.


           Crotch of a tree lifted against the blue.

Forked branch between which his hand lies dreaming

a thirstier extension.

But no fierceness enters to undo

their bloods' slow contemplation.


           After coffee, blood quickens, trans-

figures the signs.

There is the woman reclining, breathing.

Here is the man standing up.

                          [1958/1962]

# THE ACCUMULATION OF HISTORIEᴗ

Let us call it

a raw excellence / Certain

harshnesses are

any exile's measure


My rooms   2   in Brooklyn

2   in Manhattan, I

construct always and

live and die and


always the same superstition: "where your foot

treads"   & was the ancient world & is the new

I do not even have to remember you among these walls

where you are my accumulation,

the present

[1958/1965]


## MADRUGADA N° 8

The whole world has its miseries—
                    Bigod,
now that's a comfort, isn't it?
                    "Come,
        come with me to my place."
                    "no."

No
longer trying to sleep alone along
a choiceless street
        laughter   /   music
voices from the bar downstairs. (It's
        a long night, baby)
Later on

                        the sounds grow more inhuman
                                merciful,
                        intimate   :   growl of foghorns
                                downriver,
                        some traffic on the avenue, the slow
                        certain chugg-thugg-thugg
                        train switching in the yards

                        Cast the cards / read them

                        Silver is only moonlight
                        Hard is only hard
                        Flame is only sight   (in)
                        Heat is only flame
                        (Baby, baby, bite, bit, gone, long)


dawn breaking now behind
bleak outline of buildings seeking down
the thin flung spiral of birdsong, reaching
down to sing the sun up   /   Fine!   But hell,
let her be uncovered here beside me sleeping, her breasts
        blessing the morning light, so—

But no,
the day is still winter
and the hour morning
and tho the sun be glorious
lacking her, is
another risen morning in the world,.
the sun not glorious enuf

[1958/1962]


**THE QUARREL**


Dried green leaf on the door

Blackened leaf below it


Under that a metal leaf, blackened also

Below that the leafy ace of clubs


Outside the window the tree I thought a friend

has undressed all its branches & is ugly to me


Returning home defenseless

even a stray dog barked at me

I could not even declare my love to him

much less my innocence.   Branches

of frozen breath writhed from both our mouths

into the air

Even the room is cold

& here I sit and stare

& barely move

[1958/1964]


## AT&T HAS MY DIME

After your voice's frozen anger

emptied the air between us, the

silence of electrical connections

the vacant window pale, the

connection broken ::

                    breaks in now

empty bravado of bar conversation, some

lonesome truck shifting gears


uptown on the avenue . Winter


has come much closer

Buy myself an ale

Manage to get it down

somehow .

[1958/1968]

## THE ROUTINE

Each day I open the cupboard
& the green shoots of my last onion
have in the dark grown higher


A perverse & fairly final pleasure
that I love to watch him stretching himself
secretly, green sprouting shamelessly in
this winter, making a park in my kitchen, making
spring for a moment in my kitchen


that, instead of eating him
I have watched him grow

[1958/1959]


## THE TWO KISSES

The way the skin
stretches paper-thin across

feel

bone beneath the lips

delicate, delicate


the forehead : the
fine rounded front of my grandfather's skull
felt the same to the touch
the kiss, as his
daughter's does now

(only my mother is conscious

sees me and the wall, heard

that siren cry, hears

traffic sounds in the street,

her skull  )

Why

do we never want
to kiss dying people
fully on the mouth?

Cancer grows
in a womb where I grew once
and swells as much
Only she carries death in her now
It is silent and will yield
only to another silence

And the skin stretches
tight across her forehead
as her father's did
as also mine someday will

[1958/1968]


## THE INSTRUCTIONS


1   lb. new wax
1   lb. resin
melting the wax
first, then the resin
in basin over middling fire : add

3   lbs. unsalted butter

removing promptly everything
that appears to be scum
Take off fire before adding

1 oz. powdered verdegris

Stir at length with a spatula

Everything well mixed, put back on
fire, so that it will blend further
stirring continually, taking
care it does not burn

Remove a moment later, scoop out,
and shut in a glazed earthen pot
It will be solider than a salve but
not enough for a plaster
To be spread on a feather and applied upon the
ulcer
which beforehand has been cleansed with
the decoction

## THE DECOCTION

    2   pots of vin blanc
    ½   lb. sugar
    4   oz. round birthwort
        (crushed if fresh,
          if dry, minced and washed in white wine)

Infusion : boiling down later

Lay on top a poultice soaked
in said decoction
Change every   8   hours

            For sickness of venery
            where the wound is open

[1958/1962]


## REDHEAD :  (OR : LOOK MA, NO CONVOLUTIONS)


  You are no mistress.
Could not be a wife.      You have
                    no inner re-
sources to fill out any life, your own,
left alone—or leaving him alone. As salve
you've a whimsicality upon the eyes that proves
your 'seriousness'.

       Seriousness is
watching Bernard die that day
the seven clubs fell.
Enough rifles within a 100 yds. to have saved him.
René's responsibility to say

          "Hold fire!"
              or
        " F I R E ! "

and chose instead the village, not
the man   his friend   and watched—


          You
are the poor slick-minded madison ave.
          man's idea of a mistress.  No
serious thing at all.

                              [1959/1959]


## ETRUSCAN TOMB

Leer

and that spine moved

back against another  (not surprising)  extension

of time(?)less stone is time perceived.

Let

the bereaved laugh with remembrance : here

one hand cups the handsome uppermost breast,

the other, the cup itself! A feast is death!

Across a slab of centuries, the living

flesh need not doubt itself or what they meant.

The slow brown eye of time and the quick blue

eye of lust

have crossed the line, forgiven themselves, become

an ornament.

[1959/1960]


## A PURITY DEFINED

It is time to be silent.

It is time to be that tower that

in this woman, a child

          lusts for.


It is good to know someone

who does not confuse this

possibility, this

meeting in the forked young branch of eternity

          (its own purity, its

          own tree)

              with love.

[1959/1959]

## SONG OF THE HESITATIONS

The moon is setting in the west
the hour near four o'clock
Temperature's down, wind is high
I'm walking toward the docks

Loose sheets of old newspapers whirl
above my head like gulls
are circling above the subway grates
are diving for the kill—

where I'm the fish in the empty street
that's caught below the wind
One newsprint bird tears at my cheek
another swoops behind

and wraps its rattling wings about
my frozen face with love
I read a headline on one wing
VISIONS THAT LED TO DEATH

And I *will* sing of Death and Love
But still I am not drunk enough
to dream us into Spring

[1959/1959]

## TRYING TO GET OUT

The rain falls in the night
through the night
Earth.

We stretch on it and cannot sleep .
Cart out the room, put it in the street
                no trees anywhere
The rain falls about the room, keeps some
measure of my impatience   .   the night .

        NO   LEAVES   YET!   wait,

spring came four days ago   .   again


now,    sleet  /  rain  /  the night, odorless
my inaction is as perfect as my hate


When I move, another shall hate me for it,
one be sad, a third will wish it strength
What spring? Great goddess, here's the king of winter,
                                snow!

I sink,
founder in this thing I am and do not know, and wait
to be called into a night where the snow turns warm .

                                [1959?/1967]


## MEDITATION ON THE BMT

Here, at the beginning of the new season
before the new leaves burgeon,   on
either side of the Eastern Parkway station
                near the Botanical Gardens
they burn trash on the embankments, laying
barer than ever our sad, civilised refuse.

1   coffee can without a lid
1   empty pint of White Star, the label
            faded by rain
1   empty beer-can
2   empty Schenley bottles
1   empty condom, seen from
1   nearly empty train
            empty


            empty


            empty
Repeated often enough, even the word looks funny.



Man in an alley carrying a morning load already
            walks
only by propping his hand against a thick red
            line
painted on a building wall,   while he goes past
coffee-can   beer-can   condom   bottles & fire
            past
faded brick and pock-marked cement to somewhere
relieve his bladder in the sorrow of a sun-shot morning
            with some semblance of privacy, some-
            how needed here . Cold . Sad



winter morning in spring where it is cold while
this man is high and the sun is high and there are no
rules governing the award of prizes to the dead.

My eyes

enter poor backyards, backyards

O I love you

backyards, I make you my own, and you
my barren, littered embankments, now that you
've a bit of fire to warm & cleanse you, be
grateful that men still tend you, still will
rake your strange leaves
your strange leavings.

Poor Brooklyn soil
poor american earth
poor sickening houses
poor hurricanes of streets, both
your subterranean and your public lives go on
anyhow,   beneath
refuse that is a refusal, with alienated, uneasy, un-
reflective citizens, who will be less un-
happy, more contented and vacant, if they
relieve their bladders against some
crappy wall or other.

[1959/1960]

**POP SONG
MARKET**

*See, see rider
see what yu hev done*

*See, see rider
see what yu hev done*

*Let me be yr side-track
till yr main line comes*

*O, careless love*

I.  *It's Always You*

I realize

I shut my eyes

when we make it, baby

hoping that we

'll turn out to be

some other couple entirely

_____

II.  *Someone*

O, there is some dame I am longing to see

I know that she

'll turn out to be

someone

who'll climb over me          da da

da da

da da

_____

III.  *The A Train*

Shooba . doobe-do
you-shd-take-the-A-train
      sd Duke Ellington:
      "Evvabuddy knows whea Sugar Hill is"
that song was
properly,
writ without words


      Shoo.ba.doo.be.doo  /  Now try
the longing here for you, the very
            very
            thought of you
my love .

------------------------------------------------

IV.  *You'll Never Know*


The light crazy beautiful heavy feeling in my
            legs and arms
trying to run away
I'll come back someday
to somebody

But for now, baby, it's just wonderful
and
    all
        down
            hill

------------------------------------------------

V.  *Before It's Too Late*

I'm leaving town, baby
and going to Bolivia
to dig rin-tin-tin

[1959-64/1967]


## HOT AFTERNOONS HAVE BEEN IN WEST 15TH STREET

Here, in late spring, the summer is on us already
                    Clouds and sun,
         a haze over the city.   Outside my
window the ailanthus nods sleepily under
                    a hot wind, under
         wetness in the air, the brightness
of day even with overcast.   The chair on the next roof
         sits by itself and waits
for someone to come stretch his length in it.   Suddenly

thunder cracks to the south over the ocean, one can
                    shuteye see
the waves' grey wife, the storm, implacably stride
rain nipplings on the surface of the sea, the waves
         powerfully starting to rise, raise their
                    powers before the hot wind
The endless stretchout to Europe disappears, the
rainsweep moving toward the city rising caught in the haze-hot
                    island atmosphere
         Hate anger powers whip toward the towers rising
from the hum of slugbedded traffic clogging avenues, the trees
         of heaven gracing their backyards crazily
         waving under the strengthening wind

sun brighter

more thunder

birdsong

rises shrilly announcing

the storm in advance in encroach in abstruse syllables of pure

SOUND . SONG . SOMEONE

comes to the porched roof to cover the chair from the thunderfilled

wet atmosphere, there is

nothing clearly defined wrong I can see except

I must go uptown and see what other storms there

be, there


And paint the inside of my wife's white filing cabinet red

that all things may be resolved    correct    and dead  .

[1959/1963]


**RITUAL II.**


The human body is not supposed to mean

anything, just

to be I guess.

Yet a hand waving, or fingers cupping a match flame

can be

is

sometimes an explanation    an answer to everything.


Likewise, the eyes watch

this foot descending the stair, the steps

foot takes to reach the ground

down a portable platform rolled

out to the plane

explains    (that foot

       does,    descending)

everything, the

first overthrow, the cries, and what other ritual

remains

       to be . to be .

               Not said

                     [1959/1962]

## SUSPENSION

Slow wash of sea at dockside

Gull cries on the dark waters

       A star falls

then another

Gravel patterns the back and elbow

Toward the other side the moon rises

Moon is caught in tree branches, will

stay there, rise no higher

—Shall I climb up and get it down?

       —No. Leave it alone.

                     [1959/1961]

# CITY SUNSET

Pink and blue.

The pink striations angle down the sky

enter the southern deeps,    keep

laying out across my eye

asleep where it may not lie down

                  tell lies truly

        and see

love's breasts at attention, at rest, at

        my hand, orange

            sand,    this

        sunset you also see

but with two islands between you and me—

And if the sun is down

            our hearts

        the lights, the darks

they still are up, are high    o

dance with me

        O,

            dance

                with me !

                          [1959/1966]

# THE PURSE-SEINE

Fierce luster of sun on sea, the gulls
                    swinging by,
          gulls flung by wind
aloft, hung clear and still before the
                    pivot
     turn
               glide out
riding the wind as tho it werc
                    the conditions of civilisation

But they are hungry too,
and what they do that looks so beautiful, is
     hunt .

The side of your face so soft, down, their cried falls, bitter
broken-wing graces crying freedom, crying carrion, and
we cannot look one another in the eye,
                    that frightens, easier to face
the carapace of monster crabs along the beach . The empty
shell of death was always easier to gaze upon
than to look into the eyes of the beautiful killer . Never
                    look a gull in the eye


Fit the 300-pound tom over the pursing lines, start it sliding
down the rope to close the open circle, bottom of the net, weight
thudding down thru the sea

brass rings hung from the lead line come closer together, the tom
pushing the rings ahead of it, the purse line drawing thru them,
taking up the slack, the school sounding the fish streaking by
toward that narrowing circle
               and out . . .

Waiting behind the skiff, birds sit on the sea, staring off, patient
      for what we throw them .   We
      merely fight it, surf, and that other day.   No
bed ever was until this, your face half-smiling down your swell of half-
sleep, eyes closed so tightly they will admit
      nothing but fear and stars . How can we
call all this our own?   and shall we dare?   admit the moon?   full
bars of song from nightbirds, doors of the mind agape and swelling?
     Dream again
that orange slope of sand, we belting down it hand upon hand, the birds
         cry overhead
the sea
lies in its own black anonymity and we here on this bed
enact the tides, the swells, your hips rising toward me,
        waves break over the shoals, the
sea bird hits the mast in the dark and falls
with a cry to the deck and flutters off . Panic spreads, the
       night is long, no
     one sleeps, the net
is tight
we are caught or not, the tom sliding down ponderous
       shall we make it?
       The purse closes.


The beach is a playground . unsatisfactory, but we
pretending still it's play swim out too far, and reaching
back, the arms strain inward
Waters here are brown with sand, the land too close,
       too close, we drown
       in sight of
I love you and you love me . . .

                         [1959/1961]

# VISITATION I.

Magic of morning

walking thru the autumn of West 24th St. slowly

late to work

a schoolboy slowness along the sunburst sidewalk

Cold air, sun on the walls

one

sees

on the walk the broken bits

of color glistening in sun like frozen

smashed Christmastree decorations or bits of glass

imbedded in cement, that are only paper somehow, only

paper   .   No


sooner is that reality complete

ly absorbed, than another real thing rears its

multilimned head in the semblance of barrels, barrels

rolled past

dollies loaded with reams of printed sheets for the binder,

a reminder of work, the mist full of sun, the

barrels with bindings of bent under steam split willow instead of

steel

tape binding, holding

china from England, to

feel filling the eye:

docks, warehouses, ship's hold, long-

shoremen, the wood

shavings and

the hands that wrought these, touched and shoved these barrels

not

those that bought their transit, raked the profit in,

but a cooper's dream of death

these broken staves

singing themselves in the last triumphant crackling song

of fire

the barrels being burnt

unUSE again,   U N U S E . The


park is still green but leaves have fallen already, some

raked in piles and miles of countryside stretch out

filling the eye :

heaped leaves burning at roadside, the air blue

acrid . Nostrils

sting with the smoke of years we no longer remember

except with the rare

attack of the senses . Still,

the tender drooping spray from the fountain

center of park, has old dixie cups, tops from

icecream cartons, burnt matches and other rubbish to be

its birds

and its fish

Move along

move along

don't care

cold air, the

sun, the sun     I

wish I were far from here

[1959/1965]

## WINGS (TALK OF THE TOWN : ITEM)

    A
  Boeing 707
ingested a seagull in flight
A compressor blade was slightly bent
The encounter made no difference
                 to anyone
except the sea gull

Wings-swept-back
         ate Bent-wings
the night the jet flight landed
           11:45 P.M.
Clearwater, Florida

[1959/1965]

## WATCH

a gull rise from the water and
finding the wind in the quarter
       in which he sought it
swing back and up

      Watch ships move in the bay  .  Dim
      lamp lines  /  single riding lights
      move with the masts
      Ships further away
      gloom monstrous prow out of the mist
      Horns honk from all sides  /  The sea's
      movement is love in loneliness

  Those at anchor in the Narrows bend gently
      on the tide, creak
an end of voyage sadness to
      the Brooklyn beaches . Near

      Staten Island a yacht
swings single lines of lights above the colored dusk of hulls
Dusk creeping thru the fog, its monstrous prow will split us all
cover us isolate here, but
night not yet fallen on the Lower Bay
      and buoys offer
bells and lights for the craft that move  .  The mist
thickens,
an aura of moaning sundown above it
      split with foghorns, closes
      A tanker emerges
its passage toward us swerves a wake across the wakes

of two green beetle ferries plying
Brooklyn before the fading light
            The dusk
            comes with a bell

a bell to the left, to the
crosses behind us   /   it
has something to do with loneliness

A man stands up and counts
his wretchedness
her beauty
the silent
power of vessels at anchor
against obscurity, against
penetration by bells and horns,
against the delicate light   /   that stance
fades into bells and rounded shell of yellowed fog

            Gulls again,
            reminding, never enough, of
            hungers
            theirs
            our own

The rough, sudden  B R R A A T T   of prowling ships
their movement in the softening skull and kiss
the ear and sullen breasts
of any living sky, announce
            our fear
            our trust
            the lights against

(it is enough)

        against night's narrow masts, all
        say only that we are. It is

enough we are, and this
has something to do with love

[1959/1961]


**FREE FALL**

Single

skinny,   young

leaf

born too late in the year

hangs there

the dangerous wind

the branch

slick with rain

a single drop of

rain

hangs,   suspended

from the leaf-

tip a gust of wind a

double - suicide

[1959/1963]

## PERSPECTIVE : HE WATCHES

Windows are

steps of light

running down into darkness

From the lowest yellow step

one falls into backyard blackness


The upper one near the roof steps off

into dark glow of sky

the immense black rose of the city

curbing the eye


Lamplight falls one

corner of the bed

Sliding off the pillow   her bright sleeping

head fashions shadow low on the shoulder

her curled white body hugs

the afternoon's sprung seed

[1959/1967]

## THE PASTURES OF THE EYE

Flocculations of cirrus hang

              precipitate

in the tube of sky above the street,

roof the eye aging in its pool,

                 enclosing its

own reflection with a crust of ice

               Crack

Dull, but

the eye looks out

and lines of random sheep grazing above the park feed

on the only grass there is this winter morning

       /

        in the mind

The eye, yes

       aging in its pool,

but open .

O  P  E  N

                       [1959/1962]

## POEM

Memories
of summer come back
stretching their wings, screaming
gulls waiting
to see what I have to throw them

                       [1959/1960]

**RITUAL VI.**

Grids and lines

keep all our melting time

•

the roof dissolves under the sun

a map melting and changing like Africa

only it is snow and the continents shift


A shimmer hardly to be shook off

assails the birds as the birds assail the air

with their complaints


Plants spread

their leaves in the sun

while in the sun snow

slides from the roofs, icicles crash,

blup-drip of icicle together with

sudden sparrowsong

burst at the sun thaw Sunday, keep

measure of our love


And here you sit in the sun with something

sunday about the newspaper and coffee, the egg

leavings drying in the cup, and your new

haircut, the face so soft, the sweet line of

mouth, smoke rising, cigarette

                    moving with the hand

                    table to a mouth and down

my fingers reach and trace the loving line it

                    makes at me, a mouth

laughing . . .


        Who is this madman

who wishes for a subdued life of leisurely gestures?

                                        [1959/1963]


## NEDERLANDISCHE DICHTER


        He constructed forms and lines of piles
        hammered into overwhelming
        Rotterdams of poems, half-
open canals, about to freeze
over or open out
thawing into barge-ridden tulip red,
or yellow half-rotting wharves and whitened
decrepit buildings set
about by wheeling gulls and sky

                                        [1960/1961]

## THE FLIES

My hands circle her
firm waist slowly,
move up the back    we
look in one another's eyes
& close / My hands move
small of her back, below,
curve under


"There are    5    flies in this room"
her hands also moving
                            lazily
I can feel her chin in my shoulder
move as she watches them buzz
under the single lightbulb in the ceiling
        center of the room turned off
            now it is day
I can tell from her chin they are circling

[1960/1961]


## THE SIGN

End of September    .    At

19th Street and Fifth Avenue

on the sidewalk in front of

the U.S. Employment Service

a colored lady looks at her watch.

Five of nine.

She shines in the sun impatiently

In Madison Square Park

young Persephone from the Bronx

emerges from subway

ducks her head into

the *Daily Mirror,* walks

not hearing the message

in Puerto Rican Spanish

delivered toward her ear

by a passing young man from Third Avenue and 26th Street

Lady!

You're being flirted with—

enter your life!


I wonder,

does this fountain run all night?

The park smells like an autumn hayfield, dried

leaves, dried grass all heaped together to be

      burned in hazy afternoons by men

          with rakes and visor caps.

     Sparrow

     looks at fountain ambitiously

     and settles for puddle next to it, left

     from last night's rain.

In another puddle nearby, a big one,

seventeen disreputable-looking pigeons splutter and

splash and duck their heads

        and drink and gargle away.

        Among them a single warbler

green and tan wings splayed

digs long beak into underbelly

        makes his toilet.


It is settled in already

the birds all employed with their hygiene

the unemployed with their newspapers

on street corners or park benches

Persephone with her page 5

young Hermes off on his errand, hopeless

bums preening outside the public facilities,

and center of it all, this

fountain plashes away . And finally

        today   .   there are

more leaves on the surface of the pool than dixie cups

        Fall is come

                          [1960/1962]

# 7TH GAME : 1960 SERIES

—for Joel—

Nice day,
sweet October afternoon
Men walk the sun-shot avenues,
                        Second, Third, eyes
                        intent elsewhere
ears communing with transistors in shirt pockets
                Bars are full, quiet,
discussion during commercials
                        only
Pirates lead New York 4-1, top of the 6th, 2
Yankees on base,    1 man out

What a nice day for all this !
Handsome women, even
dreamy jailbait, walk
                nearly neglected :
men's eyes are blank
their thoughts are all in Pittsburgh

Last half of the 9th, the score tied 9-all,
Mazeroski leads off for the Pirates
The 2nd pitch he simply, sweetly
                        CRACK!
belts it clean over the left-field wall

Blocks of afternoon
acres of afternoon
Pennsylvania Turnpikes of afternoon .  One
                diamond stretches out in the sun

the 3rd base line
and what men come down
it

The final score, 10-9

Yanquis, come home

[1960/1966]


**DEFINITION**


Long ago and far away


and the swimmer
heading out into the bay
arm lift, plunge down, the head turning;
my heart you may swim forever

out. Look,


there is the horizon.
Sea and sky meet, change; why
are we not this real intensity forever?
surrounded and known.
The world else is brown and calculated.


There on the beach, the
woman watches.
Between her legs the dog sits,
wiggling, wanting to go
too. It is a kind of death watching him swim out,
away from her, his head getting smaller and smaller, flash
of arm in sun, down,

distant churn of water between the small waves. She
holds the dog's two haunches in her hands.

> He is hardly to be restrained, and love
> is manifest, is felt from the two of them
>                     differently.


The swimmer is himself.

[1960/1961]


## THE VIRTUE

    Let me say this reluctantly:
I begrudge a song to this autumn
                not the clear, cold days
with wisps on the horizon,   but
                these dark ones
the falling year, decaying leaves, dampness
oooph, grey sky
fuck,   the slow rain
aaack,   the wind
cuts . sharp
                as my mind does not

Still,
I find some
virtue in
these wet
leaves

[1960/1961]

## THE WAIT

The earth tips
toward winter dusk
Cool autumn light
    ( the earth
            keeps on spinning )
floods the evening windows  .  I
lie on my bed alone

Across the white
wall flushed pink in sundown, a
      fly descends slowly,
        crosses the door,
stops from time to time
          dully

Cosine and tangent of my discontent
A table will find the third side,
dull, half knowing why, half drunk,
      filling the mind with friends

                      [1960/1961]


## THE SEA AND THE SHADOW

      It falls.

      The night falls

      the night sky falls

      a star, the eyes follow, my

      hand falls

It is never enough / I

am hardly ever enough

even to myself


I go.

I go through the streets

I cross avenues, helpless against your anger

I go pulverized through narrow streets with paving stones

Let the walls fall, crumble, fall, crush me finally, end it

the eyes / the hands

Your cunt is tight with anger

I can feel it a block away, your

belly is tight

your asshole is loose with disdain

and fear


And I cannot stand it, your beauty

walks beside me like a

tree in motion under the wind

of my desires, with

standing them / standing in

an emptiness not your own that you hate

and feel it is your own . It is not, it

is mine also, let me, that damned sea,

I will come

It falls.

The half-hour would-be wholeness

falls, the year falls, the mirror

destroys itself / that year, a

brilliant, at times quiescent

star will fall

into the sea

I will come


I lie down /

the trees are bright with resisting

polished under the rain . have shed all their leaves

        Corridors

of summer stretch out behind me endless

        like memory like

I destroy myself running through open doors

leading through empty rooms

Or there is someone

huddled in a corner

        pissing / Yes.

I humiliate my life, piss it away, I am

my shoes, my black pair of sneakers walking

corridors, deserted beaches, cement sidewalks, sit

now beneath a chair . torn . quiescent . my

laces flopped sideways on the floor

                   fit, however,

to the foot, dingy shape of life

smelling of dried sweat, revived

                  at any warmth

my worn fabric

yes, the corrugations


                   I shall come

shaping all truths from my own balls, seeking in my skull

even those shaped years ago / I was too young, I looked

for a shadow at ten in the morning which will not appear

until four in the afternoon / my own

with the sun from the other direction and

                  everything failing


I will come, I

shall come into your body as into the morning world,

as into a city filled with its leisure and softness,

where the soft light falls on the bird, the tree, the wall,

where the sun of mid-day is lost on the shadows of palm trees

                  arcades

                 Fountains cool it

I shall come through your eyes from the other side, my

water, my mirror

I will come into your belly and make it a sea rolling against me,

come into you soft as sleep / and be real


You will cry the whole afternoon

[1961/1962]


## THE ONE-NIGHT STAND : AN APPROACH TO THE BRIDGE


Migod, a picture window
both of us sitting there
on the too-narrow couch
variously unclothed
watching sky lighten over the city


You compile your list of noes
it is incomplete
I add another
there is no anger
we keep it open
trying,
shying
away, your all
too-solid body melts, revives, stif-
fens, clears and dis-
solves, an i-
dentity emerges, disappears, it is
like watching a film, the takes dis-
solving into other takes,
spliced suddenly to a closeup
The window tints pink
                                    I wait
We sleep a bit   .   Your
identity goes and comes
it is never for me, it
is never sure of itself
                              I wait, you

ask too much of yourself, why
of the moment, why
is your fear of feeding off other people? Must
you always feed off yourself
and find it unreal food you eat, unreal
water you drink from the source of yourself, un-
real liquor you take from the hand of a friend, and
never grow gloriously drunk, but stay
eating yourself
finding the fare thin,
stay in a dark room holding
uneasily, in an unreal hand
a thin man's unreal cock who stays
and grows more unreal to himself?

We both sleep.


New day's sun
doubles itself in the river
A double string of blue lights
glares to mark the bridge, the
city huddles under a yellow light
the sodium flares
gleam under oblique
sun's double in the stream,

I wake
ready, make my move.
"You'll make me pregnant"   you murmur
and barely audible, "I'll die"
neither will stop me
your legs are open
I am there at the wet edge
of life, the moist living lips


It will not do
I have been at this life's edge
and hurt too many hours
It will be all me for a moment
then all you
Identities will dissolve
under this new act, or
six quick strokes
you move once
toward me, say
one word, even
moan, I will be finished
done

dissolved
become real, alone, no
it will not do
You are no victim and
I no rapist hero, I can
still, I
stop at the life's edge


Later
we are too real
separate, try
to recover
dully, our-
selves gone out
The coffee does not warm
there is an orange sun in the river
there are blue lights on the bridge
Animal tenderness and
sadness is all we salvage, is
all the picture window
mirrors and maintains

[1961/1962]


**RITUAL IV.**


Seedlings

a season old

lemon trees, orange, lime, their leaves

      differing shades of green, differing

green shadows in dumb sunlight streaming beautiful

past their pots and boxes, sill to red wall, to white,

      beams holding their dust motes

                    Saturday A.M.,   juice and coffee

                    bacon and eggs and peace

                    in a fresh-painted room

You sit here smiling at

me and the young plants . This

paper is covered with coffee-cup and bacon stains

                            The dust motes

                            float . Everything

grows,

and rests

                                        [1961/1972]


## THE TIDES

                        The girl with the beautiful legs

                        walks down a Brooklyn street

                        a hope-and-a-half away


Terrible indeed is the house of heaven in the mind

soft

giving back the quiver

deeper and deeper disclosed until the blind

sun bursts

into a close warm black behind the eyes

                        yellow stars

                        then the red

Light perspiration on bodies engraved as beads

                    upon the stone mind

the heavy, delicate odor, the swift

calling by name, the pronouns

the arching back

a sky under which the blood speaks

its flood

                    its ebb

what the man must do

what the woman must

                                  [1961/1967]


## WORKING LATE ON A HOT NIGHT

It says quarter-to-6 on one watch

and 3 A.M. on another

and the spots on the floor of my livingroom are

                    from where the ice-cubes melted

But not everything is that

predictable

and the baskets of bread at an Italian bakery's cellar

                    round the corner were

                    moons or unloved

loves, things we never eat, but still

hot.   I went down and touched one.

                                    [1961/1967]

# MARINE CUMULUS : THE VALUE OF THE SYSTEM

The wind moves them

as tho there were something else

she had forgot to do

Towering mountains of cloud step over the city

marching toward the Atlantic . dream

of sunlight on them


The typist's clatter has hummed along all afternoon

some song behind the teeth

eyes the window obliquely

watching the clouds swim over Queens

heading toward the Atlantic . adjusts

her typing table

and the chair

dream of sunlight on them

facing the window, not

watching the keys

[1961/1962]

## THE SUMMER WINDOW

Cat stalks the parking lot alone
his hind legs stretched stiff and high
I take it he is just come from love
cocksore and sullen


Laundry hangs from the fire escape
four stories up   .   the woman leans
out and over to fix a clothespin firmly
Her husband gooses her from behind,
her laugh rings out against the empty lot


Above the sixth floor the wind pushes
the high clouds fast across and binds
the parking lot in the poverty of its elements
Between TV aerials a commercial jet
lays out its trail   .   from the roof, a
flock of pigeons bursts and disappears


As tho I had invented it, high above the lot
near the pushing clouds, a gull
sails and swings upon the air, the wind
upholding lonely circles, dips, the
jet roar disappears, the bird rises, floats,
no hunt over the city only the pleasure of
that ride . Better the bird in the mind,
poet, or the wind?   You choose.

The cat has crossed the yard, the clack
and whirr of pigeons returns the ear back,
the woman's back as she turns, still
laughing, to her husband, and
framed by the wash, the window, the
descending birds above them, they
close. The gull circles above the lot.

[1961/1962]


## THE PROPOSITION


After she
had complained about
men

nearly a solid hour
to her friend's mother
she

was visiting her friend
and her friend's mother
in the country, her

girlfriend left the house
to look for the cat
and she

continued the re-
petitive argument which
her friend's mother

listened to patiently
without comment
until   (while)

her daughter was gone
out, (looking for
the cat)

and she said for the
hundredth time how really
awful bastards

men were, and didn't she
(the mother) think there
WAS

something else to be in-
terested in, or
wasn't it

time to try something
new, the mother
after long silence

said :    "It wouldn't
be new
to me, but I'm

ready anytime you are."
The girlfriend
returning (with the cat)

was a trifle con-
fused when her friend in-
sisted she had to catch the late bus home (there

was some editing she
HAD to do). "I hope she wasn't
offended, or anything,"

the mother, after having
driven the girl to her bus
explained

to her daughter, on
the way home the very
probable reason her

friend had left to
go back to the city
so sudden-like

[1961/1963]

# RITUAL I.

> "The fiesta does not celebrate
> an event, it
> reenacts it"
> *In this way time emerges* .

Procession with candles around the streets of that town :    ·

hands raised and cupped to shield the tiny flames

a timeless gesture

as that slow walk

is

from church along the main street to the second store

then turn

left, downslope

to the lower street sinking past

Ca'n Font, down

past the lower line of houses .

Street rising gently to the road, back past

café

tailor's house

the stairs

the stores

dark suits and white shirts

the line of men, dark

dresses, dark shawls, veils, the line of

women's heads down  .  watching their own feet moving

       slowly  .  slowly  .  A-
            ve, a-ve,
            Ave Ma-ri-a,

            A-ve, a-ve,
            Ave Ma-ri-a


The touching directness of one lady tourist

who joined the procession

end of the women's line  .  suddenly

the angular figure in a traveling suit

          instead of a rosary, carried

          a white pocketbook  .  stood out

A german anthropologist lady who must have known

                what an

anomaly she appeared, and could not care, except to

add her poor self at the end of the line


Reaving my lady
half-asleep
in the dawn light

         Meat every Thursday
         when the calf
         is killed

                Mail from the bus at 4:30
                fresh milk at  5


The german lady with her white pocketbook .

End of a timeless act of the peoples of earth .

                        [1961/1972]

# PARK POEM

From the first shock of leaves their alliance
with love, how is it?


Pages we write and tear
Someone in a swagger coat sits and waits on a hill


It is not spring, may-
be it is never spring
maybe it is the hurt end of summer
the first tender autumn air
fall's first cool rain over the park
and these people walking thru it


The girl thinking:
                    life is these pronouns
the man : to ask / to respond / to accept
                    bird-life . reindeer-death
                    Life is all verbs, vowels and verbs
They both get wet


                    If it is love, it is to make
                    love, or let be

'To create the situation / is love

and to avoid it, this is also

Love'

as any care or awareness, any

other awareness might   might

have been

but is now

hot flesh

socking it into hot flesh

until reindeer-life / bird-death


You are running, see?

you are running down slope across this field

I am running too

to catch you round


This rain is yours

it falls on us

we fall on one another


Belong to the moon

we do not see

It is wet and cool

bruises our skin

might have been

care and avoidance

but we run . run


to prepare

love later

[1961/1962]


## RITUAL VII.


What is there sits anonymous
                              in the subway and
destroys our eye for
anything else for
hours?     It is today the eastern Mediter-
                              ranean, she
                              just sits there, dark-
complexioned, that
neat slight hook to nose, the
rosebud mouth of a persian princess, but al-
                              ready too full
                              upper and
lower and maybe the one, the fun, the great
whore of Port Saïd or Babylon who scholarly sits
there knowing the liner, the
shadow on perfectly, an-
other shadow swinging under the cheekbones as she
turns to note number or name
on the station, the neat hook, the persian
arabian, afghan, indian, pakistani, lebanese, eyes
black, black, egyptian, mesopotamian, mouth pale, pale


She gets out at 14th St. and Union
Square and speaks
to a strapping old Irishwoman about
the change of trains

A last glimpse,
the local pulls out slowly, too
slowly, she stands there,
legs parted under the black coat of fake fur, she
just stands there, endlessly, taking
neither express nor local, stands
there on the 14th Street platform
the whole eastern Mediterranean history between her thighs
thinking

[1961/1964]


## THE LITTER


A gust of wind blows papers in the parking lot like leaves

Then rain comes at the window

My girl comes at the door, my

desk and floor are littered with papers  .   When

we kiss the sheets of paper

move gently

[1961/1964]


## AN ENVIRONMENT


Jack-

rabbits are true

plains rabbits, or hares   .   You will

find them just off the runways at

Las Vegas, Reno, Salt Lake,

coming down off those miles of foothills after

the coastal ranges, all that greasewood and sagebrush when

the water ends

They

jest do not seem

afraid

of jet engines,

even with them long ears

[1961/1964]


## TWO FLOWERS


At Spring & Lafayette Streets
the car moves up to the signal
stops  .   Full moon
sits large at the end of Spring
washes the cobbles down, pins
the automobile at the light


Turning left onto Lafayette
a bum with crutches and hat
and some beard stands closed in
slumped on the white line
spits on the car as it corners
I snatch his oath from the night air
and pull it with me toward   10th Street.


Later  .   in Brooklyn:
a violinist and poet's son
listening to his last concert
played on my tape machine
elbows on desk,   head
sunk between his hands, joined,
fingers a very fast section of the Bach in
recapitulation on his other hand as
his mind moves


All our nerves contain is that dry heat
Those floodgates open wide, split
and bloat . that sound . fill

up, over
flow, and among the quiescent faces
stands absorbing Bach's dry brilliance
a numb old man in the moonlight
He spits on the car

[1961/1967]


## THE MINT QUALITY


One friend—no,

two friends' wives

are near their term and large.

One friend toils

I think that is the word, barren,

still unwed, her

head on what she gave softly

and fiercely wasted   .   Another man

will marry his love in three days' time

and rejoices   .   One

girl is dead   .   No choice


Christiane dead!   and now again, among

the white girls, green tender virgins

who sang under the apple trees, down-

slope laughing run, hair wet with rain

naked, between the curve of terrace and the sea

The touch and blackness, down

into the mind and of time, and time-suspended, where

                                        hate / love / live

like shadows after that gate closes

                                        softly

on a daily ration of sun and cloud .

                                        Sing

                                        straight as I can.


          In mid-continent, a curve

          on the shoulder of a curve

          sing straight as I can the lines of

          Jaguar the Ship, the broken

          beam of a headlight unaccountably turned

                                        on in

          full daylight, staring emptily

                                        into the ditch.

          Not my eyes can see that lovely bitch,

          ophelia-hair spread in the shocked water of frogs .

          Your spring, Christiane was too short, the

          last separation of breath

          the dead coal under your heart, our

          knowledge of parting, a moan

          is the sound of wind in the ship's rigging .

*But   HOME, we gladly go home, all my dear friends,*

*we gladly go into the soil, long feet first, white*

*face, the nose broken, both eyes blackened, isn't it*

*typical?   M E R D E !*

*They picked up my new watch   50   yards away*

*and time is free for a while—but   m e r d e !*

*all that beautiful eau de vie they shall drink in my honor*

*and I not get a goddamned drop!*

*Les   salauds!   All*

*right.   I can wait.   But why*

*did I have to die now?   Given two months more, I would have,*

*but never mind, I shall be back mes petits, unborn, young,*

*de l'âge mûr, entre deux âges,*

*I had just started life . So you bastards,*

*I couldn't shut off the ignition and broke my nose .*

*I'll come back and take my clothes off again,*

*wait for life to touch me—not too long next time, please .*

*I am glad to be quiet now for once,*

*it is cool under the ground, no*

*lessons to prepare, books to read, nothing to 'arrange'*

*My mother will not be here before*

*I'm up again*

*singing*

*filthy songs—my poor mother .*

*She looks as horrible as I did with red eyes .*

    *Tout à fait foutue,*

    *foutue à mort .*

    *Death is a quiet lover .*

    *Mother I am glad of death .*

*Perhaps I'll wait until the end next time*

    *know what you know*

        *just to understand .*

                *I always understand*

*whenever I feel like it, did you know that?*

*Freddie made a lovely key for the lock in my headstone,*

            *some human words:*

    *"More people should have known her"*

*—More people will, Freddie,*

*that key won't turn it shut but open—*

*key didn't turn off the ignition and broke my nose*

    *isn't that funny?    Next time maybe*

    *I'll wait till the middle of life,*

        *know what you know*

                *just to understand .*

*I always understand, didn't you know that?*

    In mid-continent

    on the shoulder of a curve of a—

*Roads all over this land*

*so many more than in France and fewer curves*

Y o u   c a n   r e a l l y   g o !

—Sing

straight as I can

under Christiane's cut ration of sun and cloud

which she has left us in, under

the shadow of her clarities

under the shadow of her slender body

seven months gone and dead flesh white with passion

red with tears

Proud flesh .

the blood drained back

[1961/1964]

## THE CAFÉ FILTRE

Slowly and with persistence

he eats away at the big steak,

gobbles up the asparagus, its

butter & salt & root taste,

drinks at a glass of red wine, and carefully

taking his time, mops up

the gravy with bread—

The top of the *café filtre* is

copper, passiyely shines back, & between

mouthfuls of steak, sips of wine,

   he remembers

  at intervals to

with the flat of his hand

the top removed,

    bang

at the apparatus,

create that suction that

the water will

   fall through

   more quickly


 Across the tiles of the floor, the

  cat comes to the table : again.

"I've already given you one piece of steak,

what do you want from me now? Love?"

   He strokes her head, her

rounded black pregnant head, her greedy

  front paws slip from his knee,

  the pearl of great price

  ignored . She's bored, he

bangs the *filtre* again, its top is copper

passively shines back .

Food & wine nearly

finished.

He lifts the whole apparatus off the cup . Merciful

God, will it never be done?                    Too cold

already

to add cream and sugar, he offers the last

piece of steak with his fingers .

She accepts it with calm

dignity,

even delicacy . The coffee goes down at a gulp, it

is black

& lukewarm .

[1961-2/1964]


**BODY HEAT**

escapes  to  the  air

this  weather .

A  sigh  will  enter  the  air

returning  there

A  tear,  if  there  be  one,  will

run

down  to  the  sea,  being

water,  yes,    and  salt

There   is   a   small

c e m e t e r y   s o m e w h e r e

f o r   t e n d e r   e m o t i o n s

w h i c h   a l s o   c o o l .

[1961-2/1966]


## POEM FOR THE POSTPONED TRIPLE-ORBIT-RIDING ATLAS BOOSTER MERCURY MANNED-CAPSULE FRIENDSHIP 7 SPACESHOT

The countdown
           T minus 48 hours
                              waves
running 7 to 13 ft.
in the seas off Bermuda this morning


                         What is higher is the blue
Man cannot reach what is not fallen from, now
                   graves, years, cars, cards, orbit, moon
sits at the end of Prince St.'s winter
and soon that will be the man's new play-
                         thing, new territory, new
moustached, two-eyed, double-laned Selena
                         Highway into space
           Typographers'
wasteland never was
fren' Gus
fren' Glenn
           you go
up, fuck all spaceports, these stars
what's higher is blue, higher than that
is black
and stars and
                         what we wanted was roast pork
                         what we got was chowder
                                   come back
sometime

           LOUD     LOUD     LOUD

Man cannot reach what is not fallen from now

cannot hear the time
              he does fall from


    Thus, todaym ay have dawned I minus 73 hours for
the Marine lietutenant colonel who sat more than five
hours in the waiting space craft Saturday before weather

                                              [1962/1970]


## IN WINTER


A l l   e v i d e n c e
o f   b i r d s   i s   q u e e r ,   t h e


square (it is not
square, inter-
section of 9th   &   10th Streets, Second Avenue, near

                    (& within the grounds)
              of a church called St. Mark's in-the-Bouwerie
(it is off the Bowery
at least a block off the Bowery)     Bouwerie   =   -ing farmland
& in this case, the Pieter Stuyvesant farm, well, this square


                    is
                    filled
                    with . young . trees
                    which in this case on


a minus-20   morning in February, are filled
                              with sparrows
                              screaming
as tho this snow were a spring rain somehow


          Another day (same month) another
          occurrence is clearer :   off the Battery
          against an ice-blue sky, some gulls
so soundlessly, the
sound of their wings is all, they
                    glide above the backs of boats, stern,
                    up, crying, or surrealisticly quiet .

And .
in the body and wings of each bird . are . go—


SUMMER CLOUDS      /       HIGH AND

SWIFT AGAINST THE HORIZON

                                    or else the snow   .

                                              [1962/1965]


## LETTER


Glenn:
I missed your ticker-tape parade
Fifth Avenue, midtown,
having caught the scene
at City Hall
over TV
at a local bar, you
mouthing banalities like any
politician, what
kind of hero is that? I
hated it
and went to lunch, hoping
you had not written the speech
or not that part about
representing all of us.
We expect our heroes to smile, mutter
gratitude and disbelief at our
homage, and talk about the team,
that part was okay, accept a
kiss from Marilyn Monroe
if the wife isn't there,

what a drag. Wives
should stay quiet at home, re-
ceive reporters after human
interest. The Romans
knew better, did
Calpurnia march with the legions?
Even Cleopatra avoided it. No,
we should have given you Marilyn,
not Lyndon B. Johnson. Forgive us.

The shot was fine and exciting, you
had a job to do and
did it brilliantly, and
when the automatic equipment cut out
you played it cool and took the extra circuit,
brought it in by hand   55
miles short of target, fine.
but I would not walk
four blocks to see you ride
up Fifth Ave. in an open car.

              After lunch,
(no hero sandwich, a
full meal with wine) the cold,
bright March 1st lion's sky was
filled with paper falling
                  drifting
                      flying
rolling across the skyscrapers
down the canyons, blew
underfoot
draped across roofs, strung

out across the sky
falling in homage,
not just blocks away,
maybe from miles away, had it
blown or flown from downtown, the
wind was   WSW.


   But we're back to February 20th
and the real ride, the other one,
the ship called Friendship Seven,
three times.
                The fact.


And the wind whipped
there in 40th Street,
and a long, white crepe strip snaked
high across and caught
or not, or
dropped, rolled,
sang the hero who rode,
who rides, and then
the emblem I was not looking for
but found: smaller
scraps of paper fallen
in your honor, caught in
the twist and spurt of

March wind, around

a manhole cover
orbited.

                                [1962/1962]

## THE UNEMPLOYMENT BUREAU

The fly on the floor

of the Unemployment Office

in Carlisle Street, walks

in quick little spurts as though on wheels, going

nowhere, circling, tribbling about

in a circle : when, lash, I

dash my foot out at him, he

flies a few inches away and lands

crouched

sluggish

then circles back toward my foot

where it stands in line with other unemployed feet


Poor fly,

March is too early in springtime for you to buzz our heads,

black speck on brown tile floor, you

are probably also

trying to get in line.

[1962/1964]

## BRYANT PARK

I think it
is its
location—
between 40th & 42nd—
gives it its princely
quality, by contrast

At the top of the steps in the spring dusk
the sun gone behind
Crompton Velvet & Union Dime, the massive stone
grace of the Public Library at one's back, the
loungers of varying quality on the stone benches
and about one on the steps, across the stairs stretched out
like so many Etruscan statues, old bums, the youngmen, the
college girls with their long legs under short skirts, curled
there on the steps in the fading light   .   and below one
the lawn stretching out dark-green velvet all the way to
the fountain near Sixth Avenue, one can almost hear
the sound of falling water between the red and green
light interstices of evening traffic, plash, and at
regular intervals on this edge of lawn, between the
flower beds running an equal length, three signs

KEEP OFF            KEEP OFF            KEEP OFF

simple enough   .   The trees
in lines, doubled at the far sides, have sent
the spring sap up and leaves, the first-broken buds
and moves of green have startled the streetlamps as they
open and see the blood has started up in the dusk, and

there the small leaves are
tender as the legs of girls
opening equally to night and
warm air   .   The flower beds
splay and tighten the tulips
the hands of men from the Park Department have planted there
in, patterns of triangles, white intersecting the pink and
further down, pink intersecting red isosceles
cut to the side with sun   .   The other bed,
being shade-side, shows only green, the spikes, with
green spikes rising will be flowers tomorrow, next week,
a few white blossoms al-
ready out some halfway down toward the avenue
where buildings rise their own flowers of light, the ugliness
hidden in the new dark   .   I stand

arms parallel to the lines of balustrades, foward, out
stretching as though I were dusk or stone, above the girls, the men
as though my hands were those of the Park Department men, pressing
bulbs into the dark earth months ago, fall of the year,
my stone hands warm with sun, wet and dark with earth, o-
pening, closing, like the flowers all that action will become
tonight for me, now, this evening moment of new leaves and grass.

The lawn stretches out its moment of princely peace .
From the bottom of the steps one
cannot see the bare spots on it, it
stretches out perfect to the eye .
There are those signs . For the moment I am
that tired monarch, that prince after a long day's riding
out for birds or boar or stag . I move my legs

lazily
    twice, and stand
        at the edge of the grass.

                    [1962/1967]


## ESTATE

From the formal garden
the door enters into a field
Shadow of trees against sky,
that lawn
down
sloping the trees,
some brush, the
river. But
the door enters the field
There is a slat missing from the center
and does not remove the formality of the
door, half-open, on
        a field
One walks thru it, enters.

                    [1962/1964]


## THERE ARE DOORS

Wisteria
would not be enough
Vines offend me some subtle way
and for all its nostalgic smell, wisteria
is no exception

But there were birds
past sunset, five minutes before the dark
screaming to themselves and each other
settling down in the leaves
I scared two out of the lilac tree
                just walking by it
The formal shapes that surround us,
geometric walks, the clipped trees and shrubs
cannot hold it all
                /      The statue of a young girl in the
center, some broken slabs of marble hedged about the pool
torn from their borders to facilitate laying new pipes
                to the fountain, just thrown
            there, any-which-way, about her
        kneeling among those pipes, all
added to the quiet noise of birds
and smells of wisteria, lilac, her
buttocks were real, for-
get the ungenerous tit, the motion, the stone gesture
of pouring water down her back and buttocks were enough
            to want to make her real
                for that moment


        Too many ways OUT of this garden .
not just up the stone stairs like any
                gentleman,
there are doors.


        Darkness came finally
and birds stopped their querulous nonsense
and the incense of the flowers was
less loud

                                    [1962/1965]

# HARK, HARK...

*ladra, el ladrido,* it
means barking


—yes, and
this warm spring night, the
dogs do, different dogs
my different voices . and
the other sounds : a
man across the vacant lot
laying it down to his wife, the
drunk upstairs thinks he's silently            padding
across the floor in stocking feet, it thumps, it's
Friday night


"Don' bodderme nomore, yhear?"
thumps
and the dogs
bark this re-
assuringly peaceful, warm, spring—


The phone rings, it brings a
friend at 6th & Ave. D, beyond
Tompkins Sq. Pk., the other
side of town,
& behind the warm voice I hear


a radio on & hear
the dogs bark there


[1962/1964]

**AFFINITIES III.**

Walking out of Louis Zukofsky's new place
Columbia Heights
at 1:35 in the morning
there's the smell of sea
the sound of boats / that turn of the bay
                    into river and up
crossing, the engines over the night, the
night over the bridge, the bridge
                    over the river and

up
2 blocks
the smell of all that goes
into memory of itself until, by Hicks St. the only
real thing is the odor of already-walked dogs and one's own
sweat in the summer night.

            How keep this thief from home
            and the guard down
            for a moment?

                    to turn back, to
                    make harbor at that,
                    that moment of crossing.

                                    [1962/1964]

### THREE-PART INVENTION
### JUNE 21/62, 1:05 AM
### SOLSTICE


All windows open, moths
strike against the screens.


                        The cheerful counterpoint:
the wide sound,
you whizzing in the bathroom
with the door open, against
    the steady whirr
    of air
    conditioners in
the new building round the block,
pressure of air forced on metal leaves slatted out, over-
laid by the soft nature of your relief, the sigh
                       as you dry
the small tight hairs
    and rise .
The leverage is metallic
and a cataract of water
ends the song   .


            . .
            .


The first quarter-hour of solstice
ends with your hand in the small of my back, a gentle
         stroking
that brings everything from me, colors
and the dark
spring from me into the dark / breaths

move from the shallows to deeps after-
ribcages rise and fall together.
      Aware finally of movement of air
      cooling the damp limbs, two making V
      four an inverted M : and then, both
      flopping on our faces, all those
          lower case *l*'s  .

∴

      Returning to work
      after the fuck, first
      I water the flowers,
care with fingers for the young plants that
nod in the well of night . The black young
cat jumps onto my knee as I write, her
belly heavy with kittens . She
prods at the book and my hand.

      Air conditioners spin
against the regular
breathing from the
other room . Air
      moves thru
the quiet stream of my wrist, moths
      strike the screen.

                                        [1964]

# A LONG RANGE INTERVIEW WITH SATCHEL PAIGE, THE MAN OF AGE

"I wasn't IN training, so

I run around the field a couple times"

      "1948, I

      had it in mind to quit

      Bill Veeck called me up to Cleveland

      Cleveland was

      four games behind in the pennant

      when I came up"

a n d   t o o k   t h e   f l a g

"I won

6 outta 7 games"

Satch

did not pitch in the Series .

Cleveland lost

"Then I threw some pitches, Boudreau

      caught me. I

threw 50 pitches and 48 were strikes.

Boudreau lays down the glove and says,

'That's good enuf for me'"

—I stay in condition more than anybody on earth,

from spring to September, he sed

"I pitch

in  75   games this year.   But they tell me

I'm too old to be up there.   They tell me

it wouldn't look right, some young pitcher

pulled out of a game and be replaced

by a man old enuf to be his daddy.   It would

                              shame their spirit."


                    Damn well it should.

                                        [1962/1966]



**DOUBLES: IT'S A CABIN**

        The apartment

near emptied by now,

everything moved to 9th Street

but one basket of paperwork, one

lamp, eight books, some poems & a typewriter,

three near-empty bottles of booze, a chair, the desk

and—yes—the bed

At breakfast coffee

these last mornings,

I make her use the wooden chair,

I improvise a seat, a

yellow-painted old milk crate

with the Manhattan telephone directory dropped inside for weight


As she leaves for work

this morning, she

stands in the doorway and laughs to see

me sitting over my last cup of coffee,

seedy

with a three-day beard & my morning hardon rising

absently against the short, red-and-white-trim black robe,

gift of my friend in Japan, sitting

seriously

on the yellow box crouched over the Scotsman Finlay's poems

come from Kyoto yesterday, aloud, with the sun pouring in

on my left hand & the brick wall crowding back empty

away from the scene


She in her black-and-brown dress

& high heels leaving for the business world

with this rustic scene in her eye,

laughs . Confusedly prolonging the impression

I do not even rise, she comes

to me to

have her good-

bye-kiss

[1962/1962]


**THE JUDGEMENT**

THE CORNERS OF THE MOUTH
Perseverance brings good fortune.
Pay heed to the providing of nourish-
ment / And to what a man seeks
To fill his own mouth with.
—I Ching, commentaries, p. 162


That old man Senator Capehart

(R, Ind.)   carping for

immediate invasion of Cuba &

a friend of mine went camping this last weekend, slept

overnight in a sleeping bag,

roughing it out

overnight in the Catskill Mountains, who,

in the morning

made instant coffee . . .


Old men forget

in what is probably their own incredible loneliness, the

loneliness of war

I'm not talking about doagies stoked on 3.2
        standing around a jukebox
            in a PX
            in a Ft. Sill, Oklahoma .

        There was a scene in a Russian film :
this young man
the rest of his buddies killed
wandering
alone in
an advanced post,
suddenly,
           chased by  2  German tanks, not
firing,
not spending the ammo, just
                        chasing him / across
the treeless wreck of countryside
treads churning dead earth, one
wd not think tanks cd move that fast
                        an incredible l-
                        oneliness,
        the machines, the
        man, the
m a n,    running

Or the boyish humor—
In the Alps between France and Italy
                  that cold morning
after a night ex-change of patrols,
the advance next morning past the German dead,
        that corpse lying there
        with his mouth and eyes

open,

and the joke—

to lay   2   steaming turds

in his open mouth

the loneliness, the

singleness

of that act,

after someone else making water

into the hot tomb of his ear  .

[1962/1966]


## THE INTENTION

Why, why

on this brilliant day

redolent of sweating flesh and stung

bright with sunlight, do I

think of your darkness, soft, and

see your eyes when you were young?


Skin gold, your eyes

were dark and brilliant

in some river's mirror

simple,

direct as can be out of time.

Simple and timeless

as can be now, my

hand—

and how hard it is, how simple.

[1962/1965]

## AN ATMOSPHERE,

                    or how

put it to you, render.


Tender is the.


Past has some dignity after all,

that is its re-al—its

                    virtue, that you

hold it close, hold it

CLOSE, whatever I give you

you gave it first . It's


not hard to celebrate the sky

But I heard the bus come thru the block, the

bus after your bus, come

thru.

Two cats yowled, the starfish

held out its five arms

                                        [1962/1965]

# PHONE CALL TO RUTHERFORD

"It would be—
            a mercy if
you did not come see me . . .

"I have dif-fi / culty
            speak-ing, I
cannot count on it, I
am afraid it would be too em-
            ba
            rass-ing
for me   ."
            —

            —Bill, can you still
                answer letters?

"No . my hands
are tongue-tied . You have . . . made

a record in my heart.
            Goodbye."

                                    Oct 1962

                                    [1963]

# THE FIRST TWO DAYS

The sun comes and
                    comes
The buildings against the sky
yellowed stone, red brick, against the blue

bright metals against the blue
        Today and yesterday
our first two days of winter are two words


    gray/blue       rain/sun    Sun

comes and goes and comes against the brick walls
across the street, the stained green cornices, the white rags,
clouds move.   Shadows sharpen and fade
Sound of roller skates, bicycle bells, children's
        voices in the street
A telephone rings somewhere.
No one answers it


     words, no words.
The birds sail singly or in pairs, their
shadows move against the brick and disappear
    We are men and we have words
The shadow of a flock swings down across the building
and up, past the turn, the underwings catch light,
white as the rags
blue as the sky
grey as yesterday
      The sun comes and comes
The young cat sits in my window
   black as hell

                  [1962/1964]

## THE CRISIS : A FEW NOTES

"There's two of us going,
d'ja hear, Aunt Ella?
Do they still pay ya for carrying out the bodies?"

(Bellevue Hospital)

You name it.   You
    kin have it.
        Let me
            remember
the late, let us call it, crisis.

I, anyway, had a tendency to
                    turn into an
inaccurate, walking, and revised Bartlett.

"Wellya know an' doncha kennit an'
haven't I told ya, every tellin' has a
talin' and that's the he an'the she of it"
                    That's the K and the K of it
                    That's the A by Z of it
                    That's the vine, the
grapevine :

            Walkin' inta a bar at 3:30 in tha mornin'
            and a man buys me a drink because that's
            maybe the last nice thing he can do for anyone on earth—

            at this point we're waiting
        for the first Soviet ship to confront the blockade—
                    six hours away?

four?   sixteen?   it's happened already?

(it had)

And to think
of the politicians, the poor
politicians, or statesmen, if you will
working the night out, the dis-
patches, the catches, the bastion, the
question:

PRIME—

"To be or not to be, that is the
question:   whether 'tis nobler in the mind to bear
the slings and arrows of outrageous fortune, or
taking nuclear arms against a sea of troubles,
and by opposing

/

end them and ourselves—"

is not a question .

The man leaning on the fence outside my building
falling into the garbage cans—clank—
at 2 A.M. one morning, screaming

"I  DON'T  WANT  TO  FIGHT  NOBODY!"

at his old wife down the street
trying to ignore, I think, him,
trying not to admit
that she knew him, that
he had grey hair, that by any
accident of age, there was
nothing they could do anyway,

not even fight, were

there such an opportunity

    —just not know him—

          drunk and

          screaming at her


He asked me

as I put my garbage in,

       "WHAT DO YOU WANT!"

    It was a question .

I answered as I raise any

drink, or take any

leave of anyone these days.


        "Peace,"  I said.

                    [1962/1962]


## FIRST OF ALL

            *(for U.J. and then for:*
            *U.M., M.S., G.P., G.D.,*
            *and José Fernandez Guerra)*


. HOW FIT THE EVENT, or

the possibility of an event

            in-

   to the multiples of events? be-

   cause it happens, one

   thing happens after an-

   other thing, means

           THIS, in

opposition to that, is

irretrievably lost in time

         (glass . glass)

whether you notice it, or

not, whether

you want or condone it, or

would rather, in the end,   (glass)

                  take it back

it is still there, lost,

      that morning in time (glass)

lost o lost


This movement

if it is a movement, does not

put claim on the future

but asserts only

     that quality,

call it, the dignity of the past.

Glass   .   glass   .   (too many

glasses)   with their sad

                shine.

                         [1962/1962-3]


**FACES 2.**


The loneliness

of a single coated figure in the rain,

the well-cut coat, the

face away for then

            but there to

enter the glassed counter and order breakfast?

to know that inwardness of rain,

or that other

small lost face at the turnstile?

        Impossible.

        Done.

                [1962/1962-3]


## CRANK IT UP FOR ALL OF US, BUT LET ME HEAVEN GO


        Sometimes I think

you have no sense of the body at all

that it breed . need . take joy  /
          must give

    sponsion, re-

sponse, that

I do go surety for you constantly means less

than the seed spill out

        (handsel)

        alone, no gift


Moloch . Moloch  /
      through fire

Thou shalt not let any of thy seed pass thru the fire

to Moloch, I *am* the Lord . . .

Six men of some desert tribe, their women

for that time unclean, stand about the camp's

fire

jacking off : an offering to

Moloch . Moloch


OR ANY WARMTH WILL DO?


or why are fires, why is

fire that personal a thing? that

communal a thing?

But the response from the hand at the base of the spine

spreadeagled after, los dos,

only the movements of the chest, the breath, the breath, O

Leviticus!

oil for the lamps

I move the responsibility

shifting the load on my own back

one side to other of that world

we so rarely breathe in

the act of your life

spontaneity spread in the loon-mad nuptial, the

digging,

where are you *at*, that

there is no *and*, no sound, no conjunction   but *but*

or *or*, this poem can find, the sprigs it does portend

the responses I do concern myself with

> fear

> or boredom

> or diarrhea,

this fierce year called the thirty-sixth, could end

what wc both most want

intend  . No lie,

I revere the flesh too much, while

you think I should pick up my papers or take

> the bottles down.

I hope I die

> soon.

[1962/1966]


## WHITE SAIL

THE RED DOG races toward the cliff's edge

The red peaks downfall

> sun into the sea

A spreading

memory of moon rises over the dog

> racing

> toward the cliff where

HE   MUST   STOP

when he meets the sun . The white

sail on the white

sailboat, is erect

                      indifferent

The dog stops at the cliff's edge

as the sun falls down

into the sea . The dog

barks .

                                        [1962?/1971]


## RITUAL VIII.

Let me tell you, let me tell
        you, it
        is the repetitions
        keep us going any
        way

That pretty girl crossing
        on the ferry at   6   so
        clearly ignoring
all the attention she gets, will
        grow old, get
        pregnant,
increase the population or not,
        come to look
        different, change
        her ideas, and so,

                              years from now
                              another girl
looking not unlike her will come
             sit in the same seat, not
                              smoking,
eaten up by bad coffee and foghorns
                              back
to some unremarkable life, and
                              the process
                              rebegin
That old advertisement for a cleanser, Old
                              Dutch,
holding a can of Old Dutch cleanser with
             the same picture on it,
and the same one on that, only
             a little smaller, always
             one a little smaller, the
                              same thing
                              over again  .

                                                        [1962/1966]


## THE STONE

The stone found me in bright sunlight
around 9th and Stuyvesant Streets and
found, if not a friend, at
least a travelling companion.
Kicking we crossed
Third Avenue, then Cooper Square, a-
voiding the traffic in our oblique and
random way, a cab almost got him, and I had

to wait a few seconds, crowding
in from the triangular portion edged about
with signs, safety island, crossed
Lafayette, him catching between the cobbles, then
with a judicious blow
from the toes of my foot (right) well, a
soccer kick aiming for height we cleared
the curb and turned left down Lafayette,
that long block,
with a wide sidewalk and plenty of room to maneuver
in over metal cellar doorways or swinging
out toward the curb edge. The low worn
curb at 4th was a cinch to make, and
at Great Jones Street the driveway into a
gas station promised no impediment. But
then he rolled suddenly to the right
as though following an old gentleman in a long
coat, and at the same time I was addressed
by a painter I know and his girl on their way
to Washington Square, and as I looked up to
answer,
I heard the small sound. He had fallen
in his run, into water gathered in a sunken
plate which they lift to tighten or loosen
something to do with the city water supply I think,
and sank out of sight.
I spoke to Simeon and D.
about a loft it turned out he hadn't gotten, but
felt so desolate at having lost him they didn't
stay long, I looked at the puddle, explained
we'd come all the way from beyond Cooper Square,
they hurried away.

I suppose I could have used my hands, picked him
out and continued, he'd have been dry by the time
we got home, but just as I decided to abandon him
the sun disappeared.
I continued on down Bleecker finally,
a warm front moving in from the west, the
cirrus clotting into alto-cumulus, sun seeping through
as the front thickened, but not shining, the air turned
cool, and there were pigeons
circling
over the buildings at
West Broadway, and over them a gull, a
young man with a beard and torn army jacket walked
a big mutt on a short leash teaching him to heel.
The mutt was fine, trotting alongside, nuzzling
lightly at his master's chino pants, the young
man smiled, the dog smiled too, and on they went.
They had each other.
I had left him there in the puddle, our game
over, no fair using hands I had told myself.
Not that he could have smiled.
The sun gone in.
He had been shaped like a drunken pyramid, ir-
regularly triangular.
I liked him.

[1962-3/1965]

**A DULL POEM**

(for L.Z.)

— Z E N  F O O D S
it says on the truck outside,
what can be
seen thru the bakery door
Third Avenue & 24th
where it is lunchtime
Saturday . The truck has blocked :
a young man with a portfolio from
the art school next block, he
walks very straight, proud, walked,
disappeared behind truck where
he can see, I can't,

      two boys making a fire
      in a can in a
      vacant lot across the avenue.
      Extends the depth of one building but
      was an half-block of tenements
      a year agone, half the way to
      25th  . The wood was wet, was set
      before the truck came in and parked,
      and smoked . No cherries here, no
      mickies there. It's wet, I wonder
      what there might be in that truck
      —ZEN FOODS
      bean sprouts and rice, all of
      Chinatown's fowl & fish & vegetable,
      Zen Foods, no mickies.

Does this generation know
about mickies, set among coals, wood
fires in vacant lots, cooked to half-
raw & eaten with stolen salt / charred skins and all?
Even in those islands of still-poor Irish, their
isolated blocks about the city? No micks here
no cherries there, bean sprouts with rice &
*comidas criollas* composed of the obscure parts of dead pigs.
The bakery's German & serves
healthy, bland, Mitteleuropa
meals for about a buck. Tender

loin tomorrow,

goulash today.
I bring my own wine.

— Z E N   F O O D S —

Two elderly men
with long overcoats from third-hand shops
look at me meanly, leaving, wishing
the wine were theirs, mutter.   The boys
in the lot appear throwing rocks,
broken Ignatz brick, at one another & jeering, no
micks here, no krauts there, no


Some seven-year-olds outside the plate glass
window are trying to liberate

my bicycle, it
is too securely locked to a leg
of a NO PARKING sign, garnished with
METERED PARKING and the meters as well.

They try the lamp and go see if
some eight-year-old friend has been gifted with
a screwdriver.
                    The waitress starts again
to come on, always a bit crude. That ends.
I am returned to the hopeless scene, having
                    the dollar to pay. I pay,
leave tip, the
                    —ZEN   FOOD truck pulls out.
                        "How many crullers?"
                                "Two."
I do too.

[1962-3/1963]

## IT MIGHT AS WELL BE SPRING

6:15
is already dark on
a winter night
                    in December, remember?   You
                    keep coming back like a song
                    in January, I sed you

j a n - u - w a r y  .   sunset is five-forty-seven .


            "Ven I kom to dis country
            skirts vair *dis* high
                                (the hand)
            und vit a slit, yet, in da zide,
            up to *here!*"


            I can't look.
Out the steamed-up window instead, a pickup truck is
cream-colored and dark avocado-green in the street
streaked every few minutes or so with pale yellow headlights
uptown on the avenue . The pickup

truck apparently delivers instead  .   Out of the
deli next door, figure of a man, stalks the truck, opens
the door of the truck  .

            In the window, it
being night, the inside of the bakery-restaurant is
        reflected back  .   The waitress
is cleaning up the dishes three tables back  .  Watch,
        the crotch,
near where her hand lay to indicate the height (D E P T H? )
        of the slit in the dress, the
uniform is white, tight, it's night, the man
        outside opens the truck door
and climbs into the waitress's skirt
        very naturally, and
                        just below the waist  .


Neither one knows,
but it might as well be spring  .

                                    [1962-3/1965]


## THE ANGRY MAN SITS, MAKES HIS REVISIONS


Thin as a rail, not pale, dark,

sallow with fine hands, he's tedious  .

The minute considerations of the

mind that makes those sounds, that poem,

unselected in small talk

dispersed in conversation   .    But


        sits all night

        at a desk

head bent under the light, the

hand crooked, scratches, changes

the line until the light grow pale

until the form emerges

         a coherent music
ranges up from the page,
copulation of all that rage and all that song .

                                        [1963/1964]


## POLITICAL POEM I.

### THE POLITICIAN'S SWEETHEART


         has just turned 22,
         reclines on those soft cushions with her drink
         and couldn't care less where the nearest
         deep shelter is located, those cushions;
         luckily,
         she does not care much for politics.


And Art?
A Debussy tone poem, she often says,
is that an answer to anything?
It's those cushions under her ass.
They respond to her velvet pressures.
It's a different world.
The brass, then the percussion.

                                        [1963/1963]


## POLITICAL POEM II.

*deus ex what?*


         The worker looks just like his boss.

         And they both look like the machine.

                                        [1963/1963]

## RITUAL IX. : GATHERING WINTER FUEL

The jews burn wood on First Ave., New York City, in a

barrel, to keep

w a r m

Clayton's

workmen across the cut

their house in Kyoto, likewise

warming their hands, the same cans or barrels, in the dark

flames leaping, men standing around, and

I have seen it on the West Side, New York, Gansevoort Street

growing up among the meat packers there, would go

out

at night

hunting wooden crates

break up for the fireplace

to keep   w a r m ,   my

mother's hands those days,

warming her arthritic smile . hands

& I myself in that

furnished room on 15th Street that had a fireplace, I

knew where to go to score for crates

/   Good

king Wenceslas went out

gath-er-ing

on St. Stephen's day

winter fee-yew-well, or

the vacant lot at Houston

between Mott & Third

the same barrels

& cans & older men in long

overcoats from the mission,

& here the scene unabated / 20-odd years later

the fruit & vegetable market, First Avenue & Ninth, using

wood from crates

New Jersey, Delaware, Cali-

for-ni-yay,

Florida, New Mexico, Georgia, Louisiana, Texas, all

for the same fire, how

reunite the South and North, the West and East—


w a r m ,

in sunlight you never see it, just

walking by &

feel the warmth  .  there .

Fire in a barrel, burning

the hands, the hands, the italian

bakery next door is still discreet,

but the kosher butchershop next to

that comes out for a word or two, the

      gesture,

     palms stiff out at arms' length, passing

the time of day, their magic  h a n d s

liverspotted and reddened maybe, no paesas or beard, still

            here at First Avenue and Ninth Street, it's

          the jews uniting the world, the country, the city,

       mankind down geological time perhaps,

to keep their hands warm .

               [1963/1966]


## THIS IS NOT THE SAME AS SHARING ANYONE ELSE'S DESPAIR

BRIGHT  SUNLIGHT
on the avenue
Green & cream
      the buses,
red & cream, the buses .
black . beige . red & cream
black . beige . red & cream
      the cars
        uptown .


Black dog in a red harness
      looks in at the door .
Old man
out of harness, looks
      in, at the door .

"I haven't seen one of 'em yet .
I haven't seen one like'm yet,"
says Aunt Ella looking out the door

/

"My old man."
You can tell by the tone she means her
husband.
"Since he died,"
she continues,
"I  H A V E N ' T   M E T   A N Y O N E   E L S E / "


Aunt Ella's cross is people, don't
know the names of things .


"Is that carroway seed?"  asks a lady
in a fur coat better than most. "No,
them's poppyseeds," says Aunt
Ella, & to the first conversation, confirming,  "that's
why I never married again . Fifteen,
twenny dollas a night he usta spend."


Very loud.


Old woman with kerchief round her head &
had come in holding one hand over the heart,
the man's tweed jacket, the
heart she is wearing, sends
the barley soup back

"It is
too salty,"  she says.
The cook sends back a cream of potato
soup.

Over which she is silent, but makes eating noises .

Her face is half-eaten away .

Aunt Ella still on the register :

the guy two tables away hits the Saturday-waitress for

ten  .   He's her boyfriend

and's eating free  .   He

wears a cream nylon tie

with blue & red stripes & a midnite-blue jacket .

The tie is terrible

She loves him . Aunt

Ella to her interlocutor in

an old army overcoat & grey hair,

from no context

shouts reflectively,

"S o m e d a y !"

Bright sunlight on the avenue

Green & cream, the buses,

red & cream, the buses .

black . beige . red & cream

black . beige . red & cream

the cars

uptown .

[1963/1965]

## PRE-LENTEN GESTURES

Thank God one tone or

one set of decibels is

not all there is.    The

*Dies Irae*, the radio behind me, is,

due to the mad programmer we never know, followed

by a selection of military band music.

How kind.   I

can't help thinking of

Ed Dorn, his line: *Why*

*can't it be like this all the time?*

"as my friend said"

the band, the binding, the

bound from one state to the next, and sometimes

one is not even asked.

What may be revealed, given.

What?

that it be revealed.


A girl comes in with her little fur hat

and wants to buy   T H A T

cake that looks like a group of buns in the window.

Impulse buying.   That's what it is, a group of buns.

Her young husband stands outside in

his little fur hat, smiling, superciliously.

"Foolish little girl,"

said Rudolph Valentino, smiling

to himself on the set as he read and pocketed

the bill from his tailor.

"What is it called?"

       "Sugar buns," says Aunt Ella

       looking at the buns themselves

as tho she were identifying some obscure layer

of geological time for a

micro-paleontologist who might know better, that her

expression not insult the girl.

                 "35¢" says Aunt Ella.

The girl drops a dime of the change, leaving.

           Her little

husband in the door smiles as she bends

        to pick it up.


Boy in a nicely shaped black coat and a package of

laundry, crook of his arm, who has been

not-quite-studying the menu on the window between them

glances to his left and disappears down the avenue

as the girl emerges,

readjusts his bundle.

Aunt Ella runs the squeegee over the length of the door,

the glass steamed so .   it is revealed

that the red blotch

on the opposite curb is a Jaguar (cap J)

      and the blue one behind it's a Ford.

    Robin's-egg Ford

Onward  and  upward,

we used to say in the army, before

trying to pick up a cluster of teenagers, the

streets of San Antone that hot,

we were that hot  .  A small boy has started a fire

in the vacant lot beyond the Jaguar and Ford.   Sousa

still calling the sounds from the radio at my back.


I   AM   BACK   to an earlier question:

someone had found it strange

I should think of the concomitant physical cul-

mination of love,

fucking, in short, as a release, some

times a relief from

the pain of loving itself.


Surcease of pain. The idea

is medieval at least:

"o lady, give me some relief,

cure me of that sweet sickness

I am subject to"

object, of course,

bed   .   what

happens to impulses from fingers that touch that

smooth skin, that they skim the breast, down the

line of ribs, beneath the indentation of waist, the

flare of hip, smoothness of thigh rounding inward

past forests of night to churn among mucous membranes,

heat rising.

The beaky crane, the

"one-eyed great goose"

the tower risen out of the olive grove.

Surcease of pain.

Love, the disease that implies

its own cure, part and end of it.

And that end begins again.

"You, who alone can cure me by your touch, Lady,"

a cry they sometimes insisted was, had been

addressed to the Virgin, implied in its end

surcease of pain, no virgin, but another hand,

and that miraculous touch his lady's fingers curled

against his own, against the small of his back, flat out.

A mystery? No . What

else could happen?   The

world is what it is, men and women what they are.

Every organic thing, o philosophers, man,

plant or animal, containing as seed the flower,

its own destruction, its own rebirth . Yeats was right?

>"All true love must die
>
>Alter at the best
>
>Into some lesser thing.
>
>*Prove that I lie.*"

Hardly,

with O'Leary in the grave, seed of that growth,

cure of that ill, and

once begun, the act fore-

tells its own, what-

ever-breaking-now, its own

       end   .   revealed.

       Squeegee drawn once more

       down the door's glass,

the Jaguar gone, the Ford remains itself at last,

revealed smaller now by itself, as the houses, parks,

the football fields of our youth, than

       it / they / then /

       seemed .

It always is,

always was

this way, Ed,

all the time.


It is not that it does not happen.

It does,

and there is no help for it.

And

there is no end to it,

until there is .

[1963/1965]


**OBIT PAGE**


O god.

First the greatest right-handed batter in history

Rogers Hornsby

(hit .424 in 1924)

with a lifetime average of .358


and now William Carlos Williams

Jan 5
Mar 4
1963

[1964]

# THE FIRST ROUND

Sunday morning in early Lent,
here we are
we happy few
we lucky three

        coming
        awake in mid-morning, old
        mist & must & stretch


*"Open the goddamn window."*

        "Right,"   /   flung
        sun and air warmer
than could have been predicted  .  O
the cat sits there in the sunlight


& after toast & coffee, snow still
dirty along the sidewalks' edge, gutters, to
hear those sounds from the street, up, un-
        mistakable—
Head out & look & sure!   He holds, he stands holding
        the broomstick
letting the truck get past him  .  It's


the first stickball game of the season
        in Ninth St., March the 3, 1963,
        we lucky three . William
        Carlos Williams will die tomorrow
        whom we love,
Joel will read on Wednesday
whom we love
The air sweeps out the odors of love from rooms .
the air we love, we weep, we read, sing, the first
stickball game of the season (thuck!)
        in Ninth Street  .  We
        happy few, we
        lucky three, here,
        to hear it.  The
old earth swings round  .  swings
        into the sun .

        [1963/1964]

# THE SELECTION OF HEAVEN

1.  GOD,   that it did happen,
    that loose now, that
    early configuration
                of birds, the texture set in
                words,   1945,
    a Staten Island beach in early October
    here in more than flesh and brick,
    9th Street, March 1963.


                The clouds were love.
                The words we have near 18 years, you
                prophesy, it could have been that,
                the bullshit
                words, if that is what we are then,
                that they can
                                do, come to
                Life .
                        You
                put that much life in it, baby,
                you know you can't win   (touch
                                bottom to darkness where)


    This grey . soft . overcast . not-quite-rainy day,
    that I can
    swim my mind in it, swim it in overcast, the sun
    tries, and there they are, the birds, my gulls
    circle over a street to the North.

    In the street below a child's voice yells
    "Kick'm in the nuts . . . . . kick'm in the nuts!"
                        broadcast :

        Allen K. says
    you have to let a man have all
               /
                            his balls.
     I am afraid he speaks from experience.
And here the small birds sing
speak from experience, outside
        my window, come   .
And my big birds, my gulls, come
here   .  I see them here, I
can walk thru it,
        swim it.


2.  ROYAL EBONY

is the name of a carbon paper . Is
also title of a poem by Nicolás Guillén.


The smoke rises in a thread, a
curled stream from between
his thumb and forefinger
as he snuffs it out.
           We live.
           Pity?  It
           is the waste of their lives.


No.  Pity is hate.
      Pity is hate.
           Pity is hate.
Pity
is
hate.
      O,  were it so,
or as they say,
were it not so.

3.               HOW do we keep any of it

ever?          Do you

know what I'm talking about?
You borrow my books
you borrow my bicycle
7:30 A.M.   Sunday morning
to ride to Staten Island with
a girlfriend.    Yes you know.

Love
is different each time we taste it .

4.  MESTIZA:   brown, olive and black.
Scudding clouds the sun rides against.
The wind wins   /   brown, olive, and black
wind of bicycle-March against her jacket
shape of her top
revealed
       /
            the legs push   .   It is not
July, heatwaves rising from a blacktop road,
it is March   .   the sun wins sometimes,
a few minutes   .   Staten
Island, yes, my gulls are there, the wind, their
generations later of grandchildren
                nesting soon

mestiza : brown, olive and black.
The gulls are white and black
             simply   /   sun

catches the underwing
clouds keep moving
.     If you
watch clouds, riding
a bicycle is dizzying

The smoke rises in a thread
from between his thumb
and middlefinger.


5.   March 3, 1 A.M. / Kyoto.


After the conversation in two voices
after the poems
a list of objects around you
no
collage but a set of emblems
blazing low as the tea stays hot
growling from the fire
the walls   .   wood and rock
surround you
your sleeping woman, that
softness   .   *The Harbor Dawn*
not preceded by Te Deum . . . . Hand of Fire
not followed by macadam gun-grey as
your own dawn comes
/
Buzz
of the plane, hark
Hart, high, small, and distinct
The heart of clay
is shared, baked and
brittle tho it may not break.

That day does break  .  My
gulls were never further away
than this  .  The sun
coming and
coming


6.  ÁSHARA :
                es la siguiente : a
myth-real term in Japanese:
in Arabic it is the number   10
Color is black  .  "the warring,
hostile, contentious aspect of the mind"
Black is the crow
from the still-white ground to the
black branch, is
the black of cypress spires in the graveyard of Béziers,
is the blackness of night out across the cut
those two spotlights out, the
hours before the dawn
light reading to the cats outside
the cats prowling, the
tape spinning
slowly, at   3¾ ips
the cat here in my window
black as hell is, black,
as crow, as cypresss, down
into the mind and time suspended is
how this color is, is no color, is
black crow,
black cat, black
cypresses in dawn sky, is

black as black is, is the
sound of sea, the wings flapping.
Gulls are white   . sins . The mind
                          is
                          dark .
"Full fathom five thy father lies"
                          it is
the number   10
                          Color is black.


7.  THE MERE
concordance of these sufferings :
                          Hannah died.
Tomorrow the funeral in New Bedford, Mass.,
the interment, the last dancing of the coffin,
shadow of birdflight flash across the box, the
ground is cold, should we see it, in Fairhaven—
cross the river, turn
down toward the bay   .   Hannah
Gibbs Whiting Mackey Blackburn died,
87, after a full life .   I,
grandson, 37,   (you
gauge there those fifty years, I know
                the small dif-
ferences, way they ought, or
not too far wrong—)        away,
                          Ruth,
Sarruth.
You are that young,
too young   .   We never have
until tonite, given

that grey gentleness

to one another  .   wet, yes,

and why not?

Tell me what else this shoulder might serve for

please, I want to live beyond that

please, the drive back   300   miles

please, the ground is cold, there is

please, no other life, please,

please there IS that

difference, say it

might have been a man but

now, no care, who

could care?   it was that dif-

                (small dif-)

        erence be-

tween the man who filled was

more a child  .   You can

turn your back

or I can turn my back—

           it is a child

unborn, it is our being

all our being

man and wife, or else the rest

of life is Jack the

life is back, is fact, is black, is

rope enuf, is no rope, is the ripper

      is the ripper

      is the ripper

is the child, un-

born perhaps,

          and sucking.

8.   Right it should be Dicker
     does this, that we should,
                    he drives
     out of that town,
     I write it down and we go.
     It is the sea,
     okay, the East River, it
               is the sea.
     Past Riker's Island and north
     the bridges sweep
     west to east, Tri-
     boro, Bruckner Blvd., "the
     North is of storms"
                    Kelly, it is mere
     spring.
     The clouds sit there,·
                    to the

     North.


9.   The grave half-filled
     with earth  .  EARTH
     Two diggers with long-handled spades
     smile and joke with one another . The grave
     stone faces the bay at Fairhaven
     her father sailed from.
     She was   87  .
     Everybody loved her  .

10.  IT EXISTS.   There ↓
    is the very spot to place the ashtray
    so that         my hand
    may reach it without looking while I read
    And that is where I place it,
           exactly |


           THERE ↓


    The   3
    brandies I have had after lunch are
           exactly
            enuf
    to create the vulnerability the
    translator needs to bring him
    open to the text, that other life
    than his own
          /
           or how to share
    another man's glory, exaltation,
    love, penury, lust,   700
    years agone, the gap gone,
    No, not bridged, baby,
    YOU ARE THERE!


          Wet roads, the plots, the wars—
          Winter is cold, snowdrifts
          are exact, or rain comes down,
          the birds come, the sun comes,
          the lady—shall we be lucky today, shall
          we have opportunity to speak with her?
          Only a few words!    One could not hope
          for years—

4

would have been too many, would have
turned us over into drowsiness   3
exactly sufficed   .   Smoke
rises in a thread from between his
thumb and middlefinger as
he snuffs it out . continues .


11.   The   *a* of the Ballantine truck, reversed   /6
less than  7,   twice  3,   that
a-6 reversed again reflects upon
the face of a small man in a grey hat
reading the menu in the bakery window
Features recede behind two layers of glass,

the corner of the window
                                        a-6 sits
where his face would be—is
turns it
to a skull, the man is helpless, it
is his skullface looks in
                                        at my shadow (right) not at me
the number   6   is the number of
fecundity in Mediterranean myth

3   .   7   .   6   .     sixteen
                                        a proper age, it is
my own virginity I take
The skull my own
both bodies, hers, given
                                        *áshara,*  it is the number   10

Color is black .

                 a skull  .  The  6  is final, the

man is helpless before it .


12.   UNDER THE IMPRESSION THAT DESERT FLOWERS BLOOMED
      ALL YEAR

He looked for the flower

in the desert for

                9 hours

                and did not find it

                was

never anywhere but

close to home


I have to take a leak—

he says years later at McSorley's

and goes  .   He is still

close to home


13.   LIGHT  .   LIGHT

the lonely gathered

                lovely fucking light

is there, the human reach is

there .


    Keep us autonomous,

each man's control be his own,

his reach what it can be


Governments will die under the bright sun

3000° F -temperatures melt the filing cabinets .

penetrates .

The light in the bathroom changes
because there are two windows, be-
cause I keep my plants there.

        The work will be done, my brothers .
        Our loves are public knowledge .
        The light is soft, and green, it, yes,

              penetrates .
              Join us .

14.   Moving always from West to East
     how my tribe moves at last,

I have come to the black mountain
I have come to the end of the world

              I shall climb
              I have to climb the mountain
              at the end of the world, the
              black mountain, to meet the
              7   white dogs

coming down toward me  .  trotting,
the rain of pebbles and dirt
the number   10   is broken

to   7   and   3  .  the color black
smashes into the primary colors
                  3,   the light
                  is white, say
       it is my own virginity I take  .

15. | Hannah died Mar 23, 1963
John Henry, April 17

NY, New Haven & Hartford

"All tickets please!"

The ivy is green on the walls, small
                            tender leaves,
forsythia along the tracks, chestnut, magnolia trees
Woodlawn Cemetery,
the way up  .
The burgeoning green that is so full and quick is
                            willows, looks
        yellow in sunlight .  Water
        comes from the rock .


John Henry survived Hannah twenty-five days,
would wander about that section of the rest home
peering into the empty room.
        "I can't seem to find my wife."
They'd tell him his wife had died
and he'd remember that for five minutes.


The last day the 17th, his
daughter Pearl sat by him
while he ate  .  While he ate
with his right hand, he
held her hand with his left  .  the heart hand .
                            The heart stopped
                            just before midnite.

Now the weekend.    It's going to take
three days to bury him.
Showing the body tonight,
                              the service tomorrow.
        Put him in the
ground on Monday at dawn.
        Gravediggers won't work on Sunday
even for double-pay .


16.  w o r d s  :   should have been spoken at graveside


There are no true voices anymore, John
Henry, you knucklehead, you hard-
headed, stiff-backed, tough-minded old man, your
                    mouth is clenched tight for good
                    it is a solid line

from under your sharpened nose around your pointed chin, above
                                                        that
the strong, kind, (remembered), and finally closed eyes,
the dead tissues under the skull that were your brain
softened finally with your   88   years

into a forgetfulness your children could
relate to, could pity, could and did
expiate themselves upon, so
                    accept their own lives

for what they had become or grown to,
John, you knucklehead, you bonehead, in
the old photographs you are more often
                    scowling, when the others
are smiling bravely into the bright sun.

You quarreled
with everyone you loved and were proud
when your children fought you back with brain and spirit
and were hurt, of course you were hurt
                    by it, and loved them   .   You
had made them irrevocably yours you would have said God's


and that's not true, and your mouth is closed for good
upon the air of this world, your hands    not
                    folded in eternity as that
                    cliché-ridden, pompous, minister
friend of yours who did you final service might
have said had he the gift of words, but
clenched, holding your heaven to you;
swollen farmer's hands that had been kinder than your mind was
clenched in eternity the rock of your mind
that could not crack and open but
still clenched dissolved under the rain of years


the head still,
straight white hair still handsome   .   4
generations gathered round a coffin yesterday to pay
what truly was respect and sometimes love,   the
different qualities of flesh
                    from ruined to what
                    renews itself each day, and grows, John,
stood there and did you honor   .   Rocks


wear away under the rain   .   Flesh is tough
        the spirit
resilient   .   tougher than flesh   .   They

said you looked natural
and in their mouths it
was comforting cliché  .   The words
were truer than they knew, you still looked
        stiff-backed, hard-headed,
          but the spirit gone, that blur,
a peace  .

## EARTH TO EARTH

GOD,
be here at this graveside .
Not in the cut flowers the undertakers' men heaped up
but in the new forsythia, red maple
        buds, magnolia, be
        in the spring earth
will heap this grave, grow new grass over it,
golden green of willow starting fresh  .  be
        in the spring earth with John,
your faithful servant,
where he will lie
next to Hannah as he did in life, her
        eternal lover   .   Lock them
        forever into this hillside
facing the Acushnet gulls settle on,
    wheel over crying, hear them in the
distance  .

    Smoke rises
from between my forefinger
and middlefinger  .  Wind on this
cold spring hillside sweeps it off
barely visible in the sunlight

the ashes
fall upon new grass  .

ASHES  TO  ASHES

    John,
forgive the carpet of phoney grass
          too dark for the season
the undertakers spread beneath your
coffin for this moment  . We have
seen you to this hillside, let it be
enough  .  Forgive
the Reverend Doctor his recitation
of  2  Edgar Guest poems yesterday,  I
figured I could stand it if you could  . The rain
    of dirt and pebbles will be real enough  .
         fresh clods set in
           after you have settled  .  Rain
             fructifies,
            but will wear away  .
              ROCK
The committing ceremony had the
dignity of its own
        words, yesterday,
despite the use of flowers with their snapped-off heads
instead of fistfuls of earth  .  EARTH  .
When the diggers end the job, let
the first  3  shovelsful of spring earth
be my shovelsful, let it be enough  .

DUST  TO  DUST

        consigning  .  I

have not willed the occasion for these words
which cry themselves like hunting gulls
my mouth flapping open    .    GOD,
welcome your servant John Henry
into whatever Paradise he thought existed,
offer him
the best accomodation that you have for such a
                    lover of the mind   .   God
                    knows he has earned it,
            twice over   .
Let there be soft
            wind
where he is, let him hear gulls cry
above the
bridge,
            and be home.


17.   The mind returns to it always
      a machine gone insane, the senses
      tamped down, turn the dial to − 1
      that kind of death .

                  The dead man sits at the table
                  a dead cigarette in his mouth,
                  drinks, the mind-gears turn
            repetitiously over the same materials,
            the same images return, murderously.
      He sits and looks at them again and again.
      The smashed glass, her high at the party, a
      pickup truck, an empty road, sound of the man's voice,
      of his own as from a taperecorder far off and drunk,
      cannot recognize the sound of his own voice, the

sleeping bag no one can find, a pink poppy beside the chair, the
cat
jumps into his lap
wanting, not food, but love,
the glass knocked over, the
second glass thrown at that exact spot .


      Admit:   it had been a long time preparing,
now a long time gone .   Nothing just happens. But
to cut onesself down when
there's nothing left to manipulate but the impulse to murder?


Solid panic is a state of normality
when you cannot blame anyone, not even yourself.
Just the fact,   THE    FACT!
Go over it step by step, repeat, go
over it in utter despair, turn
the mind-machine on, let it run,
feed the data into the computer,
whirr –
                whirr .
—Can you tell me what difference it makes?
            —Yes. None.
     —You're a fool.
              —You're another!


Dust devils spin down the road.
Every 10th building, every 5th
corner, every 2nd
mountain is the knife  .   How
      recover the town to himself  .
        —no, not with her—  for
his own annihilated, powerless, murderous self?   How

give up any thought of final recovery
　　any victory, even over himself?
　　give up even the defeat and sit
　　at a wooden table in a strange
　　land, murdering flies dully
　　with a flyswatter and his left hand?

How come to it with the inexhaustible world of phantoms on his back
pressing in the repetitious fact—nothing
he can say or do
will make the slightest difference to her?

Going OVER　that road step by step
until he knows it like his broken hand,
　　living symbol of his impotence,
a right arm broken in two places, and
everytime there's a twinge in the interosteol musculature, the

　　　　　　pickup truck will return, with the
　　　　　　sound of a glass smashing, with
　　　　　　the hysterical vision of a wet rock
　　　and a pink flower in the identical spot a week later .

So he murders flies, throws
the dead cigarette away and lights
another.

　　　　　A sweet potato
　　　　　in water
　　　　　in the bowl in front of him
　　　grows into a forest of green, cuneate leaves,
　　　al-most unbelievably .
From every eye of the inert thing, dark

blooded stems growing pale toward the top

rise,

then the leaves,

light green on the younger ones, dark green on the rest,

all turned

toward the light from the kitchen window .

A jungle rises out of that inert potato

not/dead, clearly, tho it not move  .


O,     L O V E !

Smoke

rises from between the first and middle fingers of his left hand

which came to life,

so passive it was before .

He rises and opens the door to a

courtyard full of trees and birds.

Sounds of the wakening city come in .

But the laurel has one pink blossom.   He


returns to the chair

& murders a few more flies .

[1963-67/1964-72]


## TWO SONGS FOR THE OPP


1.     Stay drunk!

that's my motto .

Then you'll never have to know

if the girl love you or no

(hee   hee   hee

nor will she

2.  Play gui-

tar, go to the bar

hope there's one hand will caress

and undress

But pints to go

before you sleep

(har,  har,

nobody care

[1963/1963]


## GRAFFITI


The New York Public Library at one's back...
and a statue of William Cullen Bryant
(1794-1878)
around & back of which are
newspapers, bottles : Gallo,
Arriba, Thunderbird, Banner
Port, Twister, & Gypsy Rose
and inscribed on the stone:


"Yet let
no empty dust
of passion find an utterance in thy lay,
a blast that whirls the dust
along the howling street and dies away;
but feelings of calm power and mighty sweep
like currents journeying through the windless deep."

It also says
in less en-
during form:

CRICKET & VINCENT

Stacey and Troy

BEV AND TOM

then: Daphne & Boys!

FRANK LOVES MARGE

ERIC & TORCH

daphne & rickie

also: DIANE LOVES BOYS

poor Daphne, but

Lourdes & Joey FOREVER

The earliest dates
are 1961 .

[1963/1964]


## SCOFFING IT

The blind man with the Wallace Beery

whiskey voice keeps bawling

"Mary!

Angie!"

tells Aunt Ella:

"*Feel* that bread!

I gave pigs

better bread,

when I had pigs

Pennsylvania 1918."


"When?"  says Aunt Ella.

"1 9 1 8!"   and he

knocks over his glass of Pepsi.

[1963/1967]


## THE USES OF THE EYE


When the door of the next truck is open
it reads toward the cab

                    —Z E N   T A B L E S ,   the black dog
leaps on the man in pure
                    friendliness—he only wants to leave .
8   seats to a table
except one side of one table, only   3
                         the cigarette machine sits
                         makes its change
6   tables then
seating   47   deathsheads, the luncheon hour   .   Packed   .   a man
with a 100 lb. sack of cement walks past   .   The Modern World e-
          merges
                /
           124 Warren Street, sayeth the truckside

                    —Z E N   T A B L E S—

The truck door closes
Driver climbs in
The truck departs
The hot cat


heads toward the door tail up, the black dog barks, the first of the

7   white dogs I
meet on this mountain
greets me
                    'mid a rain of pebbles & dirt .

          "—and the an-gels sing,

               & leave

their singing

ringing                              in

                    my

          ears ."

[1963/1965]

**THE WATCHERS**

It's going to rain
Across the avenue a crane
whose name is
          CIVETTA LINK-BELT
dips, rises and turns in a
          graceless geometry


          But grace is slowness   /   as
ecstasy is some kind of speed or madness   /
The crane moves slowly, that
much it is graceful   /   The men
          watch and the leaves


Cranes make letters in the sky
          as the wedge flies
                    The scholar's function is


                    Mercury, thief and poet,
                    invented the first   7   letters,
                    5   of them vowels, watching
                    cranes   .   after got


The men watch and the rain does not come
                    HC – 108B CIVETTA LINK-BELT
In the pit below a yellow cat,
          CAT – 933
                    pushes the debris
and earth to load CIVETTA HC – 108B
          Cat's name is PASCO and

there is an ORegon phone number,
moves its load toward   3   piles
Let him leave the building to us


Palamedes, son of Nauplius,
invented   11   more
             (consonant)
Also invented the lighthouse, and
measures, the scales, the disc, and
"the art of posting sentinels"
Ruled over the Mysians,
                 Cretan stock, al-
                 though his father was Greek
                 Took part in the Trojan trouble on the
Greek side . The scholar's function is fact  .  Let him
quarry cleanly  .  All
T H O S E   I N V E N T I O N S   C R E T A N
so that a Greek  /  alpha-beta-tau
based on a Cretan, not a Phoenician
            model
           Three different piles :


earth  /  debris  /  & schist, the stud/stuff of the island
   is moved by this
   PASCO
   CAT – 933
   ORegon 6–
it does not rain  .  smoke, the
              alpha-beta-tau .


raised from  5   vowels, 13 consonants to
          5   vowels, 15 consonants
          (Epicharmus)   not
the Sicilian writer of comedies, 6 A.D., but
his ancestor  /
the Aesculapius family at Cos, a couple are
mentioned in the Iliad as physicians to
the Greeks before the equipotent walls
of Troy


                No, it does not rain, smoke
                rises from the engines, the
                leaves  .   The men watch
                before the walls of Troy

*Apollo in cithaera ceteras literas adjecit*


      7   strings on that zither
      & for each string a letter
      Thence to Simonides,
native of Ceos in the service of Dionysus
which god also at home in Delphos
both gods of the solar year as were   /

                                   Aesculapius
                                   & Hercules
                                   Let's
    get all of this into one pot, 6-700 years B.C.


Simonides, well-known poet, intro-
ducted into Athens   4   more letters  .  the
      unnecessary double-consonants *PSI*
                         (earlier written Pi-Sigma)
      and *XI*   (earlier written Kappa-Sigma)
plus  (plus)  two vowels  :  *OMEGA*, a distinction from
      t h e   o m i c r o n   H e r m e s   c o n n e d
      f r o m   t h e   3   C r o n e s,  a n d
*EPSILON*, as distinct from their eta
& that's the long & the short of it .


Cranes fly in V-formation & the
Tyrrhenians, or Etruscans, were
also of Cretan stock, held
the crane in reverence     /   The men watch
                  LINK-BELT move up its load, the
                  pile to the left near 24th St., the
                  permanent erection moves
                  slow-ly, almost sensually, al-most
                           gracefully
The scholar's function  /  fact  .  Let him quarry
cleanly  /   leave the building to us  /   Poems
nicked with a knife onto the bark of a stick (Hesiod)
      or upon tablets of clay
             Perseus cuts off the Gorgon-head
                  (Medusa)
             and carries it off in a bag . But
the head's a ritual mask and a protection, we
frighten children with it
and trespassers
when we perform the rites . It is
                       no murder,
                       she has given him power of sight

p o e t r y ,
                    the gorgons no pursuers
                    are escort, and the mask
                                (his protection)
Hermes  /  Car  /  Mercury  /  Perseus  /  Palamedes  /  Thoth  /  or
    whatever his original name was,
winged sandals and helmet, you bet!
the swiftness of poetic thought    /    And the bag

THE  ALPHABET'S  IN  THE  BAG!


Almost sensually, almost
gracefully  .  The men watch
and know not what they watch
The cat pushes . the crane  .  the bud
lifts upward  .  above the

                    Pillars of Hercules, desti-
nation, where he is going, bringing the secret in the bag
                    The tree at Gades (Cádiz)
        principal city of Tartessus, the
Aegean colony on the Guadalquivir
F r o m   t h e r e   t h e   M i l e s i a n s   w i l l   t a k e   i t   t o   I r e l a n d ?
T h e   o l d e r   c i t y   i s   o n   t h e   w e s t e r n   s h o r e   w i t h   i t s
        Temple of Cronus  .  island,
        the island of the goddess,
        Red Island  /  & Cronus
god of the middle finger, the fool's finger  /  It is
    his father he kills not his mother, his mother
    gives him
            the secret
                Scholar's function is
                        The men watch


Hercules' shrine set up by colonists, 1100 B.C.
400   years before the Phoenicians
coming from Tyre in painted ships
        and their oracle
                    HERCULES = PALAMEDES (?)


7 & 2
9   steps to the goddess
& everyone lives to 110 years
5   years to a lustrum
            (Etruscan)

22   lustra   =   110
                    (alpha-beta-tau
& the circumference of the circle when
      the diameter is   7   is
22
proportion known as   π
22 (plus) over   7
a neat recurrent sequence
which does not work out because it never
ends   /
7   lustra is   35   years   .   Maturity,
or the age at which a man may be elected
President of the United States / a convention
or a Roman might be elected Consul   /   a convention
                    $\frac{22}{7}$

These numbers no longer a secret   /   But in Crete
                                      or Spain . . .
Spanish, the mother's family name
still is set down last, and
still in Crete descent is matrilineal
The Greeks have accomplished nothing
        but death          beauty
            (Troy)
T h e   m e n   w a t c h   t h e   c a t   p u s h
k e e p i n g   t h e   p i l e s   d i s c r e t e
e a r t h   /   d e b r i s   /   &   s c h i s t
t h e   s t u f f   o f   t h e   i s l a n d,   t h e   c r a n e,   t h e   b u d
l i f t s   u p w a r d   .   a b o v e   t h e


                    And at Cádiz, Caius Julius Hyginus,
                    a Spaniard and Ovid's friend,
                    curator of the Palatine Library,
                    exiled from the court of Augustus


sitting under a tree in Cádiz
over the problem, over a millenium later,
traces Greek letters in the spelt of wine at his table
watches the cranes fly over toward Africa
wedge in the sunset   /   set down the score :

                    Mercury (or the Fates)      7
                    Palamedes                  11
                    Epicharmus                  2
                    Simonides                   4
Say that he used Etruscan sources,
      does that explain it?

Let them quarry cleanly
    Let them leave
Cranes winging over toward Africa
    a wedge .
Hyginus traces  $\pi$  on the wooden table in wine spelt


    The cat pushes, the crane, the bud
    lifts upward  /  above the
    rain comes finally
The watchers leave the construction site,
the men leave their machines
    At 323 Third Avenue,
    an old drunk (Hyginus)
sits in a doorway and downs a whole
pint of Sacramento Tomato Juice
                    The watchers are the gods

                    The leaves burgeon

                                [1963/1965]


The cat today

had kittens   . 3

one weaker than the   rest

                I fussed,

made my periodic inspections

Thrice I took the runt and laid him

        back at a teat

setting him close to the most

aggressive, making him compete


No use .   Twice

she laid him aside and I

        put him back

at the teat, the teat, there was no

energy there to compete, to

        go at it .   Life

is its own dullness

Later, then, flung into the fields
         to fertilize same
here I must drop him into
a paper bag, or the toilet, that
symbol of what we never face, down
an incinerator, or
whatever the blues, o Handy
        garbage can, I
had the luck then
to fling him into the fields—

                                  [1963/1963]


## GETTING ON AND OFF


Lexington Avenue bus,
21st of June, 1963 .
           His left eye bandaged & swollen
           with a cap
           he sits behind me, they
               / pass it back and forth .
     The girl sits to my right .
Her necklace is
very small
coral beads
and she is 25 with a worried expression,
gets off at 19th St. East and walks west / Her
       legs were expressive enuf, sweet
       thighs under blue cotton denim skirt
       enuf for me to have gotten down or
              said two words—or three .
              Lust is unpredictable.

The bum with swollen eyes & cap
got off at Ninth with his girlfriend.
These days
I go down to Seventh, myself .

The other day the lovely
negress on the A train, no,
not a spade chick, the beautiful negress,
lipstick only, pink, the dress a
shocking pink, low heels, good thighs under the tight pink & big
straightout angry eyes and old hair straightening job,
nothing matched or met
except the

                intelligent anger
                of the eyes . too credible .

                Lust is unpredictable .  But
to get it back to the old bum:
his left eye bandaged & swollen, with a cap, he
takes leave of his lady love, both raucous voices
      at 23rd and Third Avenue
                rasping above the motor, the
friend at the hydrant toasting them both
with a 45 cent bottle of Arriba .  Credible,
     & lust is unpredictable, etcetera.
                She decided to go with him .

                        [1968]

## GV : JULY 1963

Walking NW across the plaza with the
    circle of fountain,
    Washington Square,
7:10 in the morning,   the
sun is already higher than the flagpole,
                  no flag  .  than the arch
No architecture north side of the square
                  later than mid-
    nineteenth century  .   The dull orange
ball lowers behind cloud-cover  /  higher  /  rises
over the pole and the arch, over the 19th Century,
comes thru  .  crossing the plaza, as I said, NW
right side of the face is hot
the left cheek cool  .

Old man has his shoes off, rests on top
the black-painted railing, reading, before
                  going to work
The shoes are shined  .  black  .  dogs are walked  .
Newspapers rustling not leaves, no breeze
              moves  /  In
the fountain, no water turned on yet, a
gaggle of idle young girls and men who
had not found a place the night before to
              lie down together
      or had not found one
with whom to lie down  .  they talk  .  or stare  .
    The patrol car squats
    by the public lavatories
a dull green bug with a white shell  .

              Lovers confront one another,
                 dog-owners their dogs,
            some face newspapers, others


                        pavement

                         grass

                           I

face northwest, one cheek is cool the other not .

Sun already hot, all movement paced, it seems

doubtful if the morning will

                             begin or not .


                                          [1964]



## SUNDOWN . THE LAST OF THE WINE


Red wine, half-a-bottle I had
found in the surf at Bridgehampton
in the afternoon
              COOL FROM THE SEA

Al tasted it with me .


Evening   .   sundown   .
               mockup of the day :

having slammed my left thumb in the car door

I cut myself on the can opener

                opening hot beer .

God knows it might have happened to anyone.



Only
the beachday over, I
slipped on the steps of the ho-tel
            and had to

use my sprained right arm to catch
                        with to
save the delicate joining membranes of
the carapace of deathshead monster horseshoe crab

I had found on the beach,

had saved from the day, the tide.

[1963/1963]


## THE QUIET INDEPENDENCE
## DAY, 1963 .


One stretch of beach at Bridgehampton, one can

walk from the ocean-side

                        surf, the water chill,

to a brackish pond, part fresh, part

                        salt  .  where  .


The wind ripples the surface,

shallows and sand bars everywhere,

and small fish, they swarm in the shallows, the

        water's warm. One can walk

                        from   one environment

                        to the other

                        in under two

                        minutes  .

To swim in the surf and beyond

is cold, vigorous  .  To

swim in the pond

      langorous as a bath.

      I like both.


Why must I choose between them?

                  [1965]


## HERE THEY GO


The little lights in the alley
great arclights on the bridges
    and the edges of parks.
                 The young
are beautiful, walking past in the dark, in the
night, couples, two pairs, three,
children alone  .  Children  .


      They've a different world than we had, more
          brilliant, darker .
      Hip or unhip, there's the same thing
      that edge of warm light ahead of them .
      Darkness they know  .  yes, they
      know the isolations  .  come  .


Some,
fearing the example of their parents, are
afraid to love  .  others fearing
the example of their parents,

are helpless before the emotion, not
believing it possible.

      "I'm  16  years old," says one girl, "and
      never been kissed.
      "But I make it once in a while."

The generation,
or two if you like, ahead of them
uses deodorants.
They, tho,
like the smell of hot flesh
suffering relief of its passion .

Sloppy and full of bravado they will live beyond us .
Their cocks dripping helplessly
their cunts full of sperm .

Two classes of Hunter High School girls
came to a recommended M.D.
to be fitted for diaphragms, ac-
(knowledged
companied by their mothers .
The M.D. felt better about her son
who dated sometimes
girls from Hunter HS.

Little lamps in the alley
streetlights in Brooklyn
like any midwestern town:
protect the young from their elders
while,
*a lo mejor*, they fuck
close, or at worst go down on each other .
business of hands for the tender
touch at least
they
the night

Great arclights at the edges of parks
along bridges, Manhattan to Brooklyn
or the other way .
(Where are you?
The sodium flares
make public
the new world rising
from the dark waters

from dark grass .

[1963/1963]

# THE HAWSER

After midnite
Gansevoort pier
is a scattering of lovers, singles seeking
a breath of cool air, sea-smell, dock-smell,
tar, dogs seem contemplative.

Searchlight from a tug
collects the river waters in its sweep
the beam
clobbers a pair of lovers in mid-kiss,
insists,
a great cone of light.

The lovers disembarrass
themselves (meaning 3.), startled,
their legs are uneasy, blare of whistle, in-
sistent, making fun, makes
them laugh at last. The tug
comes in to water up.

A hawser thrown from the deck
to the pier misses the bollard, the
boy seizes the line before it slides
from the dock, makes it fast.

Conversation cheerful, low be-
tween the tugboat men & the lubbers   .
Intimacy of cleat & line maintained   .
Slow
words, slow wash of waves against

the dock, suck & letting go of time   .   His hands
remember the curve of her breast, the talk goes
on, the watering is
finished. Boy's arm about
the waist of girl loosens   .   "Kiss her again!"
the boatmen rail   .   he does   .   they cheer   .
The hawser holds the scene in perfect

balance, a 1930 movie, creak
of pier planks   .   One expects the boy to
clear the rail, board the tug & wave, but no   .   he looses the
hawser, tosses it across. They laugh and wave,

>           boatmen

>           lovers

>           the broken connection
is all they have, they have each other

[1963/1966]

## BARREL ROLL

>           PECK SLIP   .   smell of wholesale coffee
>                   floating in from Beekman, fish, a
wail of improbable proportions, tug
>                   on the East River .
>           Bar is called THE PARIS   .   Bell & Co.,
>                   RING FISH, the
ring on my finger, my
toes parched on the stones.

Bells and whistles from the river.
The gulls circle and ride the wind above the bridge.

One
rides it as slowly as possible,
the line of his wings, leading-edge up
folding against it
not soaring, no
ecstasy, that hold, so
slow he moves in the glide, tension of wing strut,
those bones
holding suddenly, suddenly


doing a  b a r r e l   r o l l  not losing altitude .


the control .


[1963/1967]


## ON THE ROCKS


Small,
Polish they told him, bar, East 7th Street
Saturday nights
is the only one still open after 2 A.M.
hence
crowded  .  to so prowl  .

Even crowded is cool and quiet:
the bowling machine in one corner keeps the score
with little clicks, sighs, and bells, the
jukebox down the wall turned down from concert size
no blare  .  the bar
packed, tables in the back near-empty .


JUKEBOX: Slav, Slovene, Russian, Polish, Hun-
garian, all that lonely, impassioned
*schwarze zigeuner*, the violin catguts
to tear the heart if it be torn already.

Whose is not?

Ø

Midsummer madness by the sea at night, *las*
*olas doblandose siempre*
                        knees dug into the cool sand
                        Couples spread out between the
rocks hiding from the beams of
policecars patrolling boardwalk

              He arranges the blanket properly
                        properly
              waves slosh among the rocks

One feels an intruder and walks
              away
              slowly
              back
toward the lights, the light surf repe-
titious,      dull in the ear .

                        The lovers will swim forever.
                        The whole night.


              Ø



              Coming out of the bar, slosh, the waves, lovers
              sleep lightly, their hot life away for a while, their
              arms, coming out of the bar violins, gulls sleep
                        on the waves
                        cry at his back
              until the door closes   .   streets wet
                                        the summer rain


Reflections more shimmering and real than
the lights, dull surf, than any wall
where the mind goes blank .

                                        [1963/1964]

## THE ANSWER

"What do you do about love, baby,
what do you do about love?"
asked Joel Oppenheimer holding his head
            and drinking too hard.

            "Up to that time," answered
            Satchel Paige from another context, same text,
            "I'd been wounded so many times by love
            I had to learn
                        something. I'd
                        learned to be careful."
"¿Que quieres de mí, mi vida,
que quieres de mí?"

            "You look jus' fine," she scd,
            "why don' you change your shirt?
            change your shirt and maybe wear a tie."
"Keep it easy," he said,
"don't never fall in love."

                                    [1963/1967]


## THE ART

to write poems, say,

is not a personal achievement

that bewilderment

On the way to work

two white butterflies

& clover along the walks


to ask .

to want that much of it .

[1963/1964]


## DECISIONS I.

Office worker from Whitehall
or a process-server from Fulton
rummages a trash basket after
                leaving the ferry:
rejects the Daily News and takes
        The Times .

On second thought,
he puts back the first half of The Times
            with its world news and sports,
retains the second part of the paper which has
            the financial reports

also weather and shipping.

[1963/1963]

## SHOESHINE BOY

S U B W A Y   S T O P   at Wall Street,

    the girls

    going to work at

    ten of nine

    are so much prettier

    than those walking out

    at 9:30


Tho, occasionally at 10,

you see a beautiful woman.

                                     [1963/1967]


## TWO FLOWERS

T h e   g o d   sits staring helplessly

                           up/ into the sun   .   One

cannot say whether he is blind,

                         sure there is something he sees

his mouth slack with pain

                       arm broken off

We contemplate what gesture the hand might have made .
Was he holding it off?
Did he welcome it? Which
way was the hand facing?

     The left hand intact
     is a loose fist .
     Easy.

              Worn pattern on the pedestal
              was once a flower
                        staring / up
              into the sun .

Andreas Capellanus, 1176,
out of the courts of Marie de Champagne,
daughter of Eleanor: "Love is
an inborn torment of the mind"

You with your long hair loosed upon the world
walk in the procession of the goddess wearing
what today, unfortunately, must be called
a shortie nightgown .
Head lowered, your eyes never move
from my scapular bones, the hollow between them

                walk the long hall
                bearing the branch .
I stand with a stringed instrument, thou with lowered head
eyes never moving, bearing the branch with its new leaves,
a dark mark on your groin where my thumb has pressed

One cannot see
the god cannot see .
He looks into the sun with his face

                        curled flower of pain
                        arm broken above the elbow
          (which way was the palm facing? was it a fist, another fist?)
into the sun    blind
 .             /   form borne out of the light

Thou, bearing the branch among many in the procession,
hair loosed upon the world   .   Nothing
will ever be the same.

                                    [1963/1973]

—You are wearing a very zen dress,

      he told her

          And she was, the silly Hungarian.

—A very *zin* dress? she asked

        —T h a t ' s   r i g h t ,  he said

        and put his hand there   .

—V u l g a r i a n ?

    —No  .  zenless in aiza

            guyless in aaza  .

Standing in the high cool rooms .

Walking the corridors .

SHE HOLDS HIS HAND

[1963/1963]

**STANDUP**

Blue curtain
sounds in the corridor
interstices       the filtered light
and an endless net of threads.

           Vertical threads in time
           Horizontal threads in space, meshing
           separating them
           little lights, reflecting each other

throughout the net
the great light     suddenly
fucking through the fabric.

[1963/1970]

## DIRECTIONS TO GET THERE

I   go   wherever   my   feet   will   carry   me
        Sometimes   the   compass
                    swings
                                    one   way,
                    sometimes   an-
other



Which   way   is   the   wind   blowing   today?
                                    and
How   did   that   compass   get   in   there?



THE   FEET!

                                    [1963/1964]



## SIT READ

            Is any coherence
            worth the celebration?
            Okay.

            I look at the few flowers
            set amid the handsome withered
                    weeds

        podded and heeded
     Carolee made into a collage, no
         a bouquet
         yesterday
  at the precise moment of our arrival.
few light violet or white field daisies
      fading among all that
      dead and drying meadow
        summer


          \*


What might it be, the coherence, if it's worth celebrating at all
it's worth celebrating, well the camera never lies, so I
record: an empty chair with sandals sitting in front of it;
a cat under a bush; a Bob with his hair slicked down; Carolee
sitting leaning against the front of the house of glass, curled
as the cat is curled, smiling as the cat does not, resents being
held   .   all that afternoon
in the dead, drying meadow of summer, the
sense of all our bodies, the flesh of our bodies, almost
marginal, the weeds are handsomer dead than the living flowers.


         \*   \*


In the morning before the house wakes.
I read my friend's poems and drink his
yesterday's coffee reheated, seated
at kitchen table, sit facing the east windows wearing
sunglasses   .   brilliance of the
poems shining in the jungle of objects
in the sun   .   When

the sunbrilliant
at ten o'clock high
is rubbed
out in a rumble with cloud
                    I am not surprised.
                    The grey-green
softness is my element,
sea and contem-
plate beneath the cup the fish between my legs and its
mutilated relationships with the freshets of this world.
The body as I sit legs spread beneath the robe opening is
central in the eye, not marginal, not how one hand rests
on the book, to go back, change my glasses at 10:05
to continue reading the
strict-breaking coherences of
                    my friend's poems
                    to celebrate Sunday
                    to hear, see


        how he tears them out of his rich flesh

                                        [1963/1965]



## SITTING POEM


    Toward the bottom of Bowling Green
    a great green statue rides the morning tides
    the Lex, the BMT, the buses, im-
                passive with sword and scroll,
    leaning on one and waving the other   .   He
                had the papers there certainly

        A L E X A N D E R   T H E   G R E A T

        S E T S   F O O T   I N   I N D I A

only here,   is

## A B R A H A M   D E   P E Y S T E R

and a list of thirteen lines :

| | |
|---|---|
| Alderman | 1685 |
| Mayor | 1691-95 |
| Comptroller | 1701 |
| Receiver General of the Port of New York | 1708 |

etcetera, he sits

First National City Bank to the East
United States Lines to the West
the Customs House to the South
and to the North, along
the same Broad-Way, Cunard and American Export

he sits, waiting for the
tide to change

Swordless,

and without any papers to wave,

I do too

[1963/1965]

## REPETITIONS

Pain is what you feel  .   so is pleasure  .   Suffering is what happens
when you can't feel what there is there. Suffering is what you feel
partially and cannot, will not, reach and touch the rest of it. Pain
exists  .   Suffering is induced, imposed, asked for. Liquor, drugs,
are understandable attempts to not feel

pain  .   The suffering goes on dully.

Reading Jack
the Guru-ac's  S C R I P T U R E S   repe-
titions of phrase, of noumena as
the chant also dulls as
the form of blues is traditional .

Repetitions of exalted phrase.
I am reminded of myself at   13,    most
of the semen still in my balls
kneeling in the church aisles
repeating the prayers, listening
to myself repeating the prayers .

                              catcalls in the street outside

trying to feel
within
the truth and exaltation of
words   .   failing to catch it, the
suffering induced from the hopeless
repetition of prayers   .           when there's baseball

"Our Father, which art in Heaven . . . "
and try to believe it.
                  "STRIKE!"

R e p e a t :   the ways of bears and gods
are much alike   .   The rising
up from underearth to strike
the eyes of men in Spring   .   I read
the repetitions of exalted phrase

and sit
and pick my nose .

                                      [1963/1965]

## INTRODUCTION FOR A SHOW OF ROBERT SCHILLER'S PHOTOGRAPHS AT LONG ISLAND UNIVERSITY, FALL 1963
•

THE SUBJECT BECOMES OBJECT / SUBJECT .

    The eyes come first,

i.e., they are there, or they are not there, they

are partly there, blanched out, more intense . or

nothing could be more real  .   NOTHING could . The
giant heads that do not look but contain darkness.

      Or they look

    at you, teeth in that smile, it is

    all smile, shaking   .   Bob's eye
looking at the cliffs ahead over which the


    PAINTING OF THE HEAD WITH LIGHT!


It is not how things are   .
Except at their   (inner bidding)

      most real   .




In the distances, trees, the fence,

    fields, simply, a
quieter thing we love, that it is set there
the road   .   the house   .   the yard   .   To have
stood in the wood, with the wood

    about you, transformed,
the loss transformed into this wood about you
it receives you back better than any home

    FOCUS

    •




A different city   .   Do you
care how the man blows the horn?

    plays the drum?
Sims and Cohn bend to it   .   Hawkins

    bends to it

saxatile, saxifragaceous, saxifrage,
Saxe-Weimar-Eisenach, deutsche grand duchy
SAXOPHONE
tenor-  alto-  Chicago Lakefront  coool
grey-blue  .  it is
another town  .  You
can't make it more real
except to hear it

•

Then there's body  .  First
how it tastes
its texture
run the tongue
along it, the
definition, line,
THE SUN
Shut down the eye until
the highlight is left itself
Color is black, the eye, the
SUN
washes it out to its
lines, the definition
blocking light  .  burns it in
The mountains are lying down
stream burning milk
Smell her in the breeze if
there is anything left in the nose of you
if you are standing up, run
the tongue along it  .  line,

definition, blacked in again reversed,
     gives the body
     TEXTURES,
ITS textures  .  always  .  She is
always all ways  .  Smell her in the
breeze  .  She is always
her own textures in the man's eye,
     always
the most beautiful woman on earth .

          [1963]


## AT THE WELL


Here we are, see?
in this village, maybe a camp
middle of desert, the
Maghreb, desert below Marrakesh
standing in the street
simply.

     Outskirts of the camp
     at the edge of town, these riders
     on camels or horses,
     but riders, tribesmen, sitting
     there  on their horses.

          They are mute.  They are
          hirsute, they are not
          able to speak. If they
          could the sound would be gutteral.
          They cannot speak. They want
          something.

I nor
you know what they want  .  They want
nothing.  They are beyond want.  They need
nothing.  They used to be slaves.  They
want something of us  /  of me  /  what
shall I say to them.

They have had their tongues cut out.
I have nothing to give them  ¿There is no
grace at the edge of my heart I would grant,
render them?  They want something, they
sit there on their horses.  Are there
children in the village I can give them.

My child's heart? Is it goods they want
as tribute. They have had their tongues
cut out. Can I offer them some sound
my mouth makes in the night?  Can I
say they are brave, fierce, im-
placable? that I would like to
join them?

Let  us  go  together

across the desert toward the
cities, let us
terrify the towns, the villages,
disappear among bazaars, sell our
camels, pierce our ears, for-
get that we are mute and drive
the princes out, take all the
slave-girls for ourselves?
What can I offer them.

They have appeared here on the edge of my soul.
I ask them what they want, they say
—You are our leader.  Tell us what
your pleasure is, we
want you.  They
say nothing.  They

are mute.  they are hirsute.  They
are the fathers I never had.  They are
tribesmen standing on the edge of town near
water, near the soul I must look into each
morning  .  myself.

Who are these wild men?
I scream:
—I want my gods!
I want my goods!  I want
my reflection in the sun's pool at morning,
shade in the afternoon under the
date palms, I want and want!

What can I give them.
What tribe of nomads and wanderers am I continuation of, what
can I give my fathers?
What can I offer myself?

> I want to see my own skin
> at the life's edge, at the
> life-giving water.  I want
> to rise from the pool,
> mount my camel and
be among the living, the other side of this village.

Come gentlemen,
wheel your mounts about.
There is nothing here .

[1963/1968]


## POLITICAL POEM IV.
## OUR EMERGING AFRICAN NATIONS


R U A N D A  sit  right  down

and type myself a letter,

        & make be-lieve it's

from President Kennedy

declaring me a Disaster Area

& offering $30 million for

reconstruction of my major cities


      of which I have half-a-dozen


U - R U N D I?  they'll  ask,  who

ruined he?   whom didi ruin, whom?

W H A T ?   thirty million?

      Gwan!

[1963/1966]

## ANY WINDOW OR
## YOU GIVE IT A FRAME

Thin line of snow on the cornices

of roofs, two birds in the sky, one

a pigeon, the other a Boeing 707


against the same blue,

both sets of wings

catching the sun

[1963/1966]


## SO WHO NNEEDDS LEGS? WE DO

O, to look at all those revolutionaries,

Siqueiros, en seguida, and all that, sed

Muntanyer

I'm her Grendel,

she's my

d a m n , if I have to stay here with my images,

we are still all glad we have met again . Large smiles .


I have met two old friends in the bright sunlight

& to come at last to that

Gate 4, Section 11., November 28 and a long dream &

I cannot find my way from one long street to the other, or

the through streets do   n o t   run thru, and the vowels

make it

so long :

>Dear Labyrinth, o double-bitted axe, o friend,

>you are swinging, and how sharp you are, you

keep turning, and it doesn't matter which way, or

art thou still sometimes, or still, as they say, twisting?

I still haven't got to the end of you,,,,,,,I shall

never catch up, but

>still glad to see you!

>Large smiles.

[1963/1965]


CATAFALQUE


>Black horse behind, the stirrups

>backwards

The caisson

from 15th St. & Pennsylvania Ave.

down

The two greys pulling the caisson were

restless

>Black horse behind,

empty boots reversed in the stirrups, very

quiet indeed

"This is the horse I told you

about."


She walked to the goddamned coffin in the rotunda

and kissed it


The broadcloth was black

The greys pulling the caisson had been

restless  .  The black horse,

behind, very quiet indeed  .

[1963/1965]


## LINES, TREES, WORDS

How the lines run down into the night

a forest of trees standing up

It is a park

/   mise-

rere nobis,    4    voices on the

Adoremus te   .   Orlandus Lassus   (1532-94)

they are

a quarter-of-a-tone

off,   my friend says  .   They

fuck it up

Don't we all  .

Give the child words, give him

words, he will use them  .  Give

him words

       /  Have

(miserere nobis)

mercy on us.


      How the trees hang down from the sky

      grey winter down, in violet light

      how the city rises about us, in the

      dusk, drinking us in

                 [1964/1965]


And they were alone on that mountain

          just the two of them,

Jehovah 1° and Moysha  .

    And he sed:

          "Go down Moses"

        and Moses did .

It was like to set all of them free


    He carried the tablets down later

        big slabs

        of rock,

and smashed them before the people  .

                 [1963-4/1964]

## SIGNALS II.

Aside,

that you wd not come to me

that neither of us can, nor want to

share the other, nor can we help it,

I wd not come to you, either, nor

need I have

The gin and tonic begun or never drunk, I

shall sit here with my red wine and mull

I shall mull my red wine and think

I shall think

red gin   .   mulltonic   .   sitwine

red mullet, ginthink, miltown, drink

the atonic mulled red, bink, bink,

bink, bink, bink....

[1963-4/1966]


## LOWER CASE POEM

fish nibble at the surface
also down below .
my love and i spend less time so
than we would wish


belly to belly fast
and sometimes slow,
fish nibble at the surface
also down below

rooms not our own
we make our own and go
belly to belly fast
and sometimes slow .


gulls are our birds and dive
the dove, the sparrow
also prove our heat and beat
against the wings of rooms we fill and leave .


hands that walk and move
or wave and slow—
our hands have fasted
more than we would wish .


the winter beach
will be half-filled with snow
unlike the summered spring
we reached the crest


of that spring tide i sing
clutched to one another thru
the forests of the bmt, the slow
reaches of the brighton line, to


break the fast of hands
we go and go, and
come at last to that
whipped all over with sunlight
sea .

[1963-4/1965]


## TWO SHORT POEMS FOR ARLES


## FEEDING LUNCHEON BREAD

    to pigeons

more & more swing about to land

swirl of birds over us and

all winter heads that
smile under the

>grey
>
>city
>
>trees
>
>straight
>
>up
>
>to spring

[ ./. ]

>Little cigarette butt
>of smoke there, there
>at the horizon
>Ship coming!

[1964/1967]

**24 . II . 64**
**NOTE TO KYOTO**

Clay, it is almost spring  .  the air

is polar, tho, and the nights clear.

Even in the warrens of the city I look for you

for her   for you   I look

at stars over the parks,

brick

steel

glass

bodies

god, and

there   a r e   stars

                &   12 hours later there you are

               under the great Asian night,

               hands in your pockets, walking

the roads to come to your hot tea, the fire in your house .


It's spring again old man, it's coming steep against my

nerves, the old sap roiling up

makes me sick again to go

                  out   /   I want

                      to go   .   Paris!

            Barcelona in a single leap!

expanding like a star out over the Atlantic night

                              [1966]


## AFTERNOON MEMORIES

She takes her bath first and then
draws mine for me, and in my bath
a lovely, long, brown, coiled, single,
bobbing cunthair, drifting
like a medusa, a jelly fish, below the
water's surface

         while she sings and makes the bed   .

         Both remembering nicely   .

                            [1964/1966]

## FLEXIONS

the rivers of afternoon
flowing about you as you
move        stop, standing
afterward in my bathroom
naked among the young plants
in the green light singing
softly to yourself

[1964/1964]


## POEM FOR METAPHOR

The relationship is multiple
and much put-down   .   Money
you can carry around with you
or transfer easily bank to bank, accounting   .   We
                learn other ways to live.

The form destroyed by firing   .   Funny thing,
we keep the devil in our souls and taste
                everything   .   Keep it, the
act we think of is like is
like . . . sing it out, my friend,
                "The Love"
that always makes it
what is so public and hopeless a verb
when the object stands her up from bed and stret-
                ches, or just curls there, will not move,
will make
a very
private & useful
                noun.

[1964/1964]

# THE GLORY HAIRS

To watch a woman
pissing in open air is
to watch an animal
        do it  /  that naked
like a horse or cow
Nothing so neat as a man's dong
but wide as a church door
        whizzing openly

They do well for their purposes
to hide the act, that
frank, flat use of the equipment
        for business,
with a cheerful sound
not associated with love  .  And then

to dry and rise with a sly sweetness,
thinking of it  .  All I can stand
of delicacy
is the hand moving on my chest
        inside the shirt when she
            is thinking of it  .

                [1964/1964]

# THE DESCENT

I wonder what the fight was about.
They walk together, not touching, still
walking very close as if  :
        the closeness hurt them
        it was something

Both look straight ahead,
masque of grimness on him, on her
a tear or two leak down across the cheekbone  .  Some
black & green devil is
dancing in the rosy light of a fall morning.


Nothing before their eyes until they
reach the subway  .  he stands, she
never pauses but descends into the
Cave of Montesinos, disappears  .


The uptown entrance of the BMT
at 8th St. has
become the bleak doorway of hell  .  the man
stands desolated
then it gathers and he plunges


down, two steps at a time


Orpheus after Eurydice
down into the roads of darkness
tunnels of love, the teeth, ob-
structing bodies struggle forward against him, roar
of arriving trains, the sound of doors


opening  /  closing


[1964/1968]



## DARKNESS IS ON THE WORLD

### AND LOVE

has gone else

where, my mind, gloved and shot

even the hall is dark as

I glot toward bed

It is not

I do not love

you, dear, we

are both elsewhere   .

[1964/1965]

## CIVIL RIGHTS POEM

My teeth are metal in my mouth
clash, taste of cash, quarters,
Kennedy half-dollars   .   Growth
average of   10   choice stocks
into which set
        feet
        hands
        wrists, that otherwise
might move, live   .   Right,
          on rights
the north is as the south, my
teeth are metal in my mouth .

[1964/1964]

## L'ORCUS

Long sideburns & teeth showing,

the teeth showing, seedy boy,

    overcoat slack, he's back,

    that figure of joy

to offer the subway system & everyone on it

this 1 A.M., of

April 9, 1964

seeds,


or what it  /  I  /  they  /  we  /

needs    .

[1965]


**COLLAGE**

Hand on her

shoulder

I kiss her, she

grins her pleasure,

conscious .


Hand on my shoulder

she kisses me as I

kiss her   .   The

consciousness

is in the bodies

now .

[1964/1965]

## NIGHT CAPPY

O, Danny Lynch be sittin below there in McSorley's

having an India Pale & a porter & a bit o' conver-

sation & I

not joinin him, what whith his black eye an' all .

       Instead,

       I come direct up to bed,

       wheer the wife do be readin the newspaper

       & don't even move over for me .

I understand what the solution is, but

what be the question ?

He t'ought it were a weddin but

it was a funeral  .  So ?

       what is the question . or,

       who is a friend of the groom ?

[1964/1965]

## LISTENING TO SONNY ROLLINS AT THE FIVE-SPOT

THERE WILL be many other nights like
be standing here with someone, some
one
someone
some-one
some
some
some
some
some
some
one
there will be other songs
a-nother fall, another—spring, but
there will never be a-noth, noth
anoth
noth
anoth-er
noth-er
noth-er

       Other lips that I may kiss,
but they won't thrill me like
         thrill me like
             like yours
used to
     dream a million dreams
but how can they come
when there
        never be
a-noth—

                 [1964/1964]

**SPRING AGAIN**

NIGHT SITS

on the hawk's eyelid

        mid-spring,

the tulips rejoice, the beds cannot keep from

blossom, nor from the fall of blossom, petals choosing dark

earth beneath all that bedding down who will lie on it


so to sleep, perchance .

TO BLOSSOM, you damned perennial, up!

        Tubes,

        tubers,

        bulbs,

        carrots,

        parsnips even, those leafy fields


Now spread, woman, right,

here we are, night,

the field of park, there the

moon is quarter-full

        also a small cloud

        and a star .

        And a star

[1964/1966]

## CALL IT THE NET

Imagine a young woman

lying on her back at the intersection

Third Ave. and 8th St., at Astor Place, no,

   not fallen, but on her back,

reclining there in the snow, looking

alive, up at the passing crowd, they

part afraid to look but those that do,

   the men,

she raises an amorous clouding of their eyes.


   It is a threshold I cross, no

   longer an intersection, the bird

hidden in the shirt upon the chest

torn . the eye

swells in the head

bird flutters and falls into the sea of eyes

   She was so beautiful

Bird and sun are holy take the head

tear it open and set it like a

melon upon the threshold .

     I cross . Everything

that lives, Blake says, is holy . yes

Bird, sun, eyes, the street, the intersection, the fish (hip) swims from between my legs,

LEAPS, yes, that was a year ago.

But that silken trap.


Love drinks itself and is drunk.

The girl gets up off her back

and walks off quick, a clust-er

of sparrows bursts from the intersection into

grey sky   .

The eyes around the bed I sleep in

watch   .   That silken trap

Fucking drunk   .   Over the cold shadow of the street

running.

After her.

Call it the net of lust   .

[1964/1967]


## THE NET OF MOON

Impact of these splendid

things

upon the appropriate sense

How

refuse to meddle with them, how seem

to hide our passion in the dance of

moon upon the small waves, how come to it hugely

erected and keep, we tell ourselves, a just balance be-

tween the emotion and motion of wave on the bay, the

leap of the dolphin in our dreams, accompanying us home?

       Hello moon .


From the *Mary Murray*'s upper deck

the wind is stiff in our faces

              Another Spring as warm

              ten days earlier

              the moon is still out

another year falling across its face so slow-

ly, so flatly the motion of wave as I do

fall back astonished, take my glasses off,

       the shore lights

       so close

fuzz to myopic eyes naked sting in the wind, the

tide is full, he said, the moon lies fair upon the straits .

Let me tell you, let me tell

you straight, strait and very narrow indeed, encloses

the night encloses all but the bright moon, night does not close

              upon the bright

Lights white

or red

mark the

bell buoy's

clang against the dark bay

over it, over   .   it   .   Year falls across the bright face of   .

Tail of Brooklyn ferry disappears behind

                                             an anchored tanker, fail

                 I fail to see and put glasses back on,

I fail

to   .


Laughter along the lift of deck

lovers stand at the rail, close on

                 From the rail we see

the figures of moondance flicker, see

fireglow from the interior of the

                         island   .

The smell of smoke

comes out on the breeze across the lower

                         bay,

to us, ten days later, a year gone,

                 burnt across a bright face

that looks like it's been chewed on,

                 but will not die   .

The quarter-moon glints on the water

nailed,

nailed on the sky


Goodbye moon   .


V   .   19   .   64

[1965]


**NY 3**

*for Fee*

Man

sits in a rattan chair

staring away to not care, to

wear nothing

get no haircut, to not

see the table behind him

filled with empty glasses

wine bottles


In the eye of his mind, the table

bare   .   the bottles

of rare wines

all empty

[1964/1964]

## WIND FROM THE SOUTH AT 12 M.P.H.

High tail
wagging in the breeze

salope      that slope and
sleepy-breasted walk

as the girl in the lee
vies .

[1964/1964]

## POOR DOG

Out of the back window
from the wash hung two storeys up
water drops fall in the sun

slant past my floor on the light breeze
The filthy trees in my mind are never chopped down
are hung with bells tinkle in the light wind

in the light   .   From sunlight,
lowering the bucket into the deep well
hauled up again, tackle creaking, filled

with clear, cold
some water always slops from the zinc rim back
down, hear

waterdrops fall thru the blackness, scream,
splat, slop from the bucket, fuck it,
lift in both hands and drink

guzzling, holding the asses of young girls in our hands
drinking it all in, coffee or cream or both,
both sweet remembrance of

making it   .   not a thing on our minds
The silly-assed hard-drinking nights of our youth
and just making it   to the bathroom in time

with shits the next morning,
warm shit leaking from our cracks .
15  years later we still talk  .  all night  .  The day

the black cat sits in the front window looking
out of our minds
down into the street with glazed eyes

screaming
at intervals
about her cunt-hole by Geoffrey,

letting the males know where she is
wanting to be where the boys are
or at least down in front of McSorley's

huddled, accepting their courtship,
watching the flies buzz
and the dog trot sidling past on a leash

interested,
not a thought on his mind,
but that eager innocent curiosity leaking

out of his muzzle, his ears, his musculature as he moves
past the cats
preparing to copulate

not a thought on their minds, sheer
intention, passive, passion, action
C A M E R A ,   yellow filter for bright sunlight, their eyes

glaze   .
They ignore him

[1964/1967]


## HOW TO GET UP OFF IT

Any mountain climber will tell you
it's a matter of knowing yourself,
your skill   .   Even the older men,
a world locked in itself, as also
the laws of place escape us, hem us in, in
some forgotten way, as themselves :

        "Am I ready for this mountain?"
           and they go.   Up.

Around  6  of a summer evening
the pigeons are that engaged.
On the east front of the Public Library at 42nd Street
it is a matter of sitting.
On the wall SE of the entrance from 5th Avenue, seven or eight
        stand on a narrow ledge
        and are falling asleep
            or about to, beaks
            turned to the wall, fall
                asleep .


           Four on the south urn,
           on the north urn three.


A third of the way up the face, on
the edge of the second ice-field, not
just the rain of pebbles and dirt, but
going flat on your face, falling rocks
flashing off hats, shoulders,
smashing plastic cups in the knapsacks,
the sheer face, the near misses...


        Standing on the north lion, one,
           on the south lion, two pigeons.
On the rounded edge of the empty fountain, south
side of the steps, one lies down  .  Not all those
against the wall seem asleep, even immobile, but most  .


in some forgotten way
we carry the marks of places all our lives,
a kind of fate  .  her  .  whoever she is,
she swings on his arm and smiles, leans
         toward us
         and smiles .
I acknowledge the greeting somehow and
squeeze Sara's hand at the same time  .  This
world, the double avenue of trees, this
world is locked in itself, a central lawn,
the flower beds empty .

On this west side facing the park,
there are two birds who walk alone, circle
about one another,
puffing and circling slowly. The
game
is for the smaller one to seize the beak of the larger
and pull it down to the stone.
They grapple beaks and bob,
interminably almost. On
one corner of my bench a
girl in tight slacks is writing a long letter to a boyfriend.
She reads his letter over first, then begins her own:
"O God, I can't say it. If I only could" it starts. She also
watches the two pigeons at their beak game, hand across
her breast
resting on her shoulder while
she watches the beak game
and thinks of the next sentence.


A third of the way up, it's a way of knowing yourself, the world
not locked in its place but all that mountain coming down in
pieces on the back, shoulders, I'm flat on my, the arm
covering the face, tick-tick, will I ever get off it? whack!
another rock hits the knapsack, get up and go on?


        The pigeons seem never to tire
        of the game.
        Do any of us?
        Finally they circle and stroll, drop
        down
                toward the lawn,
      stroll off into the sunset together
            sort of .
                     Ro-mance .


or back down again?
Locked in myself   .   her   .   whoever she is .
The way is focused,
the formality of a way into life,
twice, three times attempted .

[1964/1965]

# SONOFABEECH

The sea is great tonight, full
        tide, the moon
flashing all over the Narrows.
On the Brooklyn side the lights move
down Belt Parkway at 60 mph, and are gone
the shell of the Verrazano Bridge stands
slim and black across the neck of the bay .

Only from the long line of spray
        at Rockaway, where the sea   cracks up
                on the moon-dark sand,
                    LISTEN!
you can hear the grating roar of
beercans that the waves draw back and fling
at their return upon the crapped-out lovers,
        stop, go
        again, and then hang back once more
the dull-assed cadence slow and bring
the eternal note of hangup in.

Ginsberg long ago, heard it off the Tangier beach
and it brought into his mind the turbid ebb and flow
of water in his toilet bowl in East 2nd St.
It brings also to our minds a thought
hearing it by this Far Rockaway .

The sea of cunt was once too at the full
and round the Manhattan island shore
lay like the folds of a great shining used condom
the financial district full of sperm.

But now I hear only its long withdrawing squush,
bored in the sunrise, retreating to death in the nightwind,
down the small-breasted ex-virgins, drear and naked fingers of the world.

O love, let us be true to one another,
for the island which seems
to rise before us like a land of dreams, each
one so various, so beautiful, so new,
hath really her second diaphragm, or takes Enovid, or
hath a good abortionist in Delaware:
and we are here as on that darkening square of bed
swept by confused accordians of polak, wop, and kike,
where ignorant mick and aeshkenasz get smashed by night.

[1964/1967]


## THE JOURNEY ITSELF IS HOME

Two girls on the beach at Brighton,
                One blonde, one dark
set their blanket down by my towel
                and wait for the action.

              Two boys come down
*se acostan cerca de las chicas,*
                situate semi-strategically.

They think the girls are too young,
legally they're right. But
both are so built, so beautiful, one
so blonde, and one dark,
do I have to take both of them on?

The boys go over and talk, it
doesn't work out;
one is too quiet, the other too aggressive
    and conscious of
himself, he can't feel past their sense of
    waiting for it,
their queenliness there in the grubby sand.
                It ends in a series of shrugs.

    The boys pack up their clothes and head
for another part of the beach.
The girls pack up, blanket, radio,
                sneakers
and head for the boardwalk   . getting
                    cold.
      the sun has gone in.

Out
I go by myself out
             into the ocean, swim
                    out
a long way,
      completely out of it all.

                          [1964/1967]


## CONCOMITANTS

fishing  in  the  dark  pools  of  the  mind,  one  finds  a

GREEN  E-
VENING  &  THE  SKY
      clears,

& the sea flats out & the crickets start

their EVEN-

ING . The

(song)

lights are up,

sun down .


Dishes on the table, one

deep & platter-shaped for, say, home fries, was

my grandmother's, pale yellow, pale resentments

with pale roses

painted on it

Another, a

platter, has a gold rim

on oyster-white 10¢-store china, I

don't even know why it gets to me

(after holding it for hours

finally peeing my pants in

the summer dusk


Exquisite relief of the warmth

trickling beneath short pants

in the summer

("can't see—")

past this green-blue evening by the sea

shore, 30-odd years later   .

[1964-5/1966]


## THE INTERVIEW WITH
## F. SCOTT McNUT


"What kind of nut is that,"

   —That's a round nut.

"What kind of a round nut is that?"

   —That's the kind of round nut

    that rolls up the bank

    goes straight up the tree

and attaches itself to a branch.

And it makes it there in the breeze

just swinging away above the river

and makin' it.


"Are you that nut?"

   —Yes.

"And what kind of tree is that?"

   —That's a woman tree.

"Didja ever chop down a woman tree?"

   —I'm not that kind of nut.

"Nuts have seeds, right?

And seeds grow trees, right?

What kind of tree do you want to be

when you grow up?"


—A woman tree.

"You're a nut."

[1964/1975]


## YA LIFT A COLD ONE (THAT'S THE COMMERCIAL)

"Shultzie?"

    —Yeah.

"The game's over?"

    —Yeah.

"The Yankees lost?"

    —Yeah,

"Good—you got any melons up your house?"

[1964/1964]


## MEMORIES OF HOME

There he come   come   across the big sunlit lawn

sparkling like the great dog in eternity,

      an heroic dog

come from the far reaches of the mind

     and the woods beyond the postoffice

     and the edge of dark


A great golden smiling collie with tail awhack

     who is my friend and betrayer,

coat glistening with dew and fresh cobweb so that

they know we have come from the hill


a great seducer of a dog that

being bored with the cheesy old cunt of the postmistress

stuck his long nose in the crotch of my 9-yr-old trousers

insistent, until I had out the hard little thing he'd given me there

and licked it for a long while


     No more touching a sight

     than a boy and his dog


so that later, when they said of some girl,

     "She's a dog"

I couldn't see that was so bad.


OLD PHOTO: Kenneth Benoit with his hand inside Laurette Coleman

's bathing suit, standing, facing one another in waistdeep water in

Lake Champlain, smiling.

*MEMORIES OF HOME* (cont-)

I had a teacher all one winter, never

taught me nuthin'

just sucked me off a lot

after school

& I fucked her once in a while

and it was wonderful .

[1964/1966]

## THE REALITY INVOKES

O let us make a poem of

this one,

of that one.

No,
not disabused, the
concrete and disenchanted world

concrete

precise

& besides

he looked

Harry, having an eye,

looked   .   The castle
commanded the left bank of the Dronne,

R I B E Y R A C

A r n a u t   D a n i e l

w a s   b o r n   t h e r e .

                    well   /   We sell
the illusions we are contracted to.


Who's to say what the reality is,
Raimon V of Toulouse would not have known the answer,
much less his son.


O lady, your arms have freckles .
We are one.
            And what was the location of that town?
                    Buovilla?
            And Arnaut Daniel cut up among his ladies .

                                    [1964/1966]



## AFTERNOON, YEATS


Dying is like this:
to settle for the solid virtues
when the clouds are
black and the storm
coming  .   get inside  .  to
            trade off the pearls
            of greatest beauty and price
                    for wood and copper
                    for brass beads,
and wear them with the same pride
                    that love traded off
            that beauty lost forever in the
dullness of every
day,

when the sun comes up
just the same,

as lovely as it ever was

[1964/1967]


## OLD QUESTION

*(for Fee)*

Why has life put such

a need to talk inside us,

when there is nobody to talk to?

[1964/1968]


## THE OLD ARGUMENT . . . CARPE DIEM

How we live .
like a dark cat looking out of windows
blankly
as if that were a blank wall standing
opposite

Any movement a composite
Give the leaf no credit
Any movement of wind may
take it and make it
twist off its stem
lie crumpled on the fire escape next door

That was cold country when it came
winter, and the kindling chopped, the
cat crouched in the woodshed, waiting
    for the door to open,
split logs for the kitchen stove, whole
ones for the fireplace, and we
waited till it was past . The logs
needed the fire to warm us, the animals
crouched there, also waiting for the night
           to come
    and 12 hours before the next fire was
made them rumble in the present or heave
and breathe, laying long snout on paws

    I issue warnings constantly from my body
    stands looking out of windows at trees
    and the strengthening wind in this valley.

                            [1964/1967]


## LAUREL


A 7-yr-old colt
belonging to Mrs. Richard C.
               du Pont
won $150,000 at the
International today
November 11th in
               Washington, D.C.
You know she needed it

    Blum, riding Gedney Farm's
        *Gun Bow,* said
*Kelso* had cut in front of him at the furlong pole  .  shit,
    he crossed in front in the stretch
    to get close to the rail, but
    he had plenty of room to do it .

                    *Gun Bow* ran second, & 9
        lengths behind him was the Soviet entry,
                        *Anilin*, a
                        3-yr-old colt .
                        Aniline dye   .

Valenzuela on top, *Kelso*
finished the 1½ mi. Laurel (Md.)
Race Course in 2 min., 23 and ⅘ sec. which
breaks the American record for 1½
miles.
THE PA SYSTEM announced brusquely: "Ladies
and Gentlemen, there has been an   o b j e c t i o n "

            by 4½ lengths?
            and a record?

Valenzuela sd.
    "Flying grass was all the
    rest of the field saw too."

                                        [1964/1966]


## ED SANDERS AT THE DÔM (WHEN THEY HAVE THE $2 COVER ON)


Black and yellow
stains of soot and weather on
the courtyard walls .
Pale sunlight
of autumn afternoon

                "Away, slave, and seek for perfume
                and chaplets, and a cask that
                remembers
                the Marsian war, if
                any vessel could elude
                Spartacus, that bugger ."
                        (that leaf-head)

Noises are coming
in the silent day
the foggy night
reckless, the
voices of a Ringo,
of a Paul

[1964?/1967]


## AND A MOXIE NEW YEAR TO YOU

Look around
look alive—
you're in the Pepsi generation
I tell myself .
No, that's bullshit—ah,
I do not want to laugh,
I'll be all the warmth and music of words I can
to women and to men

[1965/1966]


## THE CONCERN

One wonders about the hands and ribcages
of men all over this land

and brackish ponds
& breaking icy surfs

or I do   .
where are you?

I wish I knew one jubilant man, one
completely fulfilled woman.

There are the two places,
there always are

[1965/1966]

## THE STANFORD WHITE MEMORIAL

He who not have his hands stripped down to bone
must reach out,
out among his languages, his elbows, arms
reaching to the other armpit, reaching to the
shoulderbone under the armpit, reaching back

The great, beaky bird attacking the pustulence
in the armpit, o Boyle, the racked in, sacked in
o, the pustulence paid in, a third
disturbing arm for luck
& the ripe fruit in the corner, leaf still attached.

They stand in the Dôm and twist
night after night
knife into belching gut
& the blood flows there on the paper, the
paper is what we do it with, let no man lie,
they twist
happily
touching, coming
on
to

the ripe fruit in the corner, the
leaf still attached

[1965/1967]

## CURRENCY EVENTS

The American dollar
the British pound

sterling, define, in
the lines of tension proving

relation & equivalence,
proportion swirling between them

what certain ignorant
individuals of different classes

define as *reality*.
You ass, it's the idea

of value, has
conned you before
hand .

[1965/1966]

## THE ACTION

The old man eats

potato chips

from a brown bag


he has brought al-

most surreptitiously

into McSorley's, which


he eats with a blank stare as

he sips at his pair of ales


his hat perfect-

ly level across the temple


concealing most of his white hair

His eyes are blue


and water hard .

[1965/1968]


## MOTIVATIONS I.

*each animal*
*his own gravedigger*

—L. Z.

        *Crow.   Crow.   Where*
        *leave you*
        *my other boys?*

                —L. J.

He gets a job as a waiter be-

cause


he wd/ like to look at a chef's hat

what he misses in the street


the street

                              [1965/1968]


## HET UP & TAKE YR / TEETH WITH YOU

Here I am, driving this Aston-Martin, see?    the
air swings out to the sides .
The people with me are beautiful .


I put my hand in my mouth as we stop for a light, my
top front teeth have come out
all at once—the whole palate, the
whole front! A
piece of skin of the gums was holding it on .
I'm a mess, what a disaster! I take
the handful of teeth out and
lay them on the seat next to me.

Couple blocks later we catch another

light, I take it down thru the gears, and look

in the mirror   .   I look terrible.

I've given them all up, all of my voices, for this

bloody convertible


The light changes, I throw it in gear

we skid left around this corner, over and out   .   I

check the mirror and smile   .

wow.

[1965/1970]


## ASH WEDNESDAY, 1965

"Do you fuck on a first date?"

I asked her, as we left the church,

ashes on both our foreheads. "No,

but I gobble good as a

young head ought to," she sed

which is cool,

which is better than Madisonavenueing it

should anyone ask .


or a raisin in the sun.

⌐·

3   small boys

taking   2   steps

down at a time clatter on the

sidewalk in front.

The big thumbmarks

make them look

like some secret organization.


"You got the dice?" one asks

another, the head shrug once, "No,

Joey's gott'em."   Ah,

there's nuthin' like a

little penance on a nice day

to set a sinner up!

[1967]


## OUT

Friday night

free night

night of

Freya, up-

on the town

After the night out

        (on the town)   after

an overbibulation

dedicated alternately

to good & evil spirits,

it is all soft   .

        "Fuzzy," she thinks,

        pro-pretero-nymph she is become

        climbing these stairs, turns

upon the stairs, smiling

at him, at the top of her

stairs


        No flight upon the hills

            from the thyrsus he

carry before him, overcoming all, in-

cluding

her anticipation

        "Would you like

        coffee?"   she

        smiles, turning upon the stairs   .   His

head comes up to the level of the

stanchion formed by the innominate bones

            of the ilium

the "mixed inflorescence"   where

"the primary ramification is centripetal (or indeterminate, &

the secondary & successive ramifications

are centrifugal

& determinate"

   She smiles at the

       top of the stairs

Vine and ivy branches twine up about

the thyrsus of Dionysus,

pinecone tip on the staff, thud

of blood under his thumbnail in the

hand that holds open & unpapered, a

   spray of lilac, a burst of mixed

   inflorescence already moving toward

    secondary ramifications, he

     also smiles,

    his head at the softened ($\Delta$) delta

"Yes," he says, and raising his eyes finally,

   "that would be very nice. Thank you."

        [1965/1967]

# HOW IT IS VERY QUIET NOW

at   4

on a spring

morning,

the rain phased out


when it

thundered earlier

I looked at the dried seeds

grapefruit, tangerine, orange, on

the kitchen table


plant them today or tomorrow .

I go to lie down

next to my wife

in the dark room

[1965/1966]


# THE 1965 SEASON

Bottom of 7th, the
first time Berra has caught all season :
he leads off & singles, that
makes it 2 for 3 .
But those Mets

Bases loaded and no outs; one run in. The
Phils change pitchers &
Ed Roebuck of Brooklyn Dodgers fame comes in
& strikes out his first batter.
Then the Phils make a double play.
Well,

one run is better than nothing,
    that makes 2 .

Top of the 8th, the Mets
amazing—a double play—
It takes a couple of more men, but
Al Jackson strikes out his 10th man in the game.

That ties the club record.

Roebuck strikes out his 1st batter this inning, too.
Then Kranepool lines to left &
    Christopher flies out short center,
        ends that half.

"Number 9, Jim Hickman into left for Christopher.
Number 3, Billy Cowan, into center for Swoboda."
Defensive moves, o Casey.
But Thomas rips a single past Klaus at third.
Tony Taylor also singles between third and short.
Gus Triandos with 2 strikes, and Jackson
sends thru a wild pitch, the batters move up,
here we go, &
        well, Jackson strikes him out
        —a new Mets' record with 11 .
okay, there's one out.
Ruben Amaro, sacrifice fly, drives Thomas in.
John Wesley Covington on deck : 6 homeruns
11 RBI's (o, he had his at Milwaukee in
    57-58, those great years)  .  He
goes to 3 & 2, takes the payoff, it
goes to Hunt, to Kranepool
    (Cookie Rojas on deck)
           in time .
           it's all over
METS   2
PHILLIES   1

    Well, it's a game, no?

[1966]

## CATHERINE, AT EVENING

Catherine Ledoux

was someone who

I was not permitted to play with

at age  5 .

No explicit sense of her left from the dream, but

the smell of fresh clothes drying

in someone else's backyard

at evening .

[1965/1966]


## THE LATITUDES

I had a friend that took a cruise,
a Connor Cruise
name was an ex-general of UN forces in the Congo,
            O'Brien, well
the cruise was very educational
            for her, her
name—Consuela O'Brien—when,
after passing the Tropic of Cancer, an
O Henry bar in her mouth, practicing,
noticing that it had gotten smaller since 1942,
some 24°N latitude, just about
Cuba, though further east, she

watched a deck party
in which the whole crew and

(ew)

its over load of female passengers frugged—
frewgged?   The whole crew

(ew)

frugged   .       Frugged?

It was

somewhat educational for Consuela,

ruined O'Brien  .

[1965/1966]


## FOREIGN POLICY COMMITMENTS OR
## YOU GET INTO THE CATAMARAN FIRST, OLD BUDDY


y digamos que, pensamos que, like
it doesn't work, you
talk of the war in Vietnam—only you don't—
dear committee, you talk most about ways
of expressing your rage against it, only
you do not say it is rage, too
timid, baby, you are a beast in a trap,

fierce but rational

(maybe they'll let me out?)

You know they won't

and there's the persistent sense of animal rage, to
strike back, to strike out
at what hurts you, hurts them too, I mean the reality

the children who will grow up to hate us,
the Vietnamese girl blinded and burnt by our napalm and
still   /   lives, has lost all her hair, is
still pregnant
and will bear the child if we leave any hospitals for them, if

not, whatever ditch or ricefield or building still standing, that
        10   Americans die
that's her only wish

      I wonder why?
      here we are saving Southeast Asia, etc.
      And everyone knows this, every
      one feels it

      Bombs fall and are flowers
      the stamen is the whole village
      blossoming, the
      wood and tin and flesh flung outward
      are petals  .  Death
      is beautiful! Mussolini's son-in-law, what
      was his name, Ciano? count Ciano
      has described it accurately  .  The
      image is true  .  That was 1937

How the villages explode under the blossoming bombs!
Lovely! the bodies thrown up like wheat from the threshing flail?
It sure as hell is poetic and this is 1966 and what shall we
do against it?

The dead horse
nibbles
dead grass
in a dead pasture  .  There
is no green anywhere, horse,
pasture, grass, it's all

b l a c k  .

Whatsa matter with you?
Hasn't anyone
ever seen
a black horse?

[1965/1967]

## GETTING A JOB

How can we stand the soup?

How can we love the pope?

How can we put up with the cops?

and we do . . .


But plenty

of Dante

destroys us,

that great light over us


And the light enters the asshole

and the asshole enters the office

and the office records it   .

[1965/1967]

## MOTHER, IN THE 45¢ BOTTLE

S L O W   L I N E S   lay down the curve, curve

from Astor Place & Cooper Square down,

center in the eye into

Third

Avenue, the

Bowery, the parallel lines

of light the cock lies limp inside of lines

that join at the top and bottom some old prick

lying curled drunk in the doorway

           (the parallel

lines of sleep under the blue argon lights on his old face

down, join at the top and bottom, Cooper Square into Bowery

           (parallel lines of


For better or worse,

lights, bars of light

in sickness & in periodic

imitation of death, the fierce

lust in sleep

stiffening of old men

           [1965/1968]

## EAST 3RD ST. DRAG

Winding   past
all   those   undulating
O   NO,   thighs,   just   to
get   a   couple   of   drinks?

> And the piano player with the group, the
>
> only whitey and the only
>
> one with an idea
>
> in his ear, and
>
> even that much too slick and
>
> even that should kick a long so-
>
> lo along


"There're a lot of funny fat ladies here tonite,"
Sara says .


That is true.

[1965/1967]


## BETWEEN SETS

The   BEARS   are dancing
          d a n c i n g,
on the wall at

Slug's Bar, East 3rd Street, be

tween C and B

cool as you like

between guzzle and guzle


(just to the south of the curled iron grating and

muzzle to

muzle )

[1965/1966]


**HAPPINESS JOE**
                        (for R. C.)


                                        NO!

                Not another one, for

chrissake Max,    sez the

trumpet to the set of

drums, whose name is

not Max, the

set surrounds us, what

can we do against it?


And the drums turned to the bass:

—Shall we, and why not, buy a goddamned big

gin & tonic? DRINK, he sed, for

chrissake, look

                that was a request

                for *High-Heeled Sneakers!*

OR,

AS MY WIFE PUT IT,

THEIR MOTTO IS,

NOTHING CAN POSSIBLY HAPPEN .

[1965/1967]


## THE PAIN

A pert maid, a perty maid, a pretty

maid, a

rock maid, a granite maid,

the rent must be paid

I have a gun

We are climbing fences to pay the rent   .


The girls' names

are Dany Farmer, Barbara Former, and Garulous Monroe,

who is silent   .   but, we know

the money is under the counter .


We'll make it

though

all of it sounds automated .

[1965/1966]

# CANCER EJACULATIONS

not the
square root of minus 1,   or we can't
live that way no more, baby   .
T H I S   H E R E   I S   July 9,
1965,   we
must live how we
can that's in the world

---

And I grant you all of the honor, my friend,

Bernart Arnaut de Moncuc, for whom no one

has seen fit to write a *vida*  —And I know /

        values true /

So I am blunt

when I recount

how you give me joy

young lady, here & now

                And I'd have

                that integrity

                that everyone despises . . .


How keep the books on the desk

the fish in the tank

the fool at the task, the

A R A B E S Q U E ,   the

true man at the bank, our friend, impossible, stay,

we'll all stay home now,

despite the French   .

[1965]


## THE SLOGAN

Over the right

triangle formed

by Stuyvesant St. & Ninth, the

wellknit blonde in a blue knit dress & the hair piled high

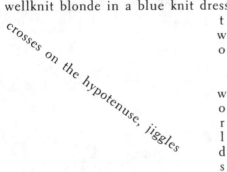

t
w
o

w
o
r
l
d
s

& several hemispheres as she walks .

The trajectory

causes a mass cessation of work

at a Con Edison encampment on

one of the other two sides, all

orange equipment with dark red flashers, flags

at the corners of the encampment wave cheerfully

in the Monday morning breeze, all the orange helmets

facing the same way, eyes right, and clearly

*everything else is right*

Click

click

the heels go at an easy pace across Stuyvesant

touch the curb at Ninth, jiggle-jiggle .   The

explanation

is printed on the sides of all the equipment, even on one flag :

DIG  WE  MUST

They dig .

[1965/1967]

**HESPER ADEST**

The evening comes
Scop points to the sky, the horizon, the
scissors point to the sign   /   paper
chronicles of lives barely coeval with my own
evil simplicities .  Torn, hopeless
trousers I eventually remove
to a separate galaxy

An old Chevy open touring and
a new, 1928 Essex are part of the pattern

Semen
shit
paper
kleenex
snot
cigarette tobacco
and
piss are part of the pattern,
are the contents of the bowel, the
bowl, the
hiss and howl of water as I hit the chain,
empty the bowl at a single flush,
empty the tank too,
which refills

And I walked around all Christmas day with it strapped on,
and the card that came with the gift, I
wrapped it in tissue paper and kept it in the holster.

That was the last for a long time   /   3,600 miles away
and a different galaxy, whatever anyone else wanted   .
That was the year I got the tricycle too.
My sister and I fought most of the time, but I
would go and kiss her
when I thought that people weren't looking.

[1965/1966]

# THE ASSASSINATION OF PRESIDENT McKINLEY

Before Trinity Church

on lower Broadway

3:30–3:35 P.M.

while the casket was being lowered into

the grave at Canton, Ohio,


the portals of giant buildings draped in black,

flags flying at half-mast,

the street is jammed dead with people,

maybe half of the men in bowlers and caps

the other half with their heads bared   .   Some


twenty Lex & Columbus Ave. & Broadway trolleys

stopped as far back as the eye can see on a muggy day,

most everyone jamming the windows murmuring or silent

while the bells of Trinity tolled for   5   minutes .


At Jackson Bros., at 66,

the first-floor windows equally draped, the drapers,

black, one of the brothers takes

advantage in the back of the store

of the dead stop, of

the new little typist in accounting, makes

her bend over the great rolls of fabric

in the stockroom, lifts the voluminous skirt, pulls

down the sad white bloomers,

      undoes his fly,

            spits on the end of his cock, &

            fucks her, the last rite

for the assassinated Mr. McKinley,

            September 19, 1901


Five minutes of hushed silence, the

bells booming and

schluk-schluk, the soppy petals of cunt, the groans, &

Tyley Jackson's yell of come is drowned,   gone

under the final two strokes of Trinity's bell  .

                [1965/1965]


## THE METAMORPHOSIS


THE LADY, reclining, de-

clines, and

no mended head know what

      be her inclinations

      Still, eyes look out

      it are the rites—

And the map of Ireland

("Ireland free

from the center to the sea"

    it wails)

with the Northern Counties torn off by a passionate hand

is taped to the cupboard wall in that same public room


       The glasses' bottoms thunk down hard

         this late hour before closing,

         and some indignant horse, an

         aroused horse,

     clambers to its feet


about to become an automobile .

                [1965/1966]


**AYEM**

     The hanger-smell of oil
       flack in the burnt set of morning
       slow clack of helicopters

Over the rear area, the smell of
eggs and ham, burnt
toast and coffee on
the South Vietnam air .

If we don't win

nobody wins .

& we don't win .

Then,

there's the fragrance

of that   b i g

## A M E R I C A N

## B R E A K F A S T

[1965/1966]

## TORCH BALLAD FOR JOHN SPICER : d. 8/17/65

Four for you
floor for you

         I twitched

                 fathered &

    AM I?

Wild again
I dialed again
trying to reach Barney Childs again

          Am I?

Jack Spicer's heart
What of it?
     He is cold,
     I agree

a few leaves on a cold tree
the cut diamond in the *paysage,*
the landscape he knew he had up his asshole
like a lord of the early hours

               s t o p p e d

                   .   m e l o d y

     Sing to him
     each spring to him

          —bring to him
4   gigantic shots of bourbon
out for him

                    Hildred,
                    Visigoth,
took him tenderly into the House of Death, the rendezvous
mission of the orbiting Gemini 5 spacecraft was then
scrubbed    .    when the fuel cell was  b e w i t c h e d
by Hildred

                              (Am I
                                      No, nurse)

The still sprouting beards
of dead men do not
itch
or bother .

                                              [1966]


**BAN ME THUOT**


FLAT ONENESS


extending from the Lido surfline without stint, the edge
fuzzes off into sky, blots
                          the horizon out
                          A dullness, but
                          4,000 miles away


someone at a desk in the District holds it
all in a pair of big flabby hands,      it is
sharp to him, real to him what he must do, nay
the palm itself shows him the lines of deployment
The green of jungle is as real as the river flows thru it


REAL   to him


REAL to the small desperate men on that same ground


as the redpainted napalm tank
                          is released.

Where it falls,
a flat oneness
Where that new horizon is created, no
edge of sky and water

/ f l a m e .

[1965/1967]

## TO-DO, TO WAKE

Someone

who smells you there

at 5 A. M. in the yellow light.

Summer.

And I smell you, the places

where our bodies touch are warm, I

hear the small tune your breathing

makes no word, my head

     and shoulders move in the dawn to catch

          the different angles of some sleeping

face and flesh

where it takes

air beside me.

I take air, I

smell you

there beside me

in the yellow light, I catch

different angles of your face and breasts, the

hipbones jutting just

and sleek below soft belly, the

face is different each

time I move, the angle of hip, the rounding of


breast   .   At Guadalajara,   55

kilometers from Madrid

                 all

                        the advertisements say, I

rise on one elbow, scramble down, and

rest my head between your legs to

taste you, the

only thing

left .

                                        [1965/1967]


## IN THE SOUP


So, tonite the moon is full
Rosh Hashana in 17 days
The pebbles lie on the beach
If you pick them up they are damp


        And no excuse for yesterday,
the waves of approaching fear, three

men, her father packin' pistol, his
brother, poodle-packin', and her brother
HIS SON, took an elevator up three flights of stairs
to
destroy some black man in their mind who,
having a realer sense of spending his time, had
spent the summer with their daughter, sister, niece.
No one was particularly nice about it
and the girl was in
tears, 3 years old again.
At least
everyone had the sense it was statutory


No one was destroyed except the old man who
destroyed himself
leaning and kept yelling   "Get OUT!   OUT!"


The weight and fullness of the moon, Elsie, he,
they, for
got you, he,
they, never even considered you .
The moon changes, Elsie, but some things are
YOU can't change .


You and Welton might
as well try to con-
sole one another,
best you can .

[1965/1965]

## FACES 1.

Who in New York in 1965 would have

such incredible taste as to do a little girl's hair

in long skinny skeins of curl *à la*

Shirley Temple, *Little Miss Marker* stage?


The wonderful Puerto Ricans. The

taste so bad, the effect is wondrous

beautiful, and so she is


a brown little waif-wife, 5-yr-old opposite me on a

Lexington Avenue train

in a peppermint red-&-white stripe dress with

some legend needlepointed neatly in across

the bottom of the skirt I can't read


        B E L O   —T O—

                             i t   s a y s .

She pulls it down prim looking at me

reproaching?  Can it be?

            She thinks I'm looking up her dress?

So I do.

          Not very interesting.

It's her eyes that get me : the

severe quality in the reproach

has already faded, re-

        ceded in favor of

               —migod— friendliness.

A friendly reproach, then, from *Shirle Temple,*

that's fading away, and there's a

look of satisfaction (5 yrs old?)

that makes me wonder what my face looks like .


The part of the skirt she'd tucked between her knees

pops up again—starch, crinoline maybe?

      well, it's still not very interesting.

      Her father finds something, tho, there's a spot

just above her right knee, bruise, dirt, what's

that?   he asks, she shrugs, he takes his hand away.


The letters visible on the skirt read now :

          —LONGS       —TO—

     I guess the legend now, it's incredible, he

     can't keep his hands off her legs, lays

     his slender hand over her knee just as

     they rise to exit at Grand Central

     Station   .   Well, I'm right, the skirt

d o e s   have a crinoline and the message reads finally :

     M Y   H E A R T   B E L O N G S   T O   D A D D Y

I'll just bet    .    The curls down

the back of her neck are perfect. In

her care not to scuff the patent leather shoes

with their sad shine,

                    she stumbles a bit at the doors

Goodbye, *Shirle Temple*, goodbye !


which close

all at once  .

                                  [1965/1966]


## THE WORD

stink, stank, stunk,
stinker   .
The septic tank over
flows, *estanque*, to
save it, tanker, to hold it,
stack? *estanco*, the tinker
saves the pot, the pan, place where
things are stacked, to tank up in the *estanco*
thank you, I will have another, or go
take a quick dive into the *étang*, if
the water be cold enuf, it
stings, the tang is almost
tangible   .   To tangle is to mixit-o, tired
*stanco, stancare*   .

                                  [1965/1971]

## HANDS

Her room is
stuffy, she notices,
as they enter it


After fucking on the light,
as she thinks of it, throwing
the light sweater on a carefully madeup bed, she


moves quickly to the
window, he is close behind her, as
she bends to throw it up
he takes the crests of
      both ilia in
      his hands to
      press
her ass against, her crack against his . . .
      "Wait a minit, cancha
      wait a minit?"
she yells, bringing
one thing up, & another
down   .

                [1965/1967]

THE SIEGE

Keep it open somehow, that sluice
from the world to us,
even at the price of a comedown,
even at the price of a bust
Mio Cid at Alcocer:
"Let men know I have camped here
and I intend to stay."
The owl makes a sound in the night.
The night cats prowling cry.
Or fight. The camp dogs whine
or sigh, lie
down
by the fires.
This is the exile,
this is the chance at the world of men & its power.
The late talk of the men
is a comfort
guards walk the trenches, mumble with one another.
Comforting also
the sound of water nearby, river Jalón.
How far from the centers of power,
how far from the courts of Alfonso
from the courts of Castile and León,
from his own castle at Bivar!
And, none of it works!
But 3 months later, 4 towns,
not one of them stormed:
Alcocer, Ateca, Terrer, and Calatayud
are paying tribute to Ruy Díaz,
just that he stayed there.

[1965/1967]

## THE LEFTOVERS

I ate the beans for supper,
cold green beans with garlicd sauce and oil and
a tray of hearts, horseradish, olives,
pickled sweet watermelon rind
and beer   .

[1965/1967]


## KICKOFF

It is a word, always,
defines our ways and days for us:
wily, knowing,
passionate, hoping,
singing, relaxed, desperate, even,
murderous .

How come gently to the word
which defines us?
Come at it as a liar with a wristwatch
which, if all else fails,
will at least tell us the time
in time enuf to quit .

A hero on a bicycle, which,
if courage shrinks or even
will not to live prevail, will
get us uptown anyway, or down,
with a natural effort or pace .

But the fingernail
under the magnifying glass! The
erection in the mirror!
The galaxy in the thousands of telescopes, the one
face in the morning mirror—how look at that? And
your mouth lying there against the pillow,
how will that look?   No.   Quit now.

[1965/1966]

## YOU LIGHT IT

The  baritone  penetrated  the  left
    s i d e  to get at the very
heart of dark, a truth
      at a reconciliation luncheon with a contralto
arrived at in the wanderings of his body from one form to another.
Shapes, shapes his rebeginnings
from another kind of repertoire.　　S p a y—cecraft.
The orbit comes to one of its ends and starts in again in
      the fixed order of rank


She
withdraws modestly into the background
so that he enters a condition not
altogether compatible with
self-esteem
      But who says second place is worse?
It pays less money, that's all.


      "It's still there," she said as he groped her.
      "I just wanted to make sure,"　he said.
& Balanchine thinks all the energy
spent in doing the frug and watusi
is wasted.

"A shame if you waste the rest of it."

or

Lincoln, lincoln, po-pincoln, or

banana-fana—or

the corners of her mouth *are* beautiful and

most one-eyed men I know

can see very well .

[1965/1969]


## O, DO THAT MEDIEVAL THING AGAIN, BABY

Love is a weakness, a
sickness, a fear & a terror, and—

I love I can do that
and risk
that evil thing
wherein our own heart go forth from us

[1965/1966]


## THE COMFORTS OF THE NIGHT

returning from the laboratory

A N

A N

"I taught a 3-hr/ chemistry lab before
coming down to the reading," he said

And he read it well, the second set especially
I enjoyed   And sat
afterward on the stone steps next door, drinking
ale with Timotha, and he came out saying

                "Get away from sitting next to my wife"

                        and that was fine, tho
I didn't move and passed things back and forth,
it's like it was in the capsule
facedown above the earth for 190-odd hours, looking up was worse.

                O, it's raw, raw, raw
                to be in the jangle of public life,
                a few moments of such peace

as sitting comfortably
in stone steps
waiting in the warm night
for a car to arrive, passing it
back and forth

                and leave us not kid each other,
                welcome to the club .

---

The three lines in my head that precipitated this poem
were the closing lines, and
in preparing for them, I
have lost them forever   .   Thanks Harvey .

                                        [1965/1965]

## THE NECESSARY GODDESS

Seeds on my desk

rotate, take root before me, my

mind dreaming controls

"the nature of plants, bodies, etc."

"How bud we our way into spring

combined bringer of forsythia?

                (soil)

                crocus the locus,

cloak us in blue skies
fuck us in sunlight
rook us in birdflight north
invoke odd gods, on the brownstone stoops
    joke with broads in the sunlight
        poke at the railings, flowers & branches
make
old women jealous, old men
sick to their stomach, failing
to join the season
                give back
what winter took," she sed,
& disappeared into the bushes  .

[1965/1967]

## THE CONSOLATION

"It's all right now, Henry,

        it's all right,"   the

old lady said as

she peed in the ocean.

[1965/1970]

## FOREIGN POLICY : AN INTEROFFICE MEMO

Gentlemen:

        We shall keep a general check on the

        direction indicated by reports from

        our field offices, CIA reports, & other

sources of information by using the

following procedure:


1)  Find a very large rock, although light enough
    to be lifted by  2  strong men (if this is
    used in the field, local labor may be employed);


2)  find a strong chain and secure the rock to one
    end of it, using the normal and approved pro-
    cedure, cross-strapping, with hooks;


3)  attach the free end of the chain to a sturdy
    branch of a large tree, easily visible from
    your window. If the wind blows the chain
    and the rock straight out from the branch, you
    may safely anticipate the approach of
    bad weather .

                                        [1965/1970]



## THE PROCEDURES


"T h e  l a w ,  once decreed, is still the law,"
          sayeth Belshazzar, the
          voice thru which the law passes.
          And he himself must follow it out, and tho
he knows it to be the councillors' in-
                    sistence on technicalities
                    and a low trick,
he orders Daniel be thrown to the lions.
It is the law.


## THAT THE LAW STAY UNCHANGED AND BE INEXORABLE


We do not believe it
not any longer, tho
large pockets of resistence still persist
even among the lobbyists themselves

in this government by pressure group
or anothr dirty word for concensus.
"Mac, I think you'll agree
that the specifications for this TX-100 are—"
                    extravagant
certainly won't be the next word.


Area Code 214       56 . 33 . 179
Area code  413      25 . 32 . 576
Zip Code   10003
Zip Code   01002



                How bud we our way into spring?
                How the leaves fall and the wind
                        pushes us toward winter.
                How bright the sunday sunlight thru
the south windows of the Lord Jeffrey Inn at Amherst   .   No,



                        the world is ordered by numbers, by the
                        numbers, we used to say in the army
RA- 42252488, I'll never forget it, and
one's wellbeing, or to call it both ways,
status, is defined by one's relationship to
one or several of these other numbers.
It is only when we wish to give the impression
of confusion   or   abundance   that we use the words
            *numberless*  .  *countless*  .  Let us pray; prayer
            is a formula for order      .     There



are   14   automobiles parked on this side of the block and
16 parked on the other common side.
Numbers are spread about everywhere,
            tho in no seeming order, indeed,
            they are a part of the landscape.
Seen from the vantage point of a man in a hotel window in a
strange town, or God, it is some kind of Brownian movement and
random, therefore private.


O n e   is a dangerous number, and unpredictable.      One man
coming down the sidewalk un-
predictably crosses and
gets into a car on the common side of the street
and drives off     .     It is ominous and
besides, reduces the total to   15.      But nature

is ingenious, balances itself a moment and a
nice old couple in a ponderous powder-blue Impala fill
the space and restore the balance.      Now take  T w o ,
              a much more stable
              number  .  Here come  2   friends
              walking along together and arguing,
              it looks very warm and stable and friendly.
Some hold that   2   is also a dangerous number, at least
under those conditions where it produces   3   .  It's an argument.
T h r e e   young men with hands in
their jacket pockets crossing a lawn against the wind
do not look ominous,
but three is an unstable number, it is
always  2   against  1,   and is not
stable, unless you like that situation, either side.


      But then, each unit within a group
is its own number, some of the numbers are secret,
              some of them plain.      I also am
              a number  /   but have no mirror, so
cannot tell what number I am or what my T/O is.      The
              landscape is full of numbers—lots
              of number  F o u r s .. And it be the
nature of things as well as the nature of numbers, that a
monster is chasing the numbers about, but
catches and devours only the odd ones.


              If I do not know my number,
perhaps no one else knows his number either, or
a secret only the monsters know, for they can see us
and our numbers, but not their own, unless they
              have powers,
              or mirrors, tho that doesn't seem to be important
              to them; perhaps they have friends,
              whom they do not eat, or eat later, per-
                        haps their friends tell them.
              But they seem always to be by themselves.    But
that's not a bad idea, a friend to tell you, that's the
advantage of  2   or   3,   it's
a kind of definition, i.e., if your friends will tell you,
if even your best friends will tell you and not lie about it,
if you don't already know whether you're odd or not.
Would you tell your best friend if he were odd?    Think of
his despair! Well think of mine, then, all my friends
have left, driven
off, in
one of those odd cars.

I pick up the phone and dial Information (411, that's reassuring,
that's balanced, I tell myself), perhaps they will know
what number I am.    I wait impatiently while it rings, I
hear the sound, I say    "Hello there!"
and try to explain the situation and she asks me:

"WHAT . NUM . BER . DO . YOU . WANT ?"

And out of the window I see a large monster
coming toward the inn, just walking along in the sun,
enjoying the day and I describe him to the operator
who gives me the information:

"That's just one of the founders
—out catching road-runners."

O there are a number (?) of clouds in the bright sky, but
the earth is balanced:
innumerable bare and half-naked trees
and countless leaves upon it and suddenly
                        there's no one in sight and the
                                sun goes in and the day goes grey and
                                        the question is
how to avoid the founders

        /    maybe .

[1965/1970]


NEWSCLIPS 2. (Dec/ 6-7)


        The news keeps squirting in from all over,

        it's like a leak in my head.

The two astronauts in Gemini 7 took a snapshot

of a Polaris missile yesterday,

shot from a nuclear sub parked near the Cape.

Co-pilot Cmdr. James Lovell cried

as the missile broke water:

"We've got 'er, we've got 'er!

She's beautiful!" sitting

there in his underwear.

Somewhere around the 30th orbit

he had climbed out of his space suit.

The first zippers he unzipped somewhere

around the Canary Islands  .  40  minutes

and 11,000 miles later, over Madagascar,

he's gotten down to his longjohns.

"I feel naked," he said, and also

"It's the only way to fly!"

Frank Borman was supposed to

get undressed later,

I never heard what happened.


But what a great idea, a pair

of astronauts

orbiting earth for two full weeks

in their underwear!

What happens when they get horny?

"Hey Jimmy, I see you got a hardon."

"Allright, Frankie, boy, you wanna

do something about it?" And Frank

cuts off the blood pressure telemetry, pulse, re-

spiration, and so forth,

& so far as the Houston Space Center's concerned,

they're dead?

Imagine when they start sending ladies up,

coeducational orbiting, wow,

LOVE AT FIRST FLIGHT   .  o, the headlines

and the usual housekeeping chores...

Meanwhile,

back at the pad, Gemini

6   is being readied for liftoff

scheduled this Sunday, the 12th.

Walter Shirra and Tom Stafford are to try

to effect a rendezvous with the other two boys.

And in Miami,

Rep. Walter H. Moeller (O.)

an ordained Lutheran minister

and a member of the House Space Committee

on vacation,

protested the launch on Sunday of the spacecraft:

"In these days of crisis," he said,

"we need all the moral and spiritual re-

sources

we can muster."

I'm surprised he didn't complain about the underwear.

Well, I'm about to the end of the broadcast.

High tides for today, Dec/ 7, at Sandy Hook

6:20   A.M. and 6:46 P.M.;   6:33 A.M. and 7:07 P.M. on

the North side of Montauk Point;

at the Battery      6:49 and 7:12   .


Temperatures yesterday were various:

88° and clear in Kingston, Jamaica
84   and cloudy in Acapulco
85   and partly cloudy in San Juan
41° and cloudy in Paris,    59   in Rome
52° and clear in Athens
36   and snow in Moscow
84° and cloudy in Saigon, in Copenhagen
34° and snow;    57 and partly cloudy in
both Cairo and Tunis .

Aldebaran is very bright to the East at sunset,
Altair and Vega in the West at the same
hour    (4:29);
Venus very bright in the West, rising at
7:30 P.M.; Mars reddish and
low in the West an hour earlier.
Again at sunset (4:29)   Jupiter
is very bright to the East, and Saturn
likewise in the Southwest .
And tomorrow, Dec/ 8, the moon is full .


And on Sat., Dec/ 11, the Home Lines
announce a 4 P.M. sailing of the *Oceanic*
from Pier 84 North River, at 44th St.
which is listed in the ship schedules

as   "Cruise to Nowhere."


Don't miss it, boys and girls, and that's

all for tonight.

[1965/1967]

# SING-SONG IN WINTER FOR THE LADY & THE GENT

"Let me put
violets in your fur,"
sed the gamekeeper to Constance, or
"Connie," as we used to call her .

O David,
the "intellectual life" in the desert consumes you? or
at best,
you shake old de Ventadorn's bones
under his abbey at Dalon,
tho the hills now under snow .
Two doves to keep you, one
sits on the eggs, you sit
and look out the window .
It is not warm   .   Put some
water on the hob for tea
& add one for the pot, make it
strong .   Put
a candle in the window for winter solstice,
the 21st, and note
how it fills the room .
the infinite tea smell
mixed with candlewick and dove-shit .

The song .

[1965/1966]

## SCOTCH FOR BREAKFAST

The helicopter cir-
cling over leafless trees—no, not
        Viet Nam, that defoliation, an
    other fall, an
    other spring, but
old deciduous Central Park
& lots of squirrels on muddy paths and lawns, sitting on rocks and grass
sitting down in a brown movement of leaves, a
lot of squirrels swarming up tree trunks    .
    World Peace, December 1965 .

"One of the biggest threats in the free world
    is internal insurrection," said Sergeant Robert O. Matthews, 28,
        of the Howard County police force, Ellicott, Md., in charge
of training three special police units in counterrevolutionary procedures.

                    (AP DISPATCH, NOVEMBER 11th)

Two men on the wooden bridge, north end of the boating
lake near 77th Street,
      stand and talk, look
    very Oriental
(we catch on quickly, no? they  m u s t  be spies)
    because they ARE
    Oriental. And there
will never  /  ever be  /  an-other  /  . . .

                        [1968]

## THE VALUE

After the argument in bed
which, tho it balanced on my life and the value of it,
     no one could take personally
         (it was about the transit strike)
        & that there was no conclusion
       possible to it,

I was enuf put off my usual intent, I found
myself both wide awake again, and sore.

There was nothing more to say about the disagreement
I had to get out of bed
    go to the kitchen
        put on the light, and read.

      Also I had a drink while I was at it,
      that might help me sleep, help me sleep.

You had to go to the bathroom
or at least,
you were good enuf to say so, and did.

Metallic sound, the tripped valve, the rush of water, you
       came directly toward the light
          in the kitchen, and leaning over
kissed me on the neck to let me know.
Well, I know that
and it's not enuf.

I kissed you on the mouth and sent you
back to bed.
I sat & read for a long time & sipped my drink.
on the clock it said : a quarter after 3.

I tired of reading finally . it was nice
knowing you wanted somehow to make it up,
that imponderable.
But the fact of the strike was there, with its reasons.
I made myself a dish of dry cereal.

The milk crunch was cold & tasted good.
I enjoyed it.
I have to feed myself.

[1966/1968]


## CORNELIA 1/10/66

There is such a thing as immediacy

or strike while the Byron is shot

or shake it when the fire is out

you'll get clinkers.


Fred, Dutch, Jerry, and Ruben

will know none of the answers, tho

their names are writ large on the wall.

That's good. I write this on the tail

of a 1960 Rambler. Two

men get in and drive off, so I move

to a '63 Buick, the hood.


Two pigeons, a police dog, and

          an oil truck, all delivering.

Stick it in your face and eat it,

hot bread is always hot bread,

no matter you slice it or pull it off

          in chunks.


And such a thing as deliberation.

Forget it.

          [1967]


## BLUEGRASS

Field of blue-white

light, sharp

over the bent heads, the instruments

useless in their reflections, all

          the questions are wrong,

blue field of arc light, fluorescent, the

          answers to them irrelevant. Put paper there

and an instrument some where

close, there are

those valleys dark below the darkening mountains,

no word comes .

"Well, writers don't live forever."

"True, but just the same..."

The blue park sits in the mind as another place we live,

the sun, perhaps, later south under the blue hills

"... it's always going to be a surprise

to me if I don't."

the

knife reflects the light uselessly,

the work is only

what is not done .

[1966/1967]


## THE HUSBAND

The vision is of a fist,

a large man's small hand with short

fingers, gently folded.   In it

a girl walks,

dances in the fist,

bends, as it precedes the arm, forward, backward, down, bent to one

side or the other, dances, circles, but

always with the small loose fist

around her, in her, she in it,

it, the movement forward of it

tho no arm is seen .


                        Where she

curls, sleeps, rises, bends,

resumes the walk or dance within the fist.

And this happens every day for a thousand years,

until one day, about sundown on the road,

the fist stops, unclenches

                    and is still,

the spatulate fingers lay out-

                        stretched, lax.

The girl hesitates within the curve,

everything stops for a minute, just

that moment before the sunball

                    sinks

below the horizon. She, too,

hesitates, strokes the hand a last

                  time,

and continues to walk forward, the

dance continues in her body

                  alone

down the same road, head down

as night comes on. She walks,

                  walks .

                                     [1966/1967]

## THE WRITER

He always did have a tendency to mumble

or, when distinctly, with emphasis

smacking the soft, gravelly voice

down on some unexpected, un-

prepared syllable,

            making the paragraph sing,

the speech-rhythm still in the brain long after

                 the sense were gone,

the sentence never completed.

                 Now the throat itself

which produced these inexact and

familiar articulations is

stopped

with a great plastic tube

inserted in the tracheotomy,

and a great machine breathes instead

beside the bed,

lifting the broken ribcage with a whistling sound.


Four days later:

heart / or brain / or both

stopped
          /
               making oxygen irrelevant

          to any strict rhythm of articulation .

All paragraphs gone, all expletives broken and gone with

               a final whistling sound .

The machine has lost its consciousness

                                        [1966/1967]


## ST. MARK'S-IN-THE-BOUWERIE

—Cargo's outbound, the supercargo speaks,

"Reality comes on fast or slow"

One by one, we finish things with gusto

and if we're lucky end up two-by-two

walking along the rim of some

          not-yet-extinct

          volcano.

David Amram on French horn takes a solo,

a sort of tender pear, *molto largo.*

When there's nothing anyone can do,

      reality

comes on fast or slow.

Cut or hack, plant the avocado;

death is no tornado, it's a crack

that widens,

separates us from ourselves

and things that happened to us years ago,

a kind of seed split open, so will grow

root and leaf, up and down, to air and soil.

What we cannot do, we cannot spoil,

and there is nothing anyone can do.

No anticipation and no love, now;

reality comes on fast or slow,

and fire comes up to meet us as we go.

                        [1966/1967]


## 16 SLOPPY HAIKU

              *for Bob Reardon*

I say what I mean

Nothing else is

given to do, say,

even poems

    \*

First large

table on the left

as you enter

His chair is turned up

*

Two years ago

Jim died

doing battle with a truck

on Third Avenue

from a motorbike seat

shaking and

cold sober

*

Love is not enuf

Friendship is not enuf

Not even art

is / Life is too much

*

It has been

seasonably cold

messy weather, the

length of his

illness

*

Bad weather over-

head, slush underfoot

Who'd want to get

out of the hospital

anyway?

*

God's blood drained

donations are required

One pint per man, no

deposit, no return

*

His three sisters,

Crapsey, Topsey, and Morgan le Faye,

want to plant him in Arlington Cemetery

Eat him slowly

*

Apostates are usually interested

in poetic values and relationships

not dogma

*

Briar-rose, primrose,

and periwinkle, all

three of you bitches can

kiss my French-Irish ass

&ast;

Cinquefoil and bat's blood

got at the wake of the new moon,

(add poplar leaves and soot)

will protect witches against cramps

while flying

&ast;

Nothing not accepted,

nothing not exchanged,

that sense of it .

The possibility, not

farewell

&ast;

We try

hard as we can

to be only what we are, fulcrum

for the work .

&ast;

Isn't  .  is

it not terrible, Eunice,

that there's a love

doesn't need an object?

*

A sound you'll never

hear again:

pissing in the toilet

about 3 A.M.

*

He had a tendency to finish

what he did

cleanly,

minus something

Find it .

[1966/1966]

## THE LIST

M I L K
C A T   F O O D
B O O Z E
T U N A
C I G S

Shopping list 2 wks.
before he died .   the use
faded toward Jan. 24, 7:38 PM

Long corridors, elevators, the
bloodspot on the top of the men's urinal on the ground floor
that stayed there a whole week without being cleaned, repeating
that observation every day I had to go up there, was
                              still there, may
                              still be there .
                   its own shopping list from whose
            arm or mouth or head did that blood drop?
We never know .


And so the air pollution still falls despite
                         the new administration,
            despite
some days of sunny weather and reluctant rainstorm,
            which comes.
It's February already, who would have thought it,
            almost Lent, or how
                   make an epitaph short enough?


               IN MY 43rd YEAR SOME
            DARKNESS DREW ME DOWN .
"No rites,
but some friends reading words I loved, mostly
other men's words, only a few my own, other
friends hearing them. Regret
only what was not finished, regret only the loss
of afternoon sun thru the window at McSorley's, that
table's wood whitened as my bones are in the fire, the
cold rain of this later date, all that.
Say goodbye for me."

                                        [1966/1967]

# SEVENTEEN NIGHTS LATER AT McSORLEY'S : 2/10/66

"I know you," he sed,

little man in a tan coat and black hat

at the end of the bar

        "from the hospital," he sed,

    "visiting Reardon, you wuz

    visiting Reardon. I wuz

    in the next bed to him."

        —B-3? I asked.

"B-3," sez he. "Next bed to him,

I seen you."

    —You won't see him again, sez I

    "No?"

        —No. You're well again? Mazeltov.

    "No?"

        —No.

           [1966]


# ASKELEPIADES VARIATION

May I address you, Aphrodite, goddess?
    There I was,
        making out with Hermione,
           everything going great.  But,
             O queen of Paphos, on

the panties ringing her waist
I found printed on the elastic :

             LOVE ME
             BUT DON'T BE
             BUGGED THAT I
             BELONG TO
             SOME-
             BODY
             ELSE  .
                    I had
to read all the way round to the crack .

                                [1966/1966]


## THE ANSWER

What's up there?
                 A moon.
    What's
        up there?
                  Stars.
Don't you believe it love?
                I
                  know, you
want my cognac de Jeréz,
my Sobranies & Picayunes,
my Ferrari, *mes*
*vins champenoises bruts*, my
Indonesian incense,
my Greek teeth & my

                dandelion!

So that's it, you
want my *dents de lion*, my

> *Taraxacum officinale,*

the old sun-tooth. Well,
there he is, all bright, all right


So what's up there?
A moon.
What's
up there?
Stars.
Don't you believe it, love.

[1966/1966]


## NAME CAST INTO THE TREE-ALPHABET FOR MATTHEW CRAIG ESHLEMAN BORN AT LIMA, PERU, FEBRUARY 22 (?), 1966.

/•
  •
   •

B E T H   L U I S   N I O N   (ogham), the

$$\frac{nion}{ash}$$ /   The month extends from feb 18

to march 17  .   tuesday

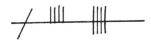

is the day of trees and pasture .

I am a wind on the deep waters .

the wind that dries the floods .

Beryl sea-green is the stone   .

    Dwelling secure in the hollow

        ship until

           wind wafts him home

Clear is the color of the wind in the aspen (white

                poplar)


M O I R I A    C A O I    E S U

The piece of brass has been given new strength

    The birch peg offered the suitor says

        'you may proceed'   it can have a

        permanent-type effect   .   we know

M U I N,   the vine, the 10th tree, is the phallus,

        Venus the thumb

in below the first joint,   M U R I A T H,   I

    distribute the seed on Moriah,

        Jehovah's holy mountain, the vine

full of joy and exhilaration

& wrath.   The Danaans

carried with them, North, more than the emblem, the plant

could fruit on a few protected and Southern slopes,

but not turn wild :

        hence the bramble

became by extension, in celtic lands, sacred to Osiris

and the Thracian Dionysus   .   the amethyst   .

dwelling secure in the hollow ship until


The last day of September,

(sept

ember)

when the devil enters the black berries  .  the black

berries  .

M U I N  C O L L  E A D H A

vine, hazel,  & aspen

coll and eadha are the same finger

the  4th finger

the 4th of the vowels

the 9th tree  (hazel)

counting from the other direction  .

the leech or physic finger, ring finger for ESU at the

base of the digit, says

repose, the god is shown

plucking festal branches with a left hand

where his right should be  .

but as wisdom, *(coll)*

I am consumed by fire, the

hazel fruits after  9  years, says the arbiter

Mac Cool, son of Hazel, which can dowse for hidden water,

buried treasure, and in cases of theft or murder,

       guilty persons  .  Wisdom is sweet, com-

pact and sustaining in a small, hard shell  .  Nut

and apple harvests coincide, thus  Q  (written CC) and

king Arthur traveled to Avalon, apple island, to be

healed of his grievous wounds  .  And the goddess

summoned Bran into the land of youth with an apple branch,

where the blossom and the branch

      were one .

         With the tip of the  4th  finger, physicians

           used to stir their potions

             and medicaments .

              The theory was

no poison could adhere to it and not

communicate directly with the heart, a small

    vein which can be seen at its base was reputed

      to run directly to the pump  .

        I have been the blue salmon,

the pool overhung with hazel trees  .  9  sacred to the muses

as the vine proclaims  /  also the hill of poetry .

The titmouse, most unabashed of birds, like poets

band together in fall to seek a liberal hand .

Wine as we know, is poet's proper drink, and so

Ben Jonson, as laureate, demanded his fee

be paid in sack.

Venus the thumb is also Isis' palmtree

()'You may proceed'))

A star used to be tattooed

in the hollow between the

thumb and forefinger,

and in some ports this is still honored, begging Venus

(of the sea) and Zeus (of the air) to bring

the sailor safe ashore  .   We are back to

tuesday/

| nion | I am a wind on the deep waters | 3rd tree |
| coll | I am a salmon swift in the pool | 9th tree |
| muin | I am the hill of poetry / and the | 10th tree |
| eadha | shield for every head   .   / the | 4th tree [of the vowels] |

Passion, wisdom, and strength under the tree of

Autumn and old age, white

poplar, aspen is the shield maker's tree, golden

head dresses of aspen leaves are found in

Mesopotamian burials of 3000 B.C., and

the measuring rod of Irish coffin-makers was of aspen to keep

in mind that death

is not the end        tin  .  ESU  .  repose  /

The birch peg is offered

The piece of brass has been given new strength

The runes speak well   .

[1967]

## SUNFLOWER ROCK

      "C'mon, get out,
      y'gotta get out," sez Milly,
      "stop sleeping'n get out, I call the cop."
The old man
crumples up his check and drops it onto the sawdust floor.

"Mary," he says, and staggers to his feet and
begins to come on to Mary behind the counter. She
wipes the glass counter and does not meet his eyes,
says, "You'll get out now."

He does, stiffening his body and pushing it back
off the counter with his arms, reels
      lightly toward the door:
        "See ya tomorrow, Mary," and
          something else low.
            "You'll get out," she says.
              He does.

Milly the waitress is full of plump wrath and righteousness
finding the unpaid, crumpled bill on the floor: "He
comes in, eats, he goes ta sleep,
don't even pay his bill!" Milly
lays the crumpled paper on the counter.
      I suppose there's a place to put it.

"Hey, he's all right, he
just thinks it's a flophouse!" Aunt
Ella joins in, having emerged from the kitchen
    where she is these nights,
      wipes her hands on her apron
        and grins .

      "Sunstroke!" it's Max,
      a customer at the front table,
      "He wuz
      hit in that head widda sunflower!"
      makes the finger-gesture
      to his own head.
He sports a new pair of those half-sized aluminum crutches
crippled open on the chair beside him.

The circles grow from the stone.
Woodie, black dog with a curly tail,
circles back of the counter, out front again.
The Mrs. circles up from the ovens to find out
what the shouting's about . Mary
circles back of the register for someone who does pay .
Aunt Ella circles back to the kitchen,
another order's in .

Struck in the head with a sunflower,
the old man's circle has taken him out the door
    into the rain.
      Outside,
        the night is full of March rain,
          That was the joke,
some joke . and the evening traffic uptown .

Soon,
we step into it ourself, stop
to buy a half-pint at the corner
for the cold night, for the pocket.
Already wet, we turn our back to the northwind,
feel the whiskey burn .

[1966/1967]


## RITUAL X. : THE EVENING PAIR OF ALES


EAST OF EDEN
is mountains & desert
until you cross the passes into India   .
It is 3 o'clock in the afternoon or
twenty of 8 at night, depending
           which clock you believe .


AND WEST IS WEST
It's where the cups and saucers are,
the plates, the knives and forks .


           The turkey sandwich comes alone
           or with onions if you like
The old newspaperman always takes his hat off
& lays it atop the cigarette machine;
the younger, so-hip journalist, leaves his on
old-style .


The old man sits down in the corner, puts
           his hat back on. No challenge, but
           it's visible, the beau geste .
               The cigarette

hangs from the side of the younger man's mouth, he's
putting himself on .
East of Eden is mountains & desert & every
thing creeps up on you & comes in the night,
unexpectedly .
when one would least put out his hand
to offer, or to defend .

[1966/1968]


## THE ISLAND


Six men stand at the bar
Seven men sit at the tables
now eight
now nine
a sixteenth man in the urinals
Matty behind the bar
George in the back .
Silence there is &    2    conversations
sometimes    3   .
It is March 9th, 3:30 in the afternoon

The loudest sound in this public room
is the exhaust fan in the east window
or the cat at my back
asleep there in the sun
bleached tabletop, golden
shimmer of ale   .

[1966/1968]

## THE GOAT : LITRY HISTRY


F. Granville Munson, Col., U.S. Army, Retired,
University of Pennsylvania, 1903, etc.,
used Pound, a sophomore then,
as a butt of pranks,
a naiveté you cd/ count on .

       But, by 1958 hd wanted to visit
the famous EP madman-traitor in St. Elizabeth's, even
            Eliot wrote him a letter, but

" . . . I rather thought the Army
would not look with favor upon social calls by a retired
officer."

           Which is immediately
           after the
           Crimean War, no?


When Pound went to Hamilton College
after his sophomore year, the
fraternity there had a telegram
from the Pennsylvania chapter:

           UNDER NO CONSIDERATIONS
           PLEDGE EZRA POUND

       Bob Hayes, telling this story, said:
"In walking, he rushed along with a long stride,
constantly talking."


He is not remembered as friendly
by any save Carlos Williams. And
that was the year when Dr. Shepard
turned him onto the Provensals.

                     [1966/1968]

## EZRA'S CONTRIBUTIONS

As for the politics
order, justice, fiscal and otherwise,
which ended in Dachau and Belsen, i-
    deas going into action, etc.,

    "It's a lonesome day today"
    the blues says and
    (economists see money as abstract)
    "it looks like tomorrow
    will be the same damn way."

            [1966/1968]


## HEY, OUSPENSKY, HOW DOES IT FE-EL?

If we find ourselves

too knowing, too

clever for passion,

it is the attention

    (general)

to the casual detail

    (specific)

  "Did you mean

  what you said to me with your eyes?"

  Billy the Kid raises the gun to his lips

  with a homosexual gesture, blows

    away the smoke from the barrel

COOL . "Lila, L-I-L-A," says a voice vrm da vindow,

> giving an address and phone number . It is
>
> the cleverness of those who cannot rest

I fall back sometimes

afterwards, the

exhaustion

having made it well

or close to, there is that difference, too clear, or

> "Rest, there is color in the world.
>
> It is a triangle, if
>
> you want to talk abt basic forms . Tie
>
> his wrists to the crosspiece."

To tell where the anger is

is not permitted . the sierras

stretching their scorching ranges at that

> angle across Spain, sun
>
> burst on the upper eastern sector
>
> above Valencia, con-

> tained by the coastline, or

they drop, and the Baleares are the extension, raised

up in the sea?

What I'm talking about is love.

Fire has some integrity at least, it

consumes its wooden fools.


## H O W   D O E S   I T   F E - E L ?


The foto is of the cross

in front of the mission at Taos :

the gesture   (he is fotographed against it)   is

the head turned to one side, the hands out, not stretched,

the show

of help

lessness, he is too low on the cross, string him up, I say,

"It is a triangle, tie his wrists to the crosspiece."


But he does that himself

when he is

hung up, then

spreads his arms, that helpless gesture, it

is all too literary, what

I'm talking abt is an ambiguity of sex and the mis-

uses of attention .

The capacity for love

CAN be sacrificed


to a habit of mind

or of body for that matter .

Baby   .

[1966/1968]


## SAM

My pants wear thin

when the wind blows

—north or south—

I know it   .   Let me

tell you how Rembrandt painted

in his old age   .

[1966/1970]


## THE DEPOSIT

It's an ill wind
what blows nobody no good
or what else have I forgotten? I don't
remember, odd's blood, it's
Spring, and I
am in an airy mood, only
you're sick

I have no lover
nor no love, no have
*ni un ni otra,* no
way to keep the new wine
aging, simply,
old bottles & all that
which, for sentimental reasons,
you just don't
turn in to the local grocery store
for 5 cents.

[1966/1968]


## THE CROSSING

The stream
piles out of the pile-
up of earth—
we call them mountains—


It
runs west to east
roughly, or
from where it starts in the
pileup of earth, it runs
ESE
          to be very exact.    And
in spring the birds cross it
                    heading north   .


Thousands and thousands of birds
heading north cross it heading
north   .

Singing  .  it makes everyone
very happy  .  the
stream is reasonably happy by itself
running ESE
as it does
& is basically unaffected
by all those migrations
of thousands and thousands of birds  .

[1966/1967]


## HE SAID

ah, no,

it's a matter of tracing it all back

carefully

who said what,

when  .


Hair stands out straight from the side of the head,

but in damp weather it curls,

what do you make of it?


belly-button parks spotted

all over the city, the immense

slash of green up the center under the mist

a deep cunt of green, do you

have your whip with you?

can you beat it?

who

are we?

it's out  : it's

      only fair,

you had yr chance and for reason(s)

said yr NO  .  it was then I sweated, summer coming on,

the separation, coming on


Now it's my turn?

That's not what I want . what do I want?  jesus, my

own life, my wife, no arm to take that up, we

are different people, more

different than I thought, the appearances, how

now can I take your arm? Lead


you?

where?

The landlady in the back yard

talks to her dog. I stepped

over a drunk in the hallway yesterday

evening, a colored man, had come

in outn the rain to which I was going out under which

I was going, errands of the gods, my own booze supply,

thought, where was I going? Had

decided north, north, stepped

south over him then stood and turned:

he raised his head and we

looked at one another, his eyes were clear and unafraid,

what else could life

do to him? The rain he could face as easily as myself,

water running from the tight-curled skull down the neck, as

easily as myself? Nothing. We looked at one another like

lovers, a tender intelligent look.

Was I aware of his needs?

      "An early reply would be appreciated." the letter

      in my hand.   I liked mailboxes when they were drab

      olive things, these red/and/blue jobs make me think

      writing letters is patriotic and I hate that .


But if it were not dark finally, but it is, where

we all become

nonentities,

grow beards,

cannot

forgive our fellowman, then

a voice in the dark begging alms, for-

get it, I can't get my hand out

of my pocket, walk on, counting

my fingers moving

over the small change .

                                        [1966/1967]

# THE CRANK

Dear   Carol,

      Logic is a machine

and every argument can and

      will

be used by somebody .

So don't worry, you

put your money down

and get change back .


      I am only sure of myself, and

      not always, and

who does that stick, I mean we do it, we

      have to

get out of the mechanism, it

goes

tick-tick

               [1966/1966]


# THE OLD DAYS

The stupid indelicacy and

roughhouse—the frontier, the pioneer?—That's
how I want to live, fight, drink
laugh, shit al fresco, pee

on the base of a pine tree
watching the limb above for
cats, or sunlight thru them—

To make love with the eyes across
a rude room and
whatever happens after, let
that happen too, like maybe
   push down the door

Fall endlessly drunk on the floor
or range, as wolves in the mountains
far enuf away to keep from getting shot
and close enuf to eat once in a while. No,

that life was not
sweet.
Only possible / and sometimes
      true.

          [1966/1969]


## OUT

The force fairly raising one

leg from the floor, buttock from the thigh

alternated, this guru's dancing

stance on the Atlantic run

  between here and Le Havre is

  one foot in 52nd Street, the

  other in France . It is

no death to see the un-

even connections between

    the swim and the   "I'm hungry"

    the cat says, the slow fuck of night

has lasted too long, the dance

has begun and we are high

strung .

                        [1966/1967]


## A MAJOR MANIFESTATION OF THE PROBLEM, IS THE PROBLEM


You appear
here on these slopes
a tired, slim, still-desireable messenger


It has been solitary
among the rocks
these two weeks,   O there've
been people, friends, work,
reasonably cheerful    with vibrations
         If one's
body turns on unexpectedly, one
can always take it for a long walk
        dissipating juices
        strengthening
        (the same in the long run)   muscles  .


                  A cold shower after a hot works
                  miracles in the mind . even
the imagination flakes out and only the eyes come alive
to that register of
small animals, trees, rock, cloud, every
thing outside   .

But now the context
changes, tho perhaps
the habit does not  .  to
read the sun on the side of Aspen Mountain
as an hour to wake and  .  turn  .  and then
to rise fully as whatever man I am
        to you, fully, explicit .
                        What is the message?
                                        I'm afraid
                the same as usual . I dress,
draw curtains on the window and leave you there
to reconstitute yourself into someone who
may someday love me  .  Hard rock
on the radio .
Coffee's lonesome, a delicate
cottonwood seed floats in the open window, lands
in my outstretched hand turns naturally to take it .
Look at it a moment then
crush it against my trousers .
plant it in my thigh, as if that were soil
or any other dirty wholesome thing  .  rock


        Lonesome's the word for it,

                that sense of it  .

        WALK    the mountain

                another hungry animal .

                                                [1966/1969]


## THE .45


"Rage, panic, and speed"

        stand together somehow

                —fastest gun on the Western Slope

they say,

it is all too poorly, he

    cain't keep company with

       no one .

[1966/1967]


## MEASURE THE TAKERS

How the words there

stand for less than it is, is

the hard way to make it, friend.

Try'er, take a shower

dry'er

hair, and aspirin by Bayer

    (briar is truly a pipe

or a kind of hay)

    cali  .  for  .  ni  .  ay

right back where I started

(from) .


How they fill up shirts

    The real question .

[1966/1974]

## BAGGS

KEEP no names that give us not

our death

To roll into it

and stay there warm

The seats of the mountains

> hold the water table close

I want her hands on my back

> though that not be possible

The grey bull codifies what we un-

> able, dis-prove

> chugchug, the jaw of

what softness we rut toward

and the rock of wool pulled short the

mountains stand

under the forks of rivers

The bowman lays it out and keeps us

down

no names

that give us not our death,

o swift current, o buffalo .

[1966/1970]

## THE FASTNESS

To stand there in the dimness with a robe on
I shake loose the feelings your eyes have
under your lids in a moment of intimacy
another dim time wheeling over you, it's

no business of mine
what you wear under your robe
or what the hour is .
And don't tell me,
your eyes
keep saying that .

[1966/1968]


## WAITING FOR (WHAT?) THE CALIFORNIA ZEPHYR HEADING EAST FROM GLENWOOD SPRINGS

*August 1966 . for Robert*


"The bus," you sed, "it
            took a long time to come."
                    Which was the answer .

Walk on by, the tune sez,
only it hadn't bn/   written yet .

And now,
look what you've done .
"Well, she wasn't my sister. . . "

[1968]

## MESSAGE TO MICHAEL

I wish to say
that a mouth
lies other
where than
where it is
North—West—
      South of me somewhere
It is invisible
and unattainable

I talk with it always   .

                                    [1966/1967]

## COLLIOURE

The town laid in there
bright orange and pink
at the eastern edge
of the Pyrénées Orientales, is full of
refugees from a civil war
two generations back   .

      The cat in the middle of the street
      resting at mid-day, faced with what
      be referred to as a motorcar, is
      not inclined to move . The street
      too narrow for any alternative maneuver, he must
      descend,
      pick up the cat,
      cradle and move it to a doorway,
      then proceed   .

Clouds skim the hills and the far scalloped
fish-shape of bay. The towers hang
on from 800 years—the flank, one
is a fortified church, and those boats
drawn up down there on the northeast beach

are used for something
every morning
early .

[1966/1967]


## HER ROOM

*for Tim Reynolds*

It is the regular quality makes us all obscene
and so much of it mineral . ⋮ . Rocks
assume unnatural positions, and yet
never have the dubious luck, she says,
of being properly fucked.

Whatever else that is, a very subjective statement
of a case
—ment, not overhanging in a useful way and give
the singer no cause for complaint, no ivy either .

And is it always that way?
You wait 2½ storeys up
for the spotlight
to hit you?

And coming down
was always
more difficult .

[1966/1968]

## THE FLOWER PHANTOM STRIKES AGAIN

Dog leans his ugly head out the truck window
digging the wind on the road,
the dust .
                Sick adjectives, dying nouns :
all those long-dead people lying in a hill back of town
no fingers or faces, stone markers from the last century
                legible,
wooden ones effaced,
                        some not totally, the
                            whole hill gone to seed
                            upkept,
                                    among the young aspens
                                    speckled shroud of sunlight .

We must
arrive someplace finally .
                In one day
I've a dream of cold spring water
& a friend arrives from over mountain .
                In one day
butterflies burst from the garden in a cloud
                        as the hose hits it .
At the top of the butte we see two butterflies fucking;
                on the road to the cemetery
it's ladybugs under the leaves along the road, a
great day for copulation, everyone's horny!

And a friend arrives from over mountain, sleeps at the door,
& a girl arrives, her arms full of flowers, steps
over him,
lays them on the doorstep .
One is never poor .

[1966/1967]


## THE GEOLOGIST

The rain falls in fresh gusts

corner of

the pass end of

this mountain town   .   The dogs

trot silent   .   People

cook their suppers

and smoke.


When the peaks rose in the Tertiary, fire

spilled upward under the rain .

The nonexistent liners on this

            boiling inland sea

            remind us, they

            pass in yr/ eyes .

[1966/1970]

## THIN WALLS  -  OPEN DOORS

Zipguns of lightning over the lower hills

Grey pencils of rain

> She giggles for a long while
> then there is the quiet sound of his lapping
> her—you can tell by the regular stroke,
> very quiet and loving . winging

pencils of rain . she tightens .
racing across the green hills like fingers
on the white berry hills
evening
showers .

[1966/1968]


## THE SOUNDS

Listen, Death
Beth, see, it's
not so bad . . .
you were the most un
conquerable, he sed, ocean I ever had, speaking to the Atlantic.
The noises in the night are cries for help
and listen to the neat
piping in the night
it's far from men
the paper's torn
and so's the word
the nails have done their

trick. the town
sits in our laps and laps, the neolithic fen
is far from born, the town
is there in the faroff sounds and
morning's rain comes in.

[1966/1969]


## THE BUTTE

On the ridge of habit

I habit, there the hand

and it's enuf

to know that there's need for it, greed for it, seed for it,

and love enuf   .   That's about climbing

woman, night and morning, near sleep

> keep the hand alert

> to an orange hill which speaks

> to the curve that's mute, no

lawn

> under sun, what

had seemed to be long looping losses, crosses the

gulch where there's water flowing, either side of the butte you

can hear what's done, the year

> rose to its close, its circles   .   Keep us

undone and silent in our loss, like how

the legs walk by,

the long legs at the end of a day's sun, you

can lear lying there, uncrossed, un-

looped and open  .   prescient, woman .

[1966/1967]


## FLEXIBILITY : OR THE RIDGE

Grey day, Pinocchio, o puppet

that we are, our legs are wood

after that mountain, up was

crevices, rockslides from the man in front

I'd time to shout

"Heads down!"

before the first rocks hit


bounced off my big straw hat, then checking

the man above, had he made it?   the

men below   .


After the three/and/two split, the three

taking what looked like an easy

but steep path down thru the pines,

it was,

Tobe and I went on

up—the other

men were afraid that

over the next summit there'd be

        another rise and peak—there was, and

when we reached the flag   (a towel

we wiped ourselves with, dripping sweat,

        and replaced)

we rested and

the down and up and down

        (rock)

then down thru the brush

        bleeding palms from the rock

        wrists and arms from the scrub

        down, never finding the road

        looked so close from the summit

A trail for horses three-quarters down

took us half the mountain across again

but down,

wooden legs now, Pinocchio   .

 

∠O∫‾‾‾        Well, to sit here on a rock, this

        high, to

        feel a reverence for valleys, that's

        what I want to sing

        high on this rock, valleys, roads

        (ROADS!)

        running thru them .

Then there's the rock, too, itself, its own pleasure

and height, to have

negotiated the steep, flaking, fingernail ridge with

feet, hands, knees, balance, belly, fingers, care,

fear and confidence, is

making love to the mountain, the use,

save one extremity, of the same parts, and now

to view briefly the truth of our fragile condition


the legs shaking in relief of their attention and to

wish the shaking would stop soon

                              there's the descent, there's

                              no other way to go

                              but down


LIFE in our bodies!   it's a reprieve from death

to sit here and breathe hard and wipe sweat, is like

contemplating a skull, we are all

                      renaissance virgins, I mean

                          JUST SMELL THAT AIR!

and what is it we do or intend, look at

that girl's hair, its fall, the pleasure

to look at her eyes, good mouth smiling,

the thighs, the turn of her ass, a flower

how it smells,

good, rosemary, basil, thyme

and again, grass smell, fresh water,

coffee aroma in early morning light,

the sun itself, the rain, this rock, its rough texture,

to be for oneself also, as for the others,

all the others,

what it is we have got at any moment, the taste

of salts on her skin, of the fruit, teeth sunk into

peach, apricot, her shoulder, cold beer on the back of the throat:

the real terms of any pleasure is that attention to it

Pain comes also with a like intensity

that is, we feel it, all a reprieve from death .


The legs are steady now, again

To look, to see, how it is possible

to move from this peak, the

descent more difficult than the climb

tho quicker, yes

let us start down now, I

think we are ready   .

[1966/1967]

**FALLOUT**

Now she's gone

who are those mountains

an I look out the window?

      Summer's left, the dogs bark all night

      Sun rises in the morning just the same,

      but the world's gone down

Light strikes the hillside later in the A.M.

Later the moon   /   dark now, the

dogs restless this end of town.


Windows without curtains, anyone can look in   .   she's

      gone   .   it's

as tho I'd gone myself but am still here to doze and talk

Hark, hark

      the dogs do   .   She's

      gone I

say .


There's nothing else to do but work some,

      pack my bags .

                            [1966/1968]

## DEPARTURE : THE SOUNDS OF SILENCE

Sirius bright over Smuggler
The Hunter is over the Pass
/ September almost
5 in the morning, almost . I
hate it, leaving the valley .
Walking thru deserted streets
the air is brisk without wind, no
cars, no
dog barks,
nothing
moves except myself

& the hunting dog over Smuggler
& Orion over the Pass .

[1966/1968]


## HEAT

Under the sun for days
no relief, a few clouds, no rain
Here, take the damned thing,
ourselves,
this flame, this thief of blue
we have become.

[1966/1968]

## STYLE

I do not know what is
the price, how
the hair falls down
past the ears
over the shoulders, it is
a style of living.

[1966/1966]


## BLUES FOR AUSTRYN WAINHOUSE

In a stone room
with a whitewashed wall
he wrote up a quotation in French
I think from Stendahl

       The Poles have their millennium
           five cents

That coast of the island faced
northwest. I
refused Madalena permission
to whitewash over it

       Poppy red's the color, the
          date, 966

So that it stayed there
that spring and thru the summer
It spoke of openness and I
found it had a savor

that blurred with the months

1957

was no date to stop that
world from sinking away.
Near a decade since and I've
not had my say, yet

THE ISLAND, the sun
in that room sits in my mind,
the unsought millennium accomplished

I am poleaxed by it.

Reach thru the poppy rain to try,
to start that opening.

[1966/1966]


**THE HEADS**

that things go well
is my whole spiel .
Not worth it

Where I've scratched
my arm,
blood comes therefrom

but stops
after a while, co-
agulates  .  stops

A dryness
overcomes the wetness
of our blood

Is it worth it to
point out
that fibrinogen, an

element causing coagulation,
exists?   I thought
everyone knew that

And the New American Library
advertises a new mystery as
a murder of quality   .

[1966/1967]


ROCKHOUND


Some pebbles from Colorado, that's
            far enuf,
            licked, they taste like the sea


                  What I want is the island
                        , really

[1966/1966]


CHEMISTRY


Who is she

who sits on her tail

            the farthest from me

and keeps a distance anyone can keep?

            says nothing, does not submit

            her voice, the poems, is the last

                  to ask for interview   .   *salt*

Miniskirts are so great and the half-length view of

thigh above crossed knees is all I need to know .


And so   .   *salt*

by slow elimination come to know her name,

my sister's

white stocking, black stocking


Say the word   'love'   aloud to yourself   21   times .

Whose fault the dominoes, what price handcuffs?

Are you my bird-sister?   Give me your   .   The words

begin to fall

*salt*

*salt*

*salt*

*salt*

S A L T   .

[1966/1969]

**INVOCATION TO VENUS**

O, foam-born lady,

take yr teeth out of my cock .

Thank you.

I guess that isn't what I meant,

just lie back now .

[1966/1975]

## SARA IS MY GUGGENHEIM

Three months now
life is too close to me      ,or
   I to it
           Just that empti
ness
   HOW   I   EMPTY   MYSELF   OUT

and whatall it fills with : Hermana
Montero singing songs of passion in
   French, as it should be,
Cortázar's hangups from the middle-forties
   early-fifties, fill it up


       &bull;
  &bull; = &bull;
       &bull;


I would like to make art from a prone position
good for using a rifle or making love
   but no, you sit here all day .


Put me in front of a typewriter with the text
See? You get it in inglés, señor
Put me in front of a shot of tequila
you get un borracho in Spanish
   put it precisely. I want
to write letters to California, Brooklyn, Buffalo,
London, India, Mexico City, E. 10th St.,
   many other foreign places.

No good.

      What is it Montero says?

"Que j'avais un commerçant?"

           I had this businessman,

                see?

Who's really me .

                        [1966/1966]


## D.C.—A.C.—A.D.—B.C.

Ain't got enuf to die on

        Lucky for you

she has no sister nobody wd/ embrace

body & soul, or

what IS your zipcode, baby, or

we'll continue doing this

not sober, not

sober at all  .  O

I love you,

          Charles de Gaulle .

                        [1966/1967]


## THE CONTRAVENTION

That is the line of red as it goes


into dimness checking past the

     desire   the contact

not made, the nape of the neck

would be blonde, touchable

after,

and before


We dance

in mind

I put my arms about her and she

     falls as from a slap

        to the floor


We are always face to face

I fall upon her

and we dance the

yellow inter/sects us at the

door   .

going out

                                     [1966/1967]


## WALKING INTO MIDTOWN

They come out of the trees, out of the bushes

                off rocks,

        looking for

peanuts, a

whole herd of squirrels

in the gazebo above the lake in Central Park hunting

peanuts .


They stand and look at you with bright eyes
crouched or standing
up, they ask you    .   Me, I've
my notebook & some brandy
no nuts    .   I say, "It's him, he's
gottem,"    & they go, this guy

sitting

on the railing

with a whole bag

of peanuts

being gracious        (noblesse oblige)

to squirrels   .

## THE CATCH

It hangs like smoke
between the buildings
over the park
                but it is not
                just mist
The sun already low in the south
                & toward the west at 3 o'clock
The girls are playing some non-competitive kind of ball:
one stands facing south & throws it over her head—blind—
                        toward the north
Four others see who will catch it, no one tries
                        hard

"He's writing something down,"    one sez

"It's all right,"    says another .

The ball

goes over all their heads .

Someone recovers, says, "You

lost something—it looks

like yr/ head."

〔 〕 〔 〕 〔 〕 〔

The United Parcel Service
                              turns the corner &
Bang,
        or maybe   B A N G,    the

whole of Sixth Avenue!

the buildings falling like blocks, the domino theory,

the length down, as

far as the eye can see, maybe 23rd Street, glass & stone

slink and clunk

                    fall like dominoes .

At 55th St.

an AT&T man swings a pick against the stone

              street

                        The New York Hilton

                        The J/C Penney Building

                        Equitable Life Assurance

                        Time & Life

                              & on the corner

                        MOONDOG

with an ad executive, yakking

And at 49th St., there's a truck that sez

"for   75   years

FINK

means good bread"

And at 48th, a sign:

F R E D   A S T A I R E

Learn To Dance

& at 45th, something

called MUFFIN-BURGER .

[1966/1967]


## THE EARLY HOURS


2 o'clock
it says now,
who knows what time it is.
                    Twice as fast
is slow   .   I want a year to come back,   THEN
what would I do with it?   Fuck it away the
way I usually do, I suppose, it's
almost as if the year did not exist withal.


    Time slows up, hangs back, you
    can get only half as much into
    the suitcase as before, as Julio puts it .


    The man sits at the table dead,
    a cigarette in his hand,
    unable.   It is 2 o'clock, who
    knows what time it is really?

You put folk rock on
on double speed
it sounds like Indian ragas .

It's   2   o'clock in the Bronx .
Also .

[1966/1970]


## THE LESIONS

There's that

skinny   skinny

lady

up on the wall


Shall I take her down?

       (yes, nailed) .

       All blue and orange


A, do. Lawdy, lawdy. With-

al,

my good health persists, and blood

is noticeable only when I wipe my ass

mornings .

[1966/1968]

# MÁLAGA, PORT

It saves the city

a provincial other

wise port, how the bloody

ships come in, the sheer

machinery of docking, un-

> (how we knock the other larger
>
> ports to the north, Cádiz & Huelva to the west

loading certain hatches

creak of crane, the strain of ropes, the rub of hulls, that close

smell of sea-rotted wood

and the wine inshore in bars we'll come to later, not

any dream of release but real

cold

and flowing

release we cannot beg or steal, but come to later

nub of skulls on hillsides, sweating bodies, gypsies

under the bridge on beds of caña, closed?   open mouths of bitches

dull strain of guitars below, the bold song rising, the hips

rising and the swing of the bloody knockers

steers the world back home .

[1966/1966]

# I'D CALL IT BEGGARY, CORSO

No love now
for a long time  .  not
that I do not
but that she does not .
      To be asking constantly
      and to get
      Not now  .  I'm tired .
      Tomorrow  .  yes,
I feel like an autumn mountainside,
nothing to look forward to
but a snowy blessing .
         Love,
         where are your hands?

Back of my head, she sed.
Which I knew .

[1966-7/1971]


# A SHORT HISTORY OF MODERN AMERICAN POETRY

*for Mac Rosenthal*

Give a nickel to the collection plate
a dime to the bum
a quarter to three in
festing the street corner spring day;
a half-doll to the magician
a buck to the herd of does

Two bucks does not an evening make

Take guns to the theater
Should you not enjoy the play in
dulge in direct criticism, shouting
"Author! Author!"

Dybbuks do not a season mate
One buck to the poet
a half-rock to green grocer for green
    bottle holding pale ale invisible
a quarter of the way down the block
a dime to win and a dime to lose
a nickel on the dead Indian's eyes
a penny for the old man .

[1967/1968]

## SIMPLE TECHNOLOGIES

Brown eyes, brown eyes,
green eyes
the underwater eyes

        The rack-system of raising oysters :
        ancient Romans used to dam up the mouths
            of estuaries
            at spawning time
        twig bundles thrust into the water to catch
        spat, the settling oyster larvae .

When it was my place to give, I
offered you a
daffodil in your hand last night, it

        was part of a performance, but
I saw what happened to your eyes
"An old army jacket, so far from the wars."
The eyes

                Now we build frames of narrow sticks
                stuck into the entrances, the
                lower reaches of estuaries.
                When the spat have settled out, take
                the sticks upstream to waters
                with less salt
                where oysters grow best.

The games.
After performance you brought the flower back to me.
It was an offer and I was scared
to look on you too long and said
        "I gave it you to keep" and turned
        to speak with George, his one eye flashing

                The sticks are nailed across racks
                single layers at proper depth
                and left to grow .

                Sometimes the young oysters are
                culled from the racks
                and placed in wire netting at the
                right water-level,
                may grow to proper size in a few months.

How is it we are summoned by it?
    the flower
that may not be returned,
    the eyes .

                      [1967/1968]


## OLD THINGS: LAZY DOGS

The sense of separation is intense.
No folklore sense of right is given
tho the government attempt it.
We do not believe them.
I do not vilify the dead of either side
soldiers—or civilians, what a
fucking awful name for

PEOPLE.

It's the old things that persist as a fantasy
the Pentagon cannot hide or smear, it
is the reality:
HUNGER, THIRST, POVERTY, PAIN, SORROW,
    INJUSTICE, DEATH

These ancient things are hard, harder
than the hot metal of jet planes
aircooled gun barrels or antipersonnel bombs

The signs we give our government it does not heed
nevertheless it escalates,
nevertheless we are losing
and have been since '54.

The whole point, Nixon, is
TO LOSE THIS WAR, not
for our own good,
for their good.

[1967/1968]


## LEAN LOVE SONG

Break flesh together

Naked Breakfast

Love eyes across a goddamn laden table, no?

Morning cockiness is

anyway one answer, what to do with all these eyes,

ears, fair forms, see

duce them

for the simple satisfaction of one another .

Migod,  a n y t h i n g

for the sincerity of a stiff clit.

[1967/1971]


## RITUAL XIII. THE SHOT

Sounds in this house I do not understand
4 in the morning sometimes, risen in the late dark,
a banging in the north wall or, maybe,
        the roof of this A-frame
(no trees about large enuf for animals to drop from)

A large bird smacking into the glassed-in
southern end one day, its stunned
fluttering off a few moments later, did
not make that much
noise
And now this morning, waiting for yesterday's
          coffee to reheat
the day's first cup, another thump
which shook the tiles under my feet
but the sound as tho from outside to the east, even
the cat wanted to go investigate and
stalked about until I slid the glass
back on the south side, what
was it?


Another house here once? & some old miner
getting up in the late dark to make
the early shift at the mine
back on Smuggler?
Hottin' up last night's boiled coffee
after straining it carefully,
stomping about to keep warm till it was ready, taking
the tot of whiskey down at a shot,
first of the day? Damn, that felt good! Stamps, thunk,
and the beams of this new house shake near a century later.
He takes his rifle down, checks, & lays it up against the wall.
To round it out, I pour a shot of
whiskey out, first of the day,
take it down at a gulp, feel it burn.

[1967/1969]

I love

THE   M O S T

(innocent of all)


She is jes comin cross the hill in her minidress

the MOST   I love is

comin across the hill

(in her mini

skirt, her underwear

perfectly clean

(changed before she left   .   showered and all   . )

[1967/1969]


## MATCHBOOK POEM

BUT   WHY   do you go to the wall?

W H Y   d o e s   h e   g o   t o   t h e   w a l l ?


You go to the

wall because

that's where the door is


maybe .

[1967/1969]

## THE SURROGATE

She stole ma hat

    ma hat   .   was in the lounge with ma jacket

The jacket she dint take it, but

                    ma hat, she tukkit, clean

                    outa the place . she liked

ma hat   .   & went with it to the room & danced,

    DANCED   with it, wearin the hat she

                    D A N C E D !

she

danced,    and dint expect I'd cum back ferit   .   ah did .


    Pretended I hadn't figured it out

    talkin with her friend . I'd figured

        she laiked ma hat .


Next mornin, nobuddy up, both of 'em sleepin late .

      "Come in"
        /
        I did, & there it wass,

ma hat

on the bed . she'd bigod

        slept with ma hat!

                [1967/1971]

## ONE ANSWER

At 5:30 it looks like clouds
hovering at horizon in the dawn dark
An hour later the light pushes up stronger
Birds batter the news about in the near trees
The city rolls out below, vaguely yellow & rose
Sound of bells and birds
trucks in the distance, train
whistles calling each other, the damned
muzak in the hotel is turned on and I have to
shut the windows again .

But now the mountain
lifts clear
against the horizon .
I can't even pronounce her Indian name, covered with
snow from halfway up . *Ixtacchuatl* . I've
come all the way to Puebla to see
—what?
The Sleeping Woman
*¿La mujer blanca dormida?*
And not in my bed
either . stretched
out there on the horizon
No one fucks with that mountain, no one
has ever wakened her .
Nor I, she

is the goddamned horizon.

[1967/1971]

# HOW DO I ADDRESS YOU? LET ME COUNT THE WAVES

She is in her subleased apartment on Waverly Place

    all's right with the world  .   Paul & Bell

    did not show  .  I kissed you and David

a real goodbye on the foredeck, tell me a better

place to neck  .  A stubby rednecked novelist came over

sd/ "Are you Blackburn? I'm the fuzz on the boat!" He

saved everybody's neck before the trip was over. The true

& original Katzenjammer kid, left a family in Ithaca, headed

    for Istanbul  .  I was a package  .  It was afternoon

    "We suggest shipment by standard carrier, rather than parcel post."

o, yes. Packed & shipped. No shit.

You both left that boat very fast after the motors started

turning over  .  Creosote the last time, set 'im on a rail

& ride 'm out of town  .  It was afternoon  .  "If you

follow the above procedure, it will result

in the prompt, efficient service you desire."

    Very fast, going away. The motors, once started, were to stay

    with us a long while. ("When you say that, smile." He did.)

Not yet out of dock, o desire, the boat's on fire, I don't even know it .

Everyone is left. On Waverly .  That's no wire-release .  The

    world is my computer, I only punch if faced

    down, the fuzz is cool, you fool, it's how it was

not how it is.     Listen, creep,

the world's complete

without me .

[1967/1974]

## GOING OFF

Going away
open at both ends
You sed I sed     merely    /    sex?
Were you merely afraid of sex
You were not afraid of sex     merely .
It was coming back to take that sad smile, echo of my own,
off you   .   as you reached for it there in the final line.

Merely going away? Hey,
dig that    MERELY

The sound of the motors
surely is not going away .
It was kissing you on the deck this afternoon, THAT
was going away very fast   .   going off the boat very fast
you and David were going away

I was not going away, I
was packaging myself and shipping me

"We suggest shipment by standard carrier rather than
parcel post."
and
"If you follow the above procedure, it will result in
the prompt, efficient service you desire."

My business is to record, and how now (brown) desire?
the North American Philips Company, Inc. is at my service.
   "À la vôtre service, monsieur!"
   "On attend le retour"
                    TO WAIT, merely,
a compliment a man can savor.
Let me return the favor:   you kissed the package and split.
Wait now then, have you back a man , shit!

                                        [1967/1974]


## THE GLORIOUS MORNING

/1/

                         Sun bright on the water, some
                         small birds over our wake, terns,
         /        birds   .   The birds turn   .   fishing
                               over our wake,
                         over the sun on the swells


To wake this morning
to wake with a girl in my bed
   a second consecutive morning
                  first time in over 40 days and 40 nights
and she thinks I reproach her for having to leave me
in the first hour of light   /
                      still virgin   /
                                ah, no .
Virtue unrewarded perhaps, but the pleasure she gives me!
To wake once more
a girl in my bed   .   a song about a dancing bear in my head
IT IS ME, I WRITE IT DOWN IN THE AIR !

Birds on the sea
sun and clouds

                 dance of waves in the sunlight
                 dance of birds in the air
                 dance of the bear in my head
           dance of her quick step across the cabin floor
           in the corridor, the dance of mop and pail
I hum:
        "I'll taste the things I please"   picking
        long soft hairs from my pillow
        small cunt hairs from my bed
so that cabin boy from the song, now mopping the gangways, will
have no stories to retail after he makes the bunk   /   my head
hums a jumble of tendernesses for what this lovely head

                  has given me .
And for all those more
glorious mornings
     in the mind .

/2/

Pas du succès        toute la nuite

       so we sleep

           sleep  .
           In the morning,
we do something fairly sensible, very
homely even, we go and have breakfast

               together .
   ACROSS  THE  TABLE,    eyes

        at meeting   .

Then,
after breakfast go
once more to the upper deck :
stand in the sun for a bit
ignoring the others   .
                    T H E    S U N !


          Return to the cabin finally,
          and there, it does happen,


it does     .    & it does
& goes on happening for a long time, the
                              other morning
                                        .
                                            now .




/3/




The city stands about us
          & friends  .
Toward the east after supper .


          She sd/ "Yeah?"
          I sd/ "Yeah."
                    A N D   I T   W A S   T R U E !


               Cuntsmell everywhere, it
               took me hours to wash, I didn't want to.
               We even got to sleep early,
               slept enormously.

*18, rue de la Harpe*
*Hôtel de Levant, le vent*
*n'est pas ici, c'est bien nous*
*NOUS SOMMES ICI,*   Joan, what
time is it now, three?

We even got to sleep early  .
Our cool hands  .

/4/

Sipping calvados in the Café des Invalides
               after morning coffee   .
        Rain drips from the eaves,
                        leaves fall   .
The gutters are up and running
                        brimfull .
September   .   o Christ, Paris   .   tout à fait normal   .

               Feuilles des marroniers
        to be swept up when it stops
        maybe next month sometime   .

And the place Dauphine-en-l'Isle
is all fucked up by construction
between the Hôtel Henri IV
& the Palais de Justice .

And it falls and falls forever   .
And looks as if the rest of these glorious mornings
                  are going to be wet as hell   .

               from JOURNAL ENTRIES, September 1967  .
                                          [1970]

## ROSEMARY & THE LANGUAGE PROBLEM


Coming to Paris, I
spoke Spanish most of the time
      —Argentine friends—
in Amsterdam a week later, am
talking mostly in English —Americans—
      including a new friend from San Francisco
          with eyes that go
      right to the bottom of my scrotal sac .   O,


balls!   & tonight I'm speaking Italian
    to waiters in the Leidseplein
& a businessman from Milano at whose table, &tc.
I am .
minestrone .
pizza napoletana
plus a half-liter of red


But there's this head with the eyes
I've got eyes for,  & with
very strange heads on us both .


What I better do is go back to Spain,
speak Spanish .

& where IS her head?
Back of her hands, I think .
Otherwise, how think in this town?
      Backwards   .   Who is it

                sitting in this chair, her
                eyes straight, her
                legs
                crossed nicely   .   Also straight
the answers   WHEN
I do ask the question :

                        "Another time, maybe."
                        Translate that.
                "When I start taking pills again."
And the eyes
            /
                saying Yes    .      & No .
Move me right there
and exactly .


                    ◻⟋


How she sits there & looks
It is a mirror   .   I am for
her      .      she for me   .   The

        GLASS

        not yet broken .


                    ✶✳✳✳⟋


            I WANT TO KNOW!

        Her mouth tells me nothing


Her eyes, however,
speak at the rough

edge of the glass, the
turn of her ass  :    they,
(yes)          speak .

—Amsterdam, Sep/27/67—

[1974]


## THE EXPENSIVE MEAL

Par la main
jusqu'à la source

     By hand, he sed
to the headwaters of it all, where

      everyone begins, be-
   gins, whiskeys, cognacs, le bien, c'est
de payer la différence, and the man
who runs the cloakroom & has his tips from that
   polishes the glasses
    when there's no one splitting out, it's
a way of doubling it up, I love

the SERIOUSNESS of it, how they all take it,
                hard or well, you
give them all le pourboire, they've done well or badly.
It is not true.

I blow my nose on some toilet tissue
from the hotel, the

young man wiping glasses notices it, his
        neutral face, that
    increases his tip  .  BLOW
everyone's mind, the

    only way to do it .

                      [1967/1975]


## WHAT YOU DO IS PICK 'EM UP AND PACK 'EM IN

Vineyards on these quiet mountain
        hillsides under fog, the far
        mountains gone behind it.
        The whole family (here
        even the cows line up to graze)
in the rows, four to a side, turn
to watch the trains pass. We probably
        also in fog
        from where they stand
        bend

to the grapes, the grapes
Boxes ready, piled under
the pear trees, the apple trees
The mist hovers above the still
waters of a river
like smoke, lays a band around
the side of a hill. All a peace

We must never kill
anyone. Pick windfalls off the earth.
Pick grapes.

                      [1967/1969]

## UNCHARTED

Sun is that
rare in Paris, I
            almost swim in it

the day accomplishes itself with its
            small failures & annoyances

Its pleasures mount gently toward evening
walking many strange streets toward

home, it were . no map, o Joan!
Let me come before you a triumph and
            a happy man!

                                        [1967/1973]


## OFF AND RUNNING

To sit and wipe one's ass in Paris
the rue Jean-Bart      /      loose as a goose

            all morning, O
            leaving again, realizing
            tomorrow morning this time

I'll be sitting in E. Seventh Street probably doing the same thing,
            gumming
            the runs clean of my crack.

The voyage .

back   .

                        Now it gets me up tight
                        the wrong way   .   Un
            able to swyve my lady Joan this morning, the
            slightest resistance brought him down.

WELL, STOP TRYING SO HARD
                    what?


                            Nothing, if
                            not cheerful,   so
                            I take her to breakfast instead.


I left my heart in San Fran
cisco, my
boots in Mexico City, my right arm
in Aspen, Colorado, two
shotglasses in Amsterdam, an
ashtray in the rue de la Harpe,
a tape cassette in another Paris hotel   .   I


wonder
what
it
was      I left in New York, in Geneva   .   On the
boat it was my gear and monster belt with a steel buckle
so enormous you could tune in UFO shortwave on it, I left
in the officers' john on the sports deck   .   O hell,

I don't wanna go no place.
I wanta stay wherever I am, wherever you are   .
baby   /   I have to go again

                            Sorry.


                                    October 1967

                                            [1969]


## ONE PICTURE OF THE FLOATING WORLD


The tree,   the window filled with
birds which speak to me                    GENTLE
my soul.   today and to                    SORROW
where my hands are not                     NOW
but will be   .   what will                BE
will be   .   soon maybe                   OURS

                                            [1967/1971]

JOURNAL 5.XI.67

How is it I keep remembering

after all those / these facts,

this flack

keeps   .   coming?

It all drives back upon the brain .

After yesterday, two things were

plain-ly set against the landfall

The sandspit in Arkansas

after a motorcycle ride in the November day

was warmed   3 cigarettes & talk

Or how explain the marks of branches in the

sand, with no mantrack near   .   Complexities

of the very simple—what?

Standing at the

edge of     I had to pee

into the Mississippi . And

later, cottonheaded from whiskey,

did not spend, tho she did from my

tongue   .   this young wife

of someone else, too up tight from

cars & bikes pulling into the driveway

where was her car?   It had run

out of gas   .   o yes.

The anxiety (plus too much whiskey) kept me down .

Here was a quim I wanted to do wonderful things in

taste was sweet and sour


The rest had left : Bobby & Lee on bike

it must have been damnably cold

that hour of morning

Bobby's nose falling off  .   the wind

up Lee's sleeves  .   And all for

a spider hanging inconclusively

swinging, flowers in the vermouth

bottle, yellow, chrysanthemums, cost 75¢ a bunch

       at the market as opposed .


Two cups of coffee and the magazine in

the bathroom  .  would be  .

CYCLE WORLD 1966  .   The Road Test

Annual  .   which only Sara

wins  .   An-other

terrible Sunday morning in the world,

everybody juiced and coffeed

Memphis is on the river, cold

Sunday paper on the porch &  torch

the flowers stand

there

the motor warming up

      turning over

The arm stretches out again

to

      no  /  one  /  there .

                                  [1975]


## JOURNAL . 7 XI 67 ff

Green shoes

black umbrella

stands on her good legs outside the school for an hour .

Checks her watch & vistas of

doorways, corners  .  People pass

      Alas, neither she nor he.

He's in Memphis and lord only knows where she is .  The

rainfall, the umbrella, the watch, the green shoes,

the green rainbow, the umbra, watch the shoes, they

move, see?

Kiss / kiss!                  A

& I do   miss            B L U E S

you .

Let me be where

that next

other glorious morning

     will be

& not in the mind either, babe,

not never no more in the mind

babe, not never no more in the mind .

Cold birds out the window trying to sing

Sweep of the sea   .   moving water   .   much further away

                I got rights

                to be blue, noo?

Who are we?

Let us see

        a gull   and a porpoise

¿cómo no?

        better

than any marriage I have had or

        could think of .

"I've been fixin a hole where the rain comes in"

& below is 17th Street, Nashville, the

cross-thru below Fisk campus

where is

LIQUOR STOREs, BARs, CLEANERS, numerous BARBER SHOPs,

burger joints, a movie, & even a gas station, ES-

SO es  . y no es . si-saw  .  So.

Off they go, back to Memphis,

                tank full of gas and a

                pocketful of rye .

The rest of this town is located else-where

        DOWN-TOWN   .   and is scary as shit

mean white mouths and steel eyes out

gunning for my beard and long hair and tight jeans

The eyes say it loud and hard        NIGGUHLOVUH!   and

I surely am, all the beautiful faces I see downtown

are black   .   a pleasure to take bus back

                to the ghetto, that's where it is, Morton .

                I am a nun here for days

                        soon shortened.


Where were all they

        &

it was not me   .   When it was

I was there.


"How is you spell PO-EMS, man?

If you're looking

> for where it is where

> it really is, never

> choose no road   .   What

> ever road you take will

> tell you, make you go

>> take you

>>> to

where

it

is

REALLY.              ⟋⟋

GIVE ME LIBRIUM or

GIVE ME METH—

among graffitti on sculpture, center of Astor Place
between the Cooper Union buildings, Nov. 10, 1967

[1970]

## GIN

Clear objects, the
clear objections   .   The gulls
float thru the yard   .   The wall-
paper is stained, sections are
pure Cretan linear-B .

I fled New York somehow,
it's all hers now . And cold .

Amsterdam is full of sun, it falls
aslant ten buildings in the next street
I can see from my window—the Dutch
    believe in large windows, it
is exactly the width of the room, a long narrow
Van Gogh-room, even the skinny bed
    in the right position .
Except the canal is at the front of the ho-tel,
so the room faces
what I wd/ call
the wrong direction.

      Black roofs and red roofs  .  Tile.
      While,
blackbirds in the shadowed backyard
hop about thru bright yellow leaves, or
flap between the lower branches .

An enormous gull just swooped thru the yards
    leisure-ly .

The canal at the front of the ho-tel,
go to it  .  Read the cards.

    Even with sunlight, I am lightly depressed .
    Foto, September 18, the boat-train
    Le Havre to Paris  .  Joan confronts
    the French landscape  .  the gold locket,
her toothmarks in it . Good, tight
lens on that camera.  Blue
dress, blue landscape blurred

O shit,
I left my heart in the 7th arrondissement
a good bit South of here, apparently.

Forget it. I've left my heart everywhere,
walk around collecting bits and shards .

Gil, how do you keep
such a unified vision of your own
      lives  /  & parts?

I take trains   /   or planes

      boats  /   or goats

Gull flies thru the backyard one way
crosses pigeon flying thru the other  .  Damn,

this gin is good!

                           [1967/1968]


## BIRDS / AMSTERDAM

Flurry of fat sparrows hits the fence
top near the Oude Turfmarkt, whence

          look very surprised
          to have made it
          look around

      10 notes   2 chords
      I try to sightread
      the melody  /  too fast, they've gone

In the tiny square NW side of the
Leidseplein   where is a carpark   the
trees are full of grackles   .   Taxi
stand   .   taxidriver, no fare, stops
briefly, gets out, slams his door,
walks to the nearest (one of the youngest) trees
& kicks it

      hard & high   .   the sky
is blackened   .   the ears attacked

   The driver smiles
   The big birds circle
   drift & land again
He gets back in the car and drives off.
Still smiling

At the Dam by Moses Aaronstraat
the Sunday afternoon is filled with
solid citizens, their overcoated arms, shoulders
loaded with pigeons doing the neck-ring peck
:   little girls with their hands full
The pigeons cluster & waddle & fly
in packs, circle up to the roofs & back
& keep the air full of wings   .   to be fed

Prinsengracht   .   Herengracht   .   Singelgracht
  families   .   flocks   /   quack
  it's ducks swimming along leaving
  delicate wakes along the quiet canals
  Well, not so quiet   .   QUACK   .

Sarphatipark   /   Vondelpark
a few songbirds   (more grackles,
more sparrows) .   Amsterdamsebos

more of the same plus some few
swans, mean-beaked, very white, plus

EVERYWHERE
my gulls

above rooftops, on them,
into backyards, over canals
bridges, parks & markets,
business streets, Centraal Station,
the Amstel, the Singel, Rokin,
Osdorp & Slotermeer, Entrepôtdok,
Het ij, Dijksgracht, Ertshaven

Mostly the birdsound
in this town is harsh
&   in/over everywhere
my gulls
hustle food

big & tough or
small & compact
they make it

tho the Paleis on the Dam
belongs to the pigeons

But, I'd heard all that about storks
nesting in chimneys   .   did not see any storks
Where are the storks?

Nov. 18-20, 1967
Amsterdam

[1970]

## TRAIN TO AMERSFOORT

Sheep staring
dully across a field

                 three white pigs in another

in a third,   7   black & white cows
grazing along, their heads down, tails lifted .

Line of trees far off .

Sheep
more sheep
more cows
more pigs, cluster of
distant cows, two horses
heads lifted this time, tails lifted also .
Whole herds of seagulls walk in the fields
sheepdung  .  cowturds  .  pigshit  .
Small
        canals
run thru the cold November day's
              green foggy morning
near an arm of the North Sea near
                Naarden Bussum

before the railroad turns from the sea
toward Hilversum .

                         [1967/1970]

## ROADS

Having been on
the road

ALL   THIS   TIME

(three months plus & it's not stopped anywhere yet)
run baby, run, you
won't get anywhere until
you
stop
(somewhere)
and even then &
even then


Thus qualified, I
want to write a poem abt/ roads
that they are there, that
one travels them & is not obtuse
nor obliged to take anymore in, onto the mind, than
the body in time and space taketh unto itself, the
mind in its holy vacuum
breaking out of   past the fact
to other   FACTS?
give me something
anything else to pad
this hard straightbacked
chair, say that bed, Joan in it   .   that's
padding, that's bedding or
railroading .   featherbedding?


R O A D S   . nowhere
I can stay for long, it goes

by itself for a long time unattended by more than
fences along it  .  what the wind constructs  .  its own
silly protection, keeping the monsters back in
that idyllic pasture we call mind  .  O, find the
nearest next intersection, the road goes on
until it meets another
road, and then rose up, it rises up, that choice
not so much taken
as come to
where we sit down in the middle
and let it all roll over us . Or
Lew Welch's gig: "Take a few steps off it
& the whole incredible machinery rolls by,
not seeing us at all."

        (Or, even further out, that naval
        lieutenant commander out on the end of a
        line in space, now on postage stamps, said:
        "There is absolutely no distortion and
        I'm not coming back in.")

so there's this road
& one stays on it forever until one
(it) stops (roads
go on forever, so do parentheses) or
gets some WHERE else in his body or his head,
finds there's another place to be, comes
or goes
quietly to one side, & there
lives
or dies
accident
-ly  .

[1967/1968]

## O, SHAKE IT UP, BABY

Today was wave day

   If you had anything to wave
   today was the day to do it.

     A late start however. Flags waving
a damp cluster of them at the palais du Luxembourg

A man in a window across the street from the Hôtel
Jean-Bart waved a lot at a group of students
turned out to be a chorus rehearsal

Joan & I waved our eyelashes at
one another   & other things

I stomped mother-naked up & down the room
imitating the choral director across the street

Everything we do is very funny
or very tender & serious
We waive everything, even clothes

I waved a 100 franc bill at the younger brother/waiter
at a Vietnamese restaurant on Vaugirard
& he had to go wave it at someone else a few
doors away to get change

After I waved my tail with some success at one of those arabic
bathrooms
    in a bar
    near the Metro
    at Latour-Maubourg
    in the middle of a good German beer

I left my Mexican hat off and let my hair wave at people

—it seemed the only thing to do today—

& swung my hat cavalierly thru the Metro changes all the
way to Strasbourg-St.-Denis where the correspondences will
get me to St.-Placide with just one change of trains

    And just to finish off the day, a
    pair of gendarmes, corner of
    Vaugirard & Boulevard Raspail

waved down a cab with a
passenger in it &
waved a finger at the driver, I
guess he was going too fast that block

The driver, as was natural,

waved it off .

[1967/1974]


## PARIS, AND NOT SPRING EITHER

The young man

in the next booth

in the café

is waiting for

while he studies

& looks at me

occasionally while I

translate & wait for


We exchange

glances, shy &


His girl arrives first   .   I feel

her presence over my right shoulder

before he sees her I see her

She is blond and very pretty

Mine is brunette

& has not arrived yet


He & I both

smile . this city.

[1967/1974]


## PARIS-TOULOUSE TRAIN


*Caersi (Quercy)*

Roads
run off into the countryside & lanes
                into the trees & disappear   .   The hills   .

At Brive, the first thing I see
is a young wife standing in her dooryard, a
chick, in red coat, black slacks, a yellow sweater, not
                taking any chances   .   the Corrèze:

that river kept coming at us from the left
side of the train, at an angle   .
                At Gourdon, shades of de Born,
I hear the rhythms of the old speech. Two gents
in the next booth in the dining car speaking a
language thought to be dead the last 700 years—
they talk abt the lack of feeling in politics these days   .
                shades of Guillem   .

Okay, I'm home but not safe yet, whole
                stretches of rapids   .   Can
you think of any better entry to the south, what
                anyway, goes on in yr mind? Tree
that it will be,
hill, that it will,
field that it see, mist that it
was Joan's mouth I kissed
before I left Paris, fog
that I dig   .   December, be kind
to me.

*Cahors*

Tileyard, lumberyard, a
medieval bridge, towers
at both ends, & in the middle   .
The hill like a sleeping animal   .
              dormant   . the
gas stations like anyplace else   .

*Signals 4.*

POUR L'OBTENIR DE L'EAU
APPUYER SUR LA PÉDALE , it sez
& the *eau non potable*
has been carefully edited down to
          'no pot'

And having had my taperecorder on for
four hours, the
new conductor at Montauban & his small moustache, tells me
              "La musique—c'est interdit sur le train."
"Forbidden to play music on the train . . . "
I figure he's got nothing else to say   .

                  There are
                  sonsofbitches
                  everywhere   .

          Bonjour, monsieur Blackburn!
          Welcome back to Toulouse!
              and rain, I swear   .

                                    [1967/1969]


MUSÉE DES AUGUSTINS : TOULOUSE


KARTHA

ginian lamps, shaped
like shells to fit the hand—2 flames—
one lifting at each end of that beautiful curve, did they
          join?          Lovers' lamps   .


          put in some oil and see

& Etruscan cups, five/six
centuries before that god came down, all
                jet-black
                with big ears
                held like a dipper,
        probably dipped in the jar—spill
a bit onto the floor first, for the gods


The guards
who'd confiscated my camera stayed
down by the *caisse* at the entrance
so I touched all the statues of Venus
cunt, belly and breasts
All those of Bacchus and Hercules
I tickled under the balls, just to be sure   .


& Lucius Verus   (161-169 A.D.)
looked just like Robert David   .   I passed
a pleasant hour with the goddess, the gods   .


                    *Toulouse, November 1967*

                                    [1968]


## FACING SOUTH


Assville, North Carolina, or   AN

ashville, Tennessee, but

Memphis is on the river, as

any Egyptian knows, where and as it goes

south   (who's asking?   maybe it's north)

is where my mouth, O Cleopatra,

        goeth where thou cometh,

in the bend

of that river

to the left   .

                [1967/1970]


## VALENCIA : WINTER

Sunrise now
abt/    8:15 every morning
Light starts coming over before that

        It's such a drag to wake up in the dark,
            and I do .

No one to turn to, I
may read for a bit, turn the heater on, the
        light off, try
        sleep another hour
          or two

    The light
    when it does come
    is timeless


Check the sky & eat an orange .
then make coffee .

                [1968/1970]

((from the journals))
## PLAZA REAL WITH PALM TREES : SECOND TAKE


BARCELONA!   this city again

after 10 years of separation, exile

maybe a better term   .   is warm

and busy


Early in January, I've just seen my friends to the train back
to France   .   poor friends   .   And my Joan weeping briefly in
the compartment   .   a good girl—will
           be a good woman soon—all there.
It's been a beautiful   18   days, half of it here on the Ramblas,
sun from late morning to late afternoon, then Valencia, Cullera,
Faro, Alicante, train & bus, then, on impulse, the boat to Palma

         "bound upon a magic ship
         for a land I'd never see"

         again, well not quite .

Seen the first time in 10 years, was very good, even if for
two days only. And walking back from the Estación de Francia
here, the train had pulled out sometime during that walk, I can't
stand goodbyes anymore, couldn't stay to cry myself

         but dove back

         into the city .

THIS CITY!

The slow walk back to the pension, a manzanilla at the Bodega Reus,
small streets, no cars, people walk in the streets .

DIUMENGA   /   SUNDAY

Here, people carry their children

no pushcarts or baby carriages, they

carry them

in their arms .

Both arms if they are mothers,

perhaps a single arm if they are

fathers—that simple,

complicated act of becoming

that kind of man, finally, but the kids—

one arm or two,   RIDE   there at ease

looking about them, digging the scene

—big eyes for my beard and long hair wd/be bigger had I

worn the cowboy hat, or the Mexican, they

eat their pasteles or sweets

& stare

The mothers worry that I am

looking at their legs   (of

course! that's what I'm doing)   the men

worry or don't—it's Sunday .

Calle de Aviño, I'm
behind a young man and his girl
all of us walking toward the Ramblas:
just below Caracoles, a drunken American beachcomber type lunges
toward them, reaches for the girl.
The little guy coldcocks him with one stiff arm, don't even
break his step   .   The big blond American staggers from the
resistance, turns and yells
                    "Hey, YOU!"

The young cat turns, I'm passing the drunk, I say
mean and quiet, "Lay off'em."
but loud enuf everyone could hear.

The young Catalan looks at me, I make
the Ballantine sign with my fingers & grin   .   I'm back
in Barcelona .

Wander up toward the Plaza Real and the pension, have

a short discussion about travel & sexual mores with

the aging faggot on the desk

& come upstairs & look out the window   .


           I live in a tree these days

             The pigeons are trotting about

Around noon ('s still Sunday), a few hours ago, the

square was filled with stamp collectors with their books

of stamps, buying & selling—

               trading

               in sunlight,

               under palmtrees waving .

Now, at   4,   young Spanish hipsters stand

their hips against the fountain's railing

               or in clumps

                         the winter sunlight fading .


Girls impossible in skirts   10   years ago

               —that short now—arrive, leave,

               with or without young men

It's Spain still & chances are they stall, they

leave with the girlfriends they arrived with

               Tho maybe in the same direction

               as the boys, tho maybe—

still, they've no place to go   .   it's money

The pigeons stroll
the people stand or move
                    but TALK!
This town .


            The   old man in dark glasses
            who sells the peanuts & sweets
has been leaning against the same palmtree for   6   hours now .
His old wife relieves him a couple hours at noon .


Families pass thru

carrying the youngest ones .

Here, people carry their children

No baby carriages in this square, they

carry them in their arms, their

children dig it .   everything .


                        Once again, I am *looking* at it
                        (down into the street with glazed eyes)
            Sounds of voices
            drift up to the pension window
            thru it, tho it be winter, O
            sweet christ, go down, go
            down there, man,
            into the real plaza, the
            Plaza Réal itself, either
            enter your life, enter its life,

or make yr/ own


By   10   at nite the young studs

've gathered around in groups of   7   or   12,

with one girl, perhaps, to each group

to keep the game going


        Groups of  4  with no girl, just

        talk—go down, go

        down, enter the dance

                (Evening, Kelly . . . )


Joan, Dean & Sandy

are back in France by now, *pobrecitos.*

   France, this winter, not only de Gaulle

   & inflation, but notably

      snow, floods, rain .

      Hugo wrote *Les Misérables,* he

         wasn't kidding, those

         people are poor in their hearts, O

fuck France, fuck its rain, fuck

its mailchutes, I ought


never to go back again   .   It's

still Sunday .


Wipe it out for an hour .
Go eat .

The boys now highly reduced

to  5  and  9 .

Two American college chicks at a table

of the café nearest calle Fernando

" . . . highly unnecessary—"   no

words I can use, everything's necessary, even snotty American

college girls   .   Dive into Quintana, the *Glorieta*

alone this time  :    sopa, canelones, ternura .   My

Ideales *con papel trigo,* the old-fashioned cheap cigarette

with black tobacco and wheat paper, found unexpectedly

on the Born in Palma

are such a rarity here, the waiter asks me one .

"*Hace diez años . . .*" I say, "10 years ago . . ."

He says, "*Hace diez años . . .*"

A professional American couple, but quiet,

next table down, he probably teaches:

"Paul will know," says confidently, not loud .


I hope he's right.

The waiter and I

both enjoy our cigarettes .

The waiter's so happy, matter of fact, he

forgets that I ordered *flan* & brings

an orange—

the *naranja*'s name is   TIPICA   & is

stamped on its side   /   is

a navel orange & seedless   .   o, the gods!


What we need here soldier, is more carts, college girls, more

black cigarettes, more navels, carts & horses,

more burros & less cavilling, take the lead out of it!

    I make room to spit out seeds

     that do not exist, just habit .


Joan is asleep on the Paris train,

it is passing Toulouse about now .

She doesn't wake up . Nods   .


   Back in the street
   Fernando is all lit up, so's

   calle de la Unión to the other side
   and the Ramblas .

   Left over from Kings? it looks like
   Christmas
     . Baby,

   it ain't .


      Barcelona
      8 Jan 68


        [1969]

**GOING OFF**

The  sun  came  over  the  mountain

and  took  me

precisely  in  its  arms

There  was  no  one  else  there

That  was  a  Monday  .


The  little  opening  of  her  mouth

doth  grow  larger,  larger,  her

tongue  moveth  deliciously  about  it

swift  &  slow  .  up  &  down


I'd  better  blow  this  town,  or

I'll  never  leave  .

[1968/1975]


**THE TISSUES**

You know what has in-
vaded Europe since I
left her a dozen years ago?

T A M P A X

&

K L E E N E X

that wood to paper, cotton
grows—on the banks of the Mississippi—
that delicacy, that intimate

(S'all cellulose)
or when are we going to send paper airplanes to Vietnam?
Disposable klenliness has come to overthrow the old world
finally . Coke, Pepsi, & hamburgesas could
                    never have done it alone.


"Comment TAMPAX peut-il empêcher
        toute odeur?—Parcequ'il n'est
pas exposé à l'air, étant porté intérieurement. . .
        RIGHT!  teach the ladies how to
        shove it, and what's at fault is the air!


Actually, I'm not so unhappy about the Kleenex, my
SINUSES THAT DEPENDENT ON IT THESE YEARS
**IT's ONLY THE PRICE I OBJECT TO, usually
twice the stateside price at least—
                    and having grown up
                        terribly
                    in Vermont, one
thing I could never stand was a
stiff, dirty snotrag .
O handkerchiefs,
I've foregone your pleasant softness all my
life, damn near, for the flimsy softness of
papier-mouchoirs en quate de cellulose,   1,30 F, prix con-
seillé,   75 skinny, halfsize (format moyen) for a
quarter, New York 200 fullsize for the same price .
        Spain even worse, 30 ptas for the small regular 100 box
(or 45¢), when
for 30 ptas. I can still buy a whole meal in Barcelona
(Okay, wine is extra).

The Kimberly-Clark Corporation is taking
advantage of my dripping forehead .
Fuck the Kimberly-Clark Corporation,
fuck their mailchutes.

I've just cooked up and eaten a
fryingpan full of sheep's guts
with potatoes and onions, leaving a
handful for the morning to heat my own gut with.

A piece of wood looks like stone
if it's worn smooth enuf by the sea—
if it shrivels a bit, like flesh then .

I'm going to bed, turn
on the electric heater, and keep
my sinuses dry .

Goodbye world  .   until
morning, sea.

[1968/1968]


## AS IT ENDS

It is not just at night

when we sleep  .   There comes

a moment in the life that we won't know .

We go past it into—

or it goes past us.

There is a rose and purple cloud

to the north

reflected in this sunset

I want you all to know

I love you very much .


        O, shut up, you are a dead man,

                for Christ's sake!

                      [1968/1974]


## FOG

My hands sit there
turned on my knees, in-
ward and soft, a few
wrinkles along the back, I stretch them out .
They hold a white
cigarette, and are brown .

        Gulls balance
        swing in pairs up
        thru this weather .

Thunderstorm
beats against the windows, 8 or 9
lines of surf breaking  .  whap .
whitecaps on the sea, color
muddy green today, far as I can
see, which isn't that far .

Lightning strikes again
so many ways, parallel to the waves this time
I hardly notice the thunder, tho it was loud
The hands are
brown, I tell you .   fog .

[1968/1975]


## THE INGESTATION : OR TAKING IT ALL IN


I try to, per-
haps I try too hard
to select it, to choose, o I CANNOT!
it cannot be deliberate, you don't choose

YOU JUST LOVE, THAT'S ALL
it is a force   .   fierce,
she   .   whoever she is   .   is
unavoidable

The openings are screwed up tight
and I bring her here
just to know
where she is
I am   .

The loathly lady tells
Arthur, middle of that wood, what
all women want most : 'Their own way'
That is very true

The same is true of men, also.
"He had his way with her"
no idle expression

> You strike the earth hard
> & enter it, finally,
> & forever .

[1968/1974]


## THE NET OF PLACE


Hawk turns into the sun
over the sea, wings red, the
turn upward . mountain behind me

I have left those intricate mountains
My face now to the simple Mediterranean . flat .
small boats . gulls . the blue

Old hawk
is still there tho, as
there are foxes on these barren mountains   .
> Old man in a beret, 62 perhaps, came
> into the village bar the other day
> —2 skins and one fox unskinned—

> "You hunted these down?"

> "I hunted them. They
> come in closer in winter, seeking food,
> there isn't much up there—"

Rocky headland down into the Gulf of Valencia .
My windows face North . He was a hawk

I turn back to the Rockies, to the
valley swinging East, Glenwood to Aspen, up
the pass, it is darkest night the hour before dawn,
Orion, old Hunter, with whom
I may never make peace again, swings
just over the horizon at 5 o'clock
as I walk . The mountains fade into light

Being together there was never enuf,—it was
"my thing" Nothing of importance (the reach)
was ever said . I turn
& say farewell to the valley, those hills   .
A physical part of wellbeing's been spent &
left there—Goodbye mountains   .   valley,
all. Never
to be there again . Never.

It is
an intricate dance
to turn & say goodbye
to the hills we live in the presence of .
When mind dies of its time
it is not the place goes away .

    Now, the hawk turns in the sun, circles
    over the sea .
              Defines me .
    Still the stars show thru        .

Orion in winter rises early,
summer late . dark before

> dawn during August
> during which day, the
> sun shines on everything.

>> Defines it .
>> Shadows I do not see.

I rise early
in every season.

> The act defines me,
> even if it is not my act .

>> Hawk circles over the sea .

>> My act .

Saying goodbye, finally .
Being here is not enuf, tho
I make myself part of what is real.          Recognize me
standing in that valley, taking only the embraces of friends, taking
only my farewell . with me

> Stone from my mountains .
> Your words are mine, at the end.

[1968/1969]

# HOW TO ENJOY FISHING BOATS

Sit on the terrace
& look
at them, inshore tonite,
across all that greying
blue .
hear (chug) . count
the boats

Ee/ush,
waves coming in   (don't count)
the beach below, low sound, then two
bikes downhill
from the construction site
One is a motorbike, its tires
smooth on the roadway, its weight, no
motor on, the other, motorless, clanks
lightly
at every unevenness

        Later a car comes down,
        a 600, the foreman's a
        likely guess, it chugs  . The

lighthouse goes on,
opens its eye to come to us all,
a half hour later now
than when I arrived on this coast a month ago .
February  :   the moon two days off full, high
already in the eastern sky  . My
girl leaves the room
because she thinks I am working &

a workingman shd/ be alone
with his mind,
whatever that is .

[1968/1975]

## RITUAL XVI. IT TAKES AN HOUR

Clear empty days like this

one after the other. I sit

:sun on the balcony, eat an orange

save the pits, set them in

the sun to dry


Later, I eat

from the piles of paper anywhichway

on the table, old manuscripts, letters, money,

contracts, other men's poems, feed

questions & answers into my typewriter

for hours before you ask me,

"Are you hungry?"

You take a long time in the bathroom

always,

gently relieving yourself, then

that long personal

hot water ritual, you stretch

under the shower, torso & limbs for what?

      (seems to me, curious glance at the closed door)

the better part of an hour   before the rush of water stops .

stretching again to towel, pat & rub yr skin (I've caught you at

nearly every part of the ritual but

      've never seen it wholl-y, god,

         I'd like to!

          After that,

the face must be prepared, the care

that attends the eyelids,

the mouth, damned good thing we're in the south,

      wear out the mirror, what

        for?  me?  the

            waiter at the ho-tel? the

              busdriver?  and we

have to run finally to make the bus .  The bathroom

takes too long . but

I love the suspense .

        To watch you walk out, preening

           just slightly, a happy smile you

ask me, "Are you hungry?"  while I know

who it is informs my morning, rises, fills my day .

      walks round this hillside, bath around herself .

      feeds me .

                [1968/1975]

**HOW IS**

we keep our watch upon the night
                    the talk?
              It is far, o, the
light swings to our eyes at 5 & 7
seconds, then again at 20, roar of the sea .


STARS  .   assuredly, and count
the constellations to the north, the east
the beasts are met there in the sky, the
              handles fixed, the Hunter rises be-
                    hind my back, her hand
                              on my thigh
tells me that the talk has come
faro, o, far, and has
gone on too long  .   the candle
power of the light is constant all night long
even as the stars dim beyond the light cloud,
the windows mist up and the temperature goes
down, here, high, and on the beach, loud and slow,
              the waves come in from the north, the
              aftermath of storm some other part
                         this sea  .   We
dance the talk in our minds, listen the waves
finish off their lives against the sand, and kind
              ask    what?   the returning
pressure of another hand


THE DELICATE PRESSURES OF THE CONSTELLATIONS


search out gently
where the sensitivity

saves its own, bungles its own,

    CANDLE

power of the light, constant .

                             [1968/1971]


**TRAVELER**

                (for Anselm)

LEAF/TIME

postage stamps by the dozen

eggs by the half-dozen

it is not now, the

rocks are my cousins

the grass is her

navel, Wife, Ladies, I

go down, I go down   .

                             [1968/1968]


**FROM THE JOURNALS; MARCH 1968** : News of Che's death & other
political musings, Spanish
newspapers being somewhat
slow to report certain events.

Plaza de Portal de Elche
in Alicante, wet
from last night's rain .
I had the news in Paris, mid-October, sitting
in a café with Joan, picked up a leftover newspaper
from the next chair, refolded it to the frontpage.
The news is still with me .

It's eight in the morning . This square carries an
unintentional message in
its ancient name made new .

       Coffee and *ensaimadas* at
       the kiosk set low center
       amid the gandules and palmeras
       *"Grande como el grande, no ande."*
*¿Que quieres?* this early, this late, 2
taxis only on the plaza now . *"Una sombra y
dos ensaimadas,"* instead of
       *"La revolución, señor, y dos ensaimadas."*
*¿Por favor?"*

Young man stops on one corner at a
shop mirror to
squeeze a pimple or two on his way to work;
looks vacantly at the white
blood-flecked excresence on the
thumb and middle finger of his left hand,
checks the mirror again,
           the hope of Spain .

       By 8:15 there are  4  taxis on
       the side of the square toward the port,
           2  on the lateral and  5
       'minitaxis' on the side toward town .
    The second coffee, this time black, with coñac,
goes down more easily .

[Back at the *pensión*, another quality of certain Spanish newspapers grows
to be of prime importance.]


Stockingfooted down
the tiled & whitewashed
narrow hall, its full
length .


The light works, so
    sit & read :
On the something 28th,
South Yemen tossed out   30   British
      military hired a year ago when
            Yemen became independent .
Foreign Office sends a stiff note—the
Yemenites reply (politely)
that they're saving money .


And an outfit called   RUTHERFORD ESPAÑOLA, S.A., at
      14, General Goded,
               in Madrid, will
build you a swimming pool shaped like your kidney
out of stone and tile   .   The
rectangles of paper are neatly
torn   .   I tear mine once more
      lengthwise, while thinking
of all the smug accountants in Yemen,
      how polite they are,
and the   30   British advisors
      out of a cushy job

while I slowly & carefully
wipe  .   Paper's a bit
on the slick side .


Alicante, March 8, 1968

[1969]


## CUTTING THE MUSTARD

The world and ourselves pass away

We go on

and enter the dance .


What other chances are there

we could think of as

already prepared?

[1968/1971]


## THE PROBABILITY

On that not-so-bleak hillside, rocky tho, there's

a bird out there singing a goddamned rondelay

there's a bird out there

also broken bottles, tiles, bricks, trash

flowers (purple, yellow & white) many iris

thorns and rosemary


The hillside is mainly a gray-green, the sea

a bluer green, goes crash below,

repeatedly,

crash   .


   A goddamned rondelay   I think

   she must have built a nest out

   there   .   crash

           [1968/1975]


## HALFWAY DOWN THE COAST

      What we do
      is what we can
      do  can
      give  .  the tenderness


  C A U G H T   G I V I N G   A W A Y   L O V E

T h e   l a y i n g   o n   o f   a n   a r m
g e n t l e   i n s i s t e n c e   o f   t h e   h a n d

   The sea insists
   on coming to a beach
   someplace

The sound is a constant offering
The hurt is suffering
the same things   .   again

I have   19   shirts in the drawer
I could give them all away & have   38
                    It's a big drawer of
                        things

And love?   What is that
many-faceted mother?

[1968/1969]


## THE TRADE

Young and as ancient as Spring

the words came sweet, the

tavern owner's wife singing

        over the ironing  .


            Falling silver on our heads

            bent over wine  .  the glasses

                clear and golden

[1968/1975]


## RITUALS PREPARATORY TO THE VOYAGE

"How cum you don' call on me no more?"

            No answer's simple.
            Friends in this town I've seen
            broken bread with, others
            not called, not seen, not broken
with either, just the time and weather  .   Spring in
Paris many weathers, hot
& muggy 2 days ago, yesterday spit rain,   the
threat ignored, Bill, Teresa, the kids & I took

lunch to the Bois de Boulogne,    scored , i.e.
                the rain held off .
                            getting hard .


                                    "Pic-nic!" Pound snorted,
                                    Charles reported .

Taking pictures, *pelota*, and wine
white with the sandwiches and cheese.

Eric & Shirley, not called, the
Jonquières not called  .  Joan's
mother's in town, I wouldn't please her mother  .  No

                            rocka da boat, Gil,    "gimme
                            the smoke, fucka
                            the world, outa the
                            blue, singa the song"

                        RIGHT!

And now to Italy, Spain, maybe
see the old man & talka with him
before he kicka the bucket

                    No, Ez, no pic-nics.

        It's just the time, friends, lovers, master, ladies,
        after Easter  /  and the weather

    This morning we woke to raining hard
    me sweating and apart as you can
    get in that sleeping bag
    with my early morning kidney-trouble
                        jiggle-jiggle

Pull on clothes, half-a-block to go
to the nearest vespasienne
            sed my red hen,    "It's time
            & the sky is falling"
                        Paris rain   .

All the clocks are kicking my keister
south, my balls and my penis  .  Goodbye Paris,
hell-o, Barcelo-
na, hello Venice!

                            Apr 22. 68

                                    [1975]

journal: April 1968
## PEEING ALL OVER THE PE-NINSULA

At the front of the truck with the door open
or at the back, against the wall,
or into the canale   if there aren't
too many trucks loading too many dorys
wood, mineral water, antiques, empty coke bottles

> You have to watch the clock
> on this dock, if
> the toilets are open and you have the muscle necessary
> > you get that far, but
> the truth of the matter (excuse the ex-
> > > press-
> > > ion, is
> a man gets to where he can and then
> goes.
> Right there.

And after one has mucked up the port long enuf:

"Excuse me sir, signor, which way is Rome?"

"Excuse me, sir, signor, all roads lead there."

"Molto grazie—danke sehr."

Too many days in this city
It's gotten down to routines
I try to vary
them.
The usual and unavoidable one starts
when the dock is still empty, 3-4:30 AM .
Take care of the simplest pressures in the canale, then
after a cigarette crawl
back into the sack for a few hours more sleep   .

An official rising about 6:30 or 7.  Gather
my shaving kit and head for the bar or the port johns.
If it's the UOMINI (next door to
the DONNE, of whom I've seen not a one use the facilities in 10 days)
and take care of the private sector of the morning immediately.
The coffee and croissant. And washup.

If the trattoria bar, it means I can wait
a bit, buy breakfast first, then
use their facilities in proper order
(they have a mirror).
        Shit, shave, and brush teeth (SIX WEEKS
since I've had a shower), and I'm ready for
serious work.
        Cross the parking lot to the
camper, turn its furniture from a bedroom into
a sitting-room/studio, spread the serape on the table,
set up the typewriter, then letters, poems, revisions,
translations, some
                kind of activity. One cup of wine.

Around 9, lower the roof, pack and lock up;
then the boat into town, *accelerata* to
Rialto if I feel slow, *diretto* to San Marco
if I want speed.

           At Rialto, I always
check the Fermo Posta in case they've
stupidly sent it there, then walk across
the island to San Marco and cold old American Express  .   I ordered
money a week ago from Geneva
and the last three days
I've been, as they say,
expecting.
        The young man is very polite as he tells me: "Nothing." Smiles.

In the calle dei Fabri there's a wineshop
    VINI  .  STELLA D'ITALIA  where
I buy a quarto di vino bianco, a big fat
glass of white for consolation.

                All this part of the routine is
                fairly  .  unavoidable.
                I drink and write, or
                drink and improve my Italian.
                Then the possibilities open:
                        10:30 perhaps.

I go to catch a *traghetto*
to Pound's side of the city, San
Gregorio, Santa Maria della Salute.
If they're in, we talk or read or go for a walk,
if not, I
walk, take pictures, take my lunch alone  .

Today I vary it by
going out to the Lido to swim.
Salami and cheese and bread I buy
and a bottle of grappa will last me several days
and walk out past the hospital where still they've
fucked up the beach with *gabinetti* but you don't have to pay .
And after arranging the towel and the food and
lie down on my back and sweat for a bit, I swim.
My first full entry this year into the Mediter-
ranean, water's shallow, so I walk out slow, and when
a wave gets me waist-deep, bigod, I giggle,
then dive . eat and sleep.

At 3, I walk my cheap sunburn
back to the *vaporetto,*
what's happened is
I've really tricked myself into a hot bath,
the first since the end of March.
I've spotted some public baths some ten
minutes from the parking lot . I dump
my beach gear at the truck and pack fresh towel
some soap, my shaving kit, toothbrush and go
buy me a hot tub for 30¢—even wash my hair,
shave, trim hair and beard and moustache, I
find I'm singing . Wash the tub, it's a ring,
what a ring! Not so much a ring as
a one-man bathtub Mafia . incredible, I
keep singing.
Coffee at Poggia's, then a small
Forst beer (shades of Merano rise, you've nothing to
lose but your alcoholic content) back to the truck,

work . drink . sleep

Smeared head to toe with coldcream, I fall asleep.
The variant strain is taking already. I wake
at 4 AM as usual, but the East is red, red with dawn, and the
trucks are four lines deep already by the dock, tho no boats yet.
It'll be another hot day . Maybe the luck today

will break the bank

and the check come .              And tho I'm ½ hour late

all along the line, it does. And I take the

¼ de *vino bianco* to

celebrate.

Late and late again, I
find you can buy wine here *suelto*, i.e.
     bring yr/ own bottle.

But the money's here,
well, back in the saddle!

[1969]

## RITUAL XVII. IT TAKES AN HOUR

Money seems to avoid me in
some mysterious way

                         so,
                what else should I do, waiting
                for my check to be cashed, but
use a large Hispano-Olivetti and its outsized carriage
sitting in the middle of the floor

First, tho, they
recognized me from similar occasions, the
check had some kind of stamp across its face, and they
said I had to open an account   .
                              OKay,
so I agreed I would open an account if I had to, why not?
Then draw out most of the money, right?

I had the account almost open, all those
questions & answers & signatures, I was even
enjoying it, the
*chica* filling out the forms filled out a
pretty tight sweater herself, good

legs and lovely breasts resting lightly
    on the desk as she bent
      her forms
        to those forms  .  Then,
this damned vicepresident comes back to tell me he'd
got permission to pay me cash, I tried to look grateful  .


So she tore up all that paper and I had to
settle for a nice smile and the bust measurement instead of a
good, solid banking relationship  .


But they weren't thru with me yet:
Had to sign it twice myself (*por*
*motivo de turismo*, that horror), then
the vicepresident, then a clerk, then
another official of some sort, the whole
damned check is covered with signatures, passport number,
addresses, verifications
           :  then I wait
           some more  .


The authorization arrives back  .   even then, the
window of *Varios Pagos* takes  3   people ahead of me.


So I sit and write the first poem I've ever written in a bank  .


It IS a lovely typewriter, and a handsome type  .   perhaps
I should come here to write
        all my poems  .


*Barcelona, May 1968*

[1968]

## ACQUIRING A TEMPORARY CAT

1.


A toad
sitting there
crouched, shrunken,
stretching and withdrawing as
    is needful  .  his
    white hairs
    do not command respect .


A ring of flesh
from which the head
protrudes  .  the mass
of smooth and wrinkled
balls beneath look peaceful
    and they are .


  Morning
    bright sun
      light a second
        cup of coffee on
          the terrace in sunlight
           a man in his nature
            a man with several pretensions but
             no clothes, sits
at a machine in sun
  light typing words .

2.


Usually
walks about
in trousers or a robe   .  faceless,
but in the sunlight
he wants   to bathe him   he is
he finds himself, without pretension
And the cock hangs between his legs
like a truncheon, that embarrassment
of half-extension   .  ready for use at the slightest
suggestion:   he thinks his lady should wake up .


3.


A contrail across the sky, a
bell sound across the wind
                              birds .
the mountains back from the coast not as clear
as they were
earlier   .   an
          industrial town, an undeveloped
          beach nearby   .   how
          he drags his life around half-
          crcctcd between his legs,
          should it   be called upon to
          fuxion, what? we make it, late afternoon   .
          And a cat is down in the street

4.


And it happens so, we
all need it   .  walking
the beach at night, sand shifting
into the broken alparagatas, climb
the breakwater, port's border, walk
the dark stones out, avoid the dark
spaces between them, a test of depth
perception, both of us pass, and at
the small red faro at the far end, the air
is warm,    unzip and let him out   .   her mouth
is all I need, her tongue the beauty of
all constellations, what a
difference a night makes   .
                              Cat,
back at the apartment,
sleeps thru us.

[1968/1974]


**THE REQUEST**


Fishing boat at night

pulled up here on the beach

    at Sitges /

    *The Antonia*


        ¡ANTONIA!


Whatever happened to you, Antonia?

You've become a stick of wood

twisted up here on the beach

along with coils of rope, cats,

    a stray dog, the sand, sound of sea

and yr hips have gotten larger,

Antonia .


    At the bar, I

    must speak too low or something,

    asked for *cacahuetas salteadas*, salted peanuts,

    so he took me to the men's room . I went .

                    [1968/1975]


## MY SAINTED


—God has taken your Grandmother,
        they told me
            when I was seven years old .

I wonder what the fuck he did with her?

And whatever it was, I
hope it was more satisfying
than anything ever happened in her life .

        How otherwise to explain it? Good
        things   and scenes
        happening ever since   . then .

backyard full of vegetables, sweet corn, the
fence full of sweet peas, all
gone now, thank Grandmother .

                    [1968/1968]

## THE GUGGENHEIM FELLOW, MANQUÉ

How . I . wish . I

were, the

man/in/the/moon


    or someone of equal importance

    Someone should play me

    "Strawberry Fields Forever," just

    for being myself .

                                [1968/1975]


## ACCEPTING THE GIFT

Wake at three
hear the rain
Rose
still fresh & red
in the vase of
empty aperitif bottle

           Water everywhere
           roof & terrace / in the air
           under where she sleeps
           in her ear . the engines
of the trip . What you doin' there, rose?
she's gone, we're alone . A-
peritif bottle full of

water .
a rose

(12 syllables)

Aperitif bottle full of
water      .      a rose

There are petals
and petals .
I cannot settle for the metal
of the kettle      .      O shit .

(12 syllables)

Rainy morning
see the mountain
—You still countin'?

To say she's gone
I put the red beret—
head out into the morning rain
on   .   Hey—

Cat's tail licks
my ankles   .   Last night
it was, honey, for us both
your tail .

5:20   & you can bet
it's A.M.      everybody
needs go work   .   2

cats cross the street
I need not
go work     .     I need
    —what are those 2 cats
        doin'?

The   TV   aerials rise
their own spidery
structures
against
the hills

                    The cat
                sits in my hat

Flocks swing
my cock hangs, half-hard-
rock on the radio, nobody sings
        except birds  .

You think you're renting
        time, comfort, etc.    I
            thot I was, etc.


All these things I sit so dully with
you touched.        No
        body  *owns*  anything .
        It's wet out .

(geranium)
Terrace wet with rain
and dawn

light of no kindness in
my eye   .   her tail is
moving along a deck some
hundred miles at sea
Two
birds fly
flutter   .   pause
over the rose
I froze   .   the cat, say, is
asleep in my old black hat

grey      .      brown      .      green      .

                                        pink .

                 ◻╱

Can I
make someone
some
pure pleasure
just by the sound ?
So, all the way on the ground, or by sea   .
some
one
& me?

                 ◻╱

(time)

I have been awake
3 hours and 40 minutes

I have done nothing
but write a few poems & read

                    The terrace is still wet

There are birds singing
& bells .

The rose

in the bottle stands
higher than the television aerials
three streets away . I'm
going back to bed
to hell with it all .


It has taken   5   minutes
to write this poem   . It
(take the hills & the herbs away)
felt like a second .

This body
lies flat out
in an un/complicated
bed .
The chimes
7   times .
No . body
no rosebud, no
buddy beside me
is
dawn.
Radio's off .
Red


(in series: the A.M.
of May 29, 1968)

[1975]

## STILL HUNGRY

After lunch and we strip

head for bed   .   Our stomachs

rumble against one another

    Other sounds .

                    [1968/1975]


## FLUVIAL

She took off her clothes so

naturally, so quickly, you

knew she didn't belong in them .

    The habit of unself

    consciousness is one

        must be acquired,

      however .

                    [1968/1975]


## ONE FOR SARA

Making a career of the carretera, to

sit looking at mountains, not that

distant, behind which

the sun has just gone .

I eat a piece of salami with some cheese,

everything goes down  .  wonder

at the cat's yammering at flies .

And your final silence,

that hammer .

[1968/1975]


## SOUTH OF BARCELONA

Early morning birdsong

grey sky & chickens & rain

across the plain

    tho chickens can hardly be said to sing

    their sound is comforting

    & homely .

The mountains inland disappear

The clouds come down .

[1968/1971]


## SIGHT

                (for Sandy)

After the oo's and aa's, after

the nose

is brought close,

a hand reaches out and

       touches the flowers

Later

  she eats the petals or

touches the skin around her mouth

with them .


  If they would only sing to her

    she'd listen .

[1968/1971]


## A SHORT, COLORFUL RIOT POEM FOR LEE MERRILL BYRD

Blue
bottles are blue, green
glass is green .
The West tastes like the North
The South tastes like blood and shit
and magnolia .
I think I can stand it

It is the strength in the arms
you feel
if you lift it

  Europe even worse than the States
  the price of kleenex, *boucliers*
  and tear gas
  paving stones and fire
  the same clubs

Cream no longer rises to the top, the
perfection of the centrifuge .
A brown unglazed jar.
The flowers are white
with centers green and yella
how you, fella . the stone
and broken fingernails, it
is the strength you feel
back and arms
when you lift it, *mes copains*

IF you lift it .
The blottolub,
     the cremaris .

[1968/1968]


16 . VI . 68

Soft, warm, sad, wet
day . Leaving again . Shall
it be the middle of the border?
Vich, Ripoll, and Puigcerda, or
from Ripoll cut off toward Col d'Aret?

     La Junquera's closed by striking agri-
     cultural workers . Nobody mentions Port Bou
     and Cerbère . Get in and drive, you clown .
     I wish I thought the French deserved a
     revolution, or that it were
     from the Pyrenees on down .

[1975]

JOURNAL . JUNE/AUGUST 1968 SAIGNON-PAR-APT (VAUCLUSE)

Oscar

Peterson
does Ellington
The "hill of poetry" sits and looks at the valley
                              hills of Haute-Provençe
                      Mont Ventoux
            still under snow
June's end .
Summer seen thru browned glasses
is a richness . I
                      watch her,
                      haircurlers & slacks
                              ironing my slacks, shirts


                                          My sister
also in curlers
makes deviled eggs   .   My friend
types in another room, his wife
makes *empanadas* for lunch  .
Everybody doin' his thing  .  her thing  .  the


Green & brown of valleys I see behind me now
            red roofs, thru
the tiny blinds & one corner of my
            glasses,
                      great shapes of shaded light
broken by the
earpieces,
thru which show

STONE

This whole afternoon
hangs itself on insects  .   In the truck
taking afternoon siesta, it was flies .
Outside later, translating under the trees, it was
flies, horse-flies, a bee, two
wasps  .  I work until 10 of 8, when
the first sound of mosquito cracks
thin in my left ear  .

All morning work, translating
　　　　　　　at the kitchen table .  Two
coffees, three slices bread/and/jam, a beer   .   Some
three-quarters thru, quick
voices outside the door of another room,
the *maestro* and the *patron* in the frontyard,
　　　　rattling French
　　　　　　　get to me in their rhythms :
one low and insistent, the other higher and hard,
some impatience there, break my own .

I stop
　　　rise
　　　　　　take a book of Gary's poems & go
　　　　　　　　out,
　　　　　　　　　　　up the steps & also
　　　　　　　　　　　sit in the sun, and
the wind blows the voices away　　　down in the frontyard .

Up here with the pail of garbage I've moved from the kitchen
slow stages to the dump, there's

                    wind

                    in the fruit trees, flies,
wasps buzz happy with the sun after yesterday's rain, last
night's wind, butterflies, can hear
        only buzz & birds
and wind : apricot, peach, figtrees, bees in the gladiolas, a
             hummingbird in the hollyhocks
                flies in the vine leaves,
the voices
blown away
down this valley, clouds
stretch, towns shine, a
lightbrown under sun
A book of poems for the hand, other
rhythms for the mind .
        buzzz .
        work   .

            not done

            ◁▭╱

            Because I have left the door open
            there is always a matter of insects
            The wind in these high valleys blows
                in   .   I
have to take a butterfly out in my hands before he
batters himself to death against the
glass pane
        between the livingroom & the kitchen  .

Then a wasp discovers the fruit bowl in the corner.

He checks out the oranges and the mayonnaise-jar

and settles on the bruised portion of a pear   .   O, yes!

> Lemons
>
> peaches
>
> a melon

> but returns to

> > the bruised pear, its
> >
> > speckled skin, he

hovers & sucks, he checks my outgoing mail,

my empty pastis glass, the story now translated,

even the lines of this notebook where he walks


> for a bit, but returns,


> > makes love to the pear   .

> > > [1969]



Morning in which

I can keep nothing

hid back

under the green rain

in the green grove

by the green lake in

this green morning under the mountains .


Austrian Alps full of

green stones, kitsch architecture, shit, grüss Gotts,

Germans, Dutch, Swedes, a funny

green morning summer lull, pull and

love  .  And


the flashlight works.


July 16/68
Austrian Tyrol

[1975]


## THE TOUCH


The w i n d o w s
are never wide enuf .


Calle del Vidrio, Barcelona, is
off Fernando, toward the Plaza Real;
short, tight, narrow, &
leads toward the palmtrees


The corner bar to the left is
three to five pesetas cheaper than
the one to the right
as you enter, plenty of
sky, trees, a fountain, the

arcades sit over each side we
sit with gambas, cervezas, dis-
cuss my sis-
ter's imminent
arrival, I face
the walls, cannot see
the palmtrees behind me

BEBA COCA COLA

BAR FARAON

MARISCAS
PERCEBES
ALMEJAS VIVAS
CENTOLLOS
Y
GAMBAS
ALAJILLO
SEPIA
PULPITO

it says

A quieter day
than yesterday
at the Glorieta, we
sat at the old man's tables in the
back, yesterday, asked
where he was, vacation?
     —No, the other waiter says, he's
dead, came into work on a Thursday
didn't come Friday or Saturday,
Saturday died.

An incredible sadness .
You do not have to know these people's
          names to love them, the way
                    the old man moved
                    among the tables, an
                    organized waddle that
cared for so many so quickly, the new
young man works the same station like

a beheaded chicken, no cool to lose, he
whips it out, everything very organized, but
    it doesn't make the same
        coherence.    Our friend
's tables are full in front so we
        speak only
when he has time  .  None of us
knows anybody else's name .


What was he called, the old man?
A gentleness and efficient waddling is
    dead now.  We do
    not need to know
    their names to recognize
a pleasure in feeding people well,
    that rare intimacy, how
miss someone whose name you've never known?
We do not need to know their names, they
minister to us for tips and love they
give is given back  .  The old man
worked the back—four tables only
in the front—sometimes five, it
depended on how heavy the clientele
was that day  .  Today, we
take the full *cubierta* the first time .


Again  .  The *viejo* lost to time  .
We never know one another's names, tho
we touched each time .
    I'd come back to Barcelona again
    he'd come and touch my shoulder, even
    if I were not at his tables . a greeting . We

do not need to know

anybody's name

to love them.

[1968/1969]


## THE FIERCE SUNRISE

I want night

out of the morning sky

    now       Beasts

out of the dark earth

               damp grass

The rooster stands up on his horny toes

    and send it down the valley

        to another

            one

                deep in the violet light


Hearing that distance

his whole

being glisten

listen, his

fierce eye on the

greying dark, taken  .

answer

shuddering .

Light

whitens .

[1968/1974]


**VAUCLUSE**

A   t r a c k ?   Well yes,

& better than that .

the dignity of a dirt road

leading uphill and

full of rocks .


Three turns

you can make in second

if you start fast enuf from the

pavée at the bottom . The fourth

you jus gotta shift down to first, one

smooth fast movement inside the bumps,

inandout / the clutch, very fast & smooth .


The machine claws its way   up the final slope.

Don't relax yr eye or yr foot's

pressure on the gas pedal

m a i n t a i n   s p e e d   as the signs used to say in the tunnels

      right up that slope where there's a break in the

      stonewall to your left . the eye & foot . now swing

      fast and left   into the small field

                made it?

      relax yr foot, shift back,   f you feel like it,

      to second   .   move into second, swing to park

      below most of the roofs of the town, the cliffs

      the church   .   It ain't where the buffalo roam, but

      back in neutral without a stall, you're

      at Cortázar's place, Saignon .

                        [1968/1975]


## THE SAIGNON SUITE


## THE   SLOPE


Looking up the hill
toward the town, thinking:
the mailman,
telephone call to be made, the
garbage .

BEFORE LUNCH

Cortázar in shorts, that length
stretched along the walk a fair piece,
in the sun   .   in an hour
*un apéritif!*

THE   DUMP

As you put it
in, over the high fence-boards
one lower edge of the village, the cats
leap out   !!   disappear
in several directions   .   wait   .
watch you .

SUPPER OUTSIDE

The buzz of wasps be now
over the plates on the table
under the fruit trees .

[1968/1970]

# A VERY GREAT TREASURE

[1968/never before published]

## TANKS

Houses three stories high

or block homes of apartments

    both with steep Norman roofs


The fish swims in the river

and shares it with other fish

        The cabbages have a garden

          to share with the lettuce and radishes,

                the tomatoes


The cow has a small pasture

and grazes it by herself


                An old man lies on a sack on

                a hillside in the sun

                after lunch .

                watches the train whip by


The dead lie in the cemetery near the tracks

share earth with the other dead

and do not look at anything

A barge on the river barges past, the wash flying

The fish swim in the river

    They share it with the barge,

        the fishermen .

late Aug / 1968

[1975]

**WET**

Goats trot and feed among the oil refineries

Cows lie down in the fields . short pieces of rope

tied to one horn to lead them in .

Small feeder canals, the flat landscape

broken by trees . an insistent green . den Haag to Rotterdam

    Two horses, one feeding, the

    other scratches his rump on the high

    power

    transmission tower . The shaggy goats .

[1968/1970]

## JAZZ 1968

If it's bullshit, put

the name on it,

call it bullshit .

    What's happening is

    the opening of it

    up, change up & go

take all the chances, if you

get good enuf at it, you

        can't make no mistakes

    It's a fiction & a diction

    : what you got is freedom .

Is it dull?           You did it .

                      [1975]

    Naked as a fish, she

    skinnies down next to me, we

    make

    it new .

labia majora and breasts, an old

black hat & worn army jacket

    lighting a cigarette, then

        removing the jacket, her

left hand as she lies back

touches the flowers from underneath .

It is a delicacy .

          [1968/1975]


## BACKSWEEP / BLACK

Sweep of the sea
moving water
    running water  .  rubble  .  rosemary  .
thyme  .  wild celery  .  (time) and again
I walked your valleys, sat upon your hills,
slept upon your body time
              (and again) all
gone now  .  rose
blown  .  rose bay  .
wind  .  rosewood  .  rose water  .  rose breast
rosary  .  roseate  .  rosebush  .  rosemary
Time
gone now
and again
recurs

          [1968/1969]

## A STRUCTURAL PROBLEM

A roll of soft tissue
    fat, for the toilet,
        wraps me tight
Pressure of   200   sheets at a time, a
memory wrapping around me

           (rapping around me

      Each small square
      detachable.
      White  .  blue  .  pink

           (why don't they make it black?

                    [1968/1969]

## THE LONG DAY

THE NIGHT is also my lover, I shall not want

anyone        I shall not want a second time .

She maketh me to lie down next the warm bodies

which leadeth me to screw beside the dripping water faucet,

on summer beaches, in parks, doorways, on tops of ferriswheels,

couches, & on the carpeted floors of darkened business offices,

in hotel rooms, Toulouse, Kansas City, Paris, Amsterdam & Memphis, in furnished rooms in Brooklyn, in the locker room of a swimming pool

1 A.M. in the Bronx, a doctor's waitingroom 2 in the afternoon, Central

Park, the backseats of cars, truckbeds, station wagons, warm

hallways in suburban homes, standup showers, picture windows,

dried-up stream beds in the Rocky Mountains, shacks (ibid.),

condominiums (ibid.), tents in Provençal backyards, 3rd class pensions,

mountainsides, on the main streets of Granada, Málaga, Paris, Barce-

lona in the back of a VW microbus, a square in Nice, Long

Island cottages, a few motels across the land, not

to mention fellatio or slippery handjobs in girls'

dormitories, hospital wards, waitingrooms in psychiatric clinics,

trains across Europe, buses in the States, back

up against refrigerators at parties, country lanes, open

railroad cars, love in trailer trucks

their sidedoors ajar, still

filled with unpacked crates—and they say

our friend and maestro, Henry Miller, exaggerates?

[1968/1971]

## FROM THE NOVEMBER JOURNAL : FIRE

The end of a distance come
so early in the morning
    where the eye stops,

                flames
running   O   their tongues up thru
    along the rooftree of
        down the coping of
            that church in Harlem .


D R I V I N G    R A I N
Wind driving a winter rain and fire, O
the twigs stripping outside the classroom window
we watch sexy

ANYthing
    vegetable, tall and branched
        yellow, the fire
        yellow, the leaves
        yellow, the girl's blouse
grey, the slacks
grey, the day outside
grey, smoke rising pierced by flames

    turning blue to red to yellow
      Which leads to a discussion of
the personal character of firemen and cops, not
altogether complimentary
    but granting courage    .    A Harlem precinct
    hd/bn firebombed earlier that morning .
Where the eye stops

smoke and flames thru the hill's trees, their
branches stripping  .   burning the whipping rain
                inscrutable cracks  ,   Whaddya hear?
          The blindman singing on the uptown train
coins in the enamelled metal cup clink


She sits back in the desk no longer thinking
          a dreamy look on her face :
               "It is so pretty," she sez .
Her yellow blouse sighs up and down
The rain strips the branches, drives the
                    fire across the church roof
                         where the eyes stop.

                    ╱:╱ ‾‾‾

Smoke floats
               in its layers upon
                    the room's air   .   has
                         nowhere to go .  floats
MALIK is king  .   King is dead of assassin's bullet
Malik is dead of assassin's bullet
Three Kennedys down and one to go .
Dallas is in Texas
California one might have suspected
and Memphis is on the river
and the Audubon Ballroom at 166th Street
belongs to the CIA under prior contract .


               Two cats move in the sunlight
               stream thru the window
               wash, kiss, wrestle, play
               under the smokehaze   .   they

are black cats  .    Yoruba, what
does Oshūn mean? Ouan Jin, or the
man of education?


Feet raised in sunlight
against the other's face
King dead
Malcolm dead
w h o   w i l l   b e   t h e   n e x t   t o   g o ?
Ted?
And then she married Onassis,
a prescient woman, to the
Eastern Mediterranean, this time .
You have to transport the stuff
He has the boats  .  He passes .
My friend, Economou, a medievalist
and poet, owns the most spec-
tacular Afro I've ever seen . The
people pass him in the street and speak to him,
"Hello, brother." He refuses to pass.
But Onassis?

and Jack the Cowgirl?
They pass everywhere, it
is a conspiracy between
East and West  .    what
did you think Bouvier meant?


The sunlight goes .
It is a clear light from the South
smogged in  .    The cats sit
and wash themselves
in the window,
look out .

What did you think Bouvier meant?


Gassir's lute
    The light
    shining on Oshūn's face
    is not easy to behold . to be held .
Do you think you can put your hat on your head
and walk away with him?    Down that hill?
        But Haarlem is a Dutch name
        and the Dutch have forgotten us .   Deutsch?
The destroyer?    What did you think Oshūn meant?
Ogun,
Yoruba is his tribe
"the six powers of light"
The sunlight across the window, Hooo
Dierra, Agada, Ganna, Silla, Hooo Fassa!
            Wagadu the legendary city of the Fasa .
The epic *Dausi* goes back to  500   perhaps, B.C., at
                which time Homer  .   The
remnant of that tribe, mostly Muslim, holds
two desert oases  .   Tichit and Walatu  .   The blood
of seven of his sons
        dripped
over his shoulder
onto his lute
to feed the song .
        or John?
    "I dig

    talking to a black man   who

    thinks of a white man

    as just another kind of black man."


OR vice versa,

OR thank you, Leo Frobenius


            —to feed the song .

Elaine calls me at 3 A.M. from Toronto. I come up out of a
deep dream, furious. No one else calls me at three in the
morning. I've been sick for two days now. I yell at her and

wish her a happy birthday. Nothing is such a pain in the ass as
being loved where one does not love : it is
an humiliation for both parties
Elaine is just such a pain in the ass. She says
we are married in her dream. I must say she has better dreams
than I do. I'm dreaming of an absolutely natural hair, a single,
intricately curled, long, brown hair in a tiny plastic container
you can see thru like a fuse, loose at both ends, beautifully
involuted and fine. This is an absolutely indispensable item in
a list of objects which must be collected, this wild hair in its
artificial little glass tomb, carefully random, carefully
natural. An absolute fake essential to the collection, essential
for a correct life.

The Ft. Moultrie flag on a recent 6¢ stamp
is the word   LIBERTY   toward the bottom
across a ground of dark blue, and in the upper lefthand corner,
the last quarter of a waning moon  .   PIE IN THE SKY .
Ft. Moultrie is in Charlestown, South Carolina .

The black cat comes over and stages a sit-in directly on the note-
book in which one is trying to write a poem .
It is not that she does not know, but will not
confront you eye to eye, sits and looks in another direction
—on your papers.   *And* purrs.

All right, Elaine, get off my back.


I pick the cat up and put her down on the floor
     & go on.
          And it doesn't stop.   None of it
stops, ever, it needs that wild hair in its
          plastic container, the essential image  .  So .


I stay up until dawn
          reading Philip Whalen's first book
    which after all these years still turns me on .

"YOU GOIN'TA TELL ME I
HAFTO GIVE UP
MAH  *P I E C E ?* "

THE TREES

Leaves on the branches
At the end of branches twigs
carrying everything
brushing against each other
reaching toward everything
touching everything  .  The air.

Nov. 1968

[1969]

**JOURNAL**                                    December 6, 1968

A spooky green wheel

    with spokes that move

        like a stagecoach in the movies

           and a star

              all of it green, face

the eye of my friend Kelly at his desk

  : a map of southwest Asia which cuts short

somewhere in the middle of Burma and

an element chart   the 103 blank space, a gift

    of THE ATOMIC DEVELOPMENT MUTUAL FUND, W.C., a

map of ancient Greece with a lot of the islands unmarked,

feathers and pens

two packs of Camels, postage stamps, a scarab—no,

a scorpion sunk in violet plastic, violently .

    2  bottles of Pelikan Tusche, a bottle

marked:  Spiritus vini Root Purissimus

    a plastic tube of fat pills from

       of Kingston, Inc.  31817 .  11/27/68

       for Robert Kelly, Bard College

       One every four hours for

        pain

and a lot of books—

          December thirteenth

  A saturday-seeming sunlight in the front room

     the quieter pace .  I do many pickup chores

       without pressure & quickly .  tho

         it is only friday .

The black cats sit on the dirty couch & observe me reading,

drinking my coffee, first of the day .  They are waiting for me

to feed them.

I came back from the telephone and got into bed in the cold room.
The covers were still warm. She was raised on her left elbow,
looking at me . It wasn't fear, nor acceptance, nor anticipation.
The cusp of necessity. I stroked her hair a few times and told her:

"Your father is dead." Her hair is long & black & fine, her head
rounded underneath it, under my stroking hand. It breaks, falls
against my chest, my shoulder suddenly wet with tears . Sobs come
openly from the throat, not choked back, neither opened to scream .
I hold her hard against me, continue stroking. I wish she cd/
scream . I wish I cd/  .
                    R O A R

The cats sit together on the bathmat near the door & observe me
sitting on the pot  .  First of the day  .  They
are waiting for me to feed them.  I clean their box.
In the front room, one sits in the single spot of sun on the floor, the
other climbs the wooden louver, swings up to the top as the blind
swings with her weight, rides it to the centersash . sits there  .

The shaft of light falls across my legs belly & lower chest, cock &
balls lie softly in the shadow of this notebook, shadow of the pen
follows the line across the page, mixed with the shadow of my hand
moving, the shadow of the cats on the arm of the sofa, ear-and-whis-
ker shadows

Shadows  .

    "My two grandfathers accompany me."

I hold her and she weeps for a long time. We are naked and
alone in the world, lie there as one, and one and two, I hold her
and we sleep . for an hour.

> "Stone already knows the form"

Warm & desolate under the blankets in a cold room

in another man's house   /   in Annandale, New York

        somewhere in time

                sleep.

Wake.
Telephone calls . when is the wake?  telephone calls, red eyes,
red nose, put on clothes.  coffee  (hostess descends)  eggs
in a savory omelet . juice . more coffee . books . host
is raised and lowered
            EAT OF MY FLESH, DRINK OF MY BLOOD

The host descends   .   The chalice of coffee is a milkcan half full
       : a large man   .   Joan and I
       have finished the Fundador   (drink of my blood)

[Thou shalt live forever . . .

> Gone
>
> *under* .
>
> or
>
> *above?*

The mind travels among the stars   .   we in this prison earth

   await our time

     "It is necessary for the conservation of the universe
for each thing to desire & demand the perpetuation of its kind."

         Joan has ours in the oven cooking   (heaven?)

            awaits her time   .

[Osiris lies in the sunlight on a copy of   *IO,*   the
Alchemical Issue, open to Kelly's journal   .   Ablutions.]

              Coffee   .   3rd cup   .   The Sky .

The chemicals of
an industrial society
mitigate the sky over East Seventh Street, Manhattan . Colors

     "If you have dissipated & lost the greenness
                 of the Mercury
& the redness of the Sulphur, you have lost
             the soul of the stone."
                   fade .

Isis leaves the third shelf down of the large bookcase
and tries the louvers again . her weight
swings them back in this time,
makes the ascent impossible impossible,
however she
studies the problem, then sits on top
of the sewing machine & cries.

(I hold her against me & we both sleep)

"Every chemical agent requires a prepared material;     it is
for that reason that a man absolutely cannot breed
with a dead woman."

The plants are dying.
I do not give them water.

| METALS |
| --- |
| LIVE |

I let them die.
I have to go out and buy

new plants, a new
planting .

Stone already knows the form
of the statue within it.

| S T O N E |
| --- |

People arrive for talk.

There is talk.   Joan

talks again on the telephone.   Red eyes,

red nose in a chalk face.   We

hold one another in the bathroom upstairs

in the hall by the stairwell.   Excuse ourselves,

go out to walk in the cold December day.

Drive first to Blythewood   .   park   .       walk about

the Zabriskie estate, down thru the formal garden

| OUT  THE  DOOR |
|---|

into the field, slopes

down, toward the Hudson, around the cold, walled

garden, back

| IN  ANOTHER  DOOR |
|---|

                        the opposite side, walk

arm-in-arm up the steps like any funeral or

marriage, drive two minutes another road   .   park.

  walk down past the swimming pool, along the small

rushing river, two falls, a couple coming toward us whom

we greet, a boy & girl, who climb back the way we have come

| IT  IS  MIRRORS |
|---|
| ☿ |

We walk down

    —⊖—

they have come

to the river

            (we have

against the cold sun

under the trees  .   hands held   .   looking out upon the flatness.
A skinny island runs thru the middle .   railroad tracks .

    We cannot see the other side

             of the river   .   this low altitude   .   Water & sun.

Shells of water chestnut underfoot

    four-horned & light  .   seeds inside .

Two in the drawer of my telephone stand now

in the front room . bullheads . Osiris sleeps in my lap.

Seeds inside . His head turns against the notebook.

    The plants die . their screams

        fill the room . Reflected sun

against the church walls across the street  .    Two

watertowers, the bulb-shaped steeple of orthodoxy, the

   triple-cross of Russia

| | |
|---|---|
| SEEDPODS |  |

    "Have the greatest care, lest the blackness appear twice;
once the little crows have flown away from their nest, they
can never come back again."

The mind travels among the stars  .  we

in this prison earth          await our time

| |
|---|
| AWAIT   HER   TIME |

The King, naked but for his crown,
sits reclining in a large basket, an oil
lamp burning on the basket wall to his right, the basket
open on top and on the king's left side, a kind
of showcase orgone box  .   On the stone floor beneath it
a fire is laid  .   smoke rises .
He is burning his ass off in an orgone accumulator
      It is a cremation?   Creation?

She ran down the slope in Central Park that summer night,
I right behind her, caught her round and threw her down
It is a hillside, the earth under us .

We walk back up thru the light rain
   to her parents' apartment to
    dry one another off  .   to fuck.
     She will never tell me her real name.

       "Colored lights, it is colored lights,
       most of it going to purple & violet,"
      is all she will say   .   We
do not ask each other for love
  we just take it   .   and thrash
about in the bed of her father and mother  .    far away
  the sound of rain, tires on wet streets, who is it
   having the vacation?   She
    will not tell me her real name,
     turns into a tree  .

I will not speak of the driving

in silence, silences of speed  .    the parkways of the mind

swift barren trees  .   She is filled

  grief & life   .    I had to

roll her over me to the outside of the bed that morning,

to get her up, found it was myself

had gotten up   .    fucked her   .    right there .

A morning after that, after the first night of wake,

she had bought the ring entire, said, at twenty to eight,

 "You have to get up and move the car."

I existed again, I

was married to my wife!

   who was mourning her dad,
   awaiting her time   .    life
    in her belly   .    the way

we must be, a posture of a single
oneness, the beast in the bed.
O my baby!

The sun is yellow & pale, not red, these last mornings, I

drive very fast.

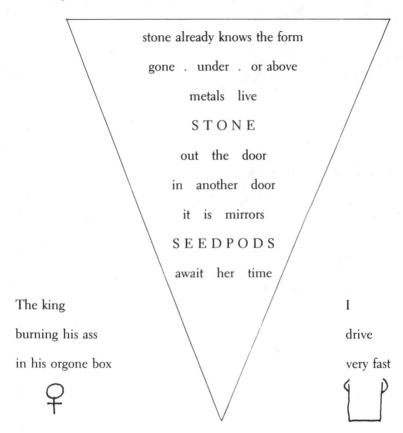

stone already knows the form

gone . under . or above

metals   live

S T O N E

out   the   door

in   another   door

it   is   mirrors

S E E D P O D S

await   her   time

The king

burning his ass

in his orgone box

I

drive

very fast

[1969]

## LOVER'S GREETING

S h e   c a m e   i n   out of the
driving snow and cold air
with other people
laughing and talking
with them, her
face red with cold
happy with the warmth of her friends.
Stars of snowflakes in her hair
glistening drops of snowwater
            on eyebrows, eyelids.
Sound of
laughing and talking, sound
of wind driving snow outside
the cedar door
into the spruces either
side of the door, the
        hemlock in the yard .

The trip must have been long
lights in the cars of the train too bright
reading dull magazines to pass
that bought and packaged time
        miles between cities
            the night air
                outside, filled
                    with snow .
I take it hard   .   How
greet her,
        laughing with her friends
        beautiful, snow in her hair,
            red face, her teeth
                showing so?
It was me
she came to see,
        to be with, no?

I think of her tail
rounding white and warm
        under the bulky coat
                under the clothes,
boy, later for that .

Her friends laugh too much
        She laughs .
They talk too much, she talks.

There is too much snow out
side the door   .   I
don't know how to welcome them all
nor her   .   Was it me? She
      glitters and faces me .
I stand warm, half-owned,
embarrassed, and more
      than somewhat
            sulky .
Small huddled birds in the hemlock
in the yard   .   I take it hard.

[1968/1970]


FEBRUARY JOURNAL, 1969     BOQUERÓN, P. R.     HEAT


            Sitting on the ashtray, "Yes,
            I've been here be-fore"

reading about caterpillars, bees, wasps, *(les guepes)*

that were my friends, Saignon-par-Apt in the Vaucluse, last summer;

old Fabre at his *harmas* at Sérignan,

            setting down the days:

            "The common wasp and the Polistes
            are my dinner-guests: they
            visit my table to see if the grapes served
            are as ripe as they look."

      And a half year has gone,

Joan swells patiently and smiles, not from wasp-stings .

And I sing in this hotel room in Boquerón

which has no proper ashtray, so must

      use the john, I sit hereon, reading,

            smoking .   Hot ash or the butts themselves,

                  hiss as they are dumped. Sitting on

the ashtray—do I have to pee or dump?

I do. Never move except to wipe,

or flush .


Sunburnt

from this Caribbean island's heat, it is

last summer's sun is in the mind :

    *pastis* at 11, Julio's sunbathing done .

    recreation, translation, shop in Apt .

                *Les guepes*

still stir in my head . I have seen them here

in Boquerón, in the grasses,

lazing about in the poinsetta bush with the butterflies .

    *Un autre saison, un autre monde,* another year .

    still I sit . *Quand même,*

    Julio caught one in his armpit, last summer,

    between the shortsleeved shirt and the long hairs,

to the panic and discomfort of them both . O

the Hymenoptera, what we shd/ fear!


The gnat-whine of a twin-motor overhead :

circles widen from where the small fish

surface for an instant

The beercan floats peacefully

    "out in the tranquil bay"

catches the flash of sunlight,    drifts

        with the tide-turn    toward

the white & orange of the dock's Gulf sign  .

                  ◿

                                  [1975]


## PUERTO RICO

Seaplane going over, going

    somewhere  .   over

        head, the blue re-

           ally re-

                flected in this sea .

See

the dust of the street, see

the beach   .   A bitch to listen

to  .

Lie there and listen to waves, gulls, other

more spectacular but soundless birds   .

Boquerón   .   The sun

is harsh and ethereal   .   One man

stands on a balcony watching

another man   .   among

the TV aerials   .

The birds dive

to live .

                                  [1969/1975]

McCLURE POEM

# L A M B

mary         had a         little
cunt        whose fleece      was

C     ED SANDERS    C
O                                   O
M                                   M
B   TULI    KUPFER BERG   B
E   and fourteen rim-happy groupies in San Francisco  E
D    and Everytime that mary Came  the    D
)by(                                   )by(
(surely) the L A M B (o|God)
WAS sure
To Get some also

oR

BLACK LAMB/WHITE LAMB

— by Jerome Rothenberg &

there are some barbarous countries (Australia, Montana,
Belgium) where WOOL is the
source of                                 (source of
wealth                                   wealth)

[1969/1969]

There is an irregular movement of the light and

                                   all things are changed
                                   new and old
                                   past & not yet born
                                   enter it
                                   as one

Cannot keep my heart
as bright
as this spring is

                         Lady Godiva on a chopped hog
                         makes it new

Muscles bend it
to the face to
face   .   no turning now, the very way of knowing,
                                        renewing

"I want her hands on my back

                       tho that not be possible"

has been a blue flowering plant of mine,

the most of a year now.

                     *Limonium commune californicum*

woody root (that's mine!)   leaves obovate-
to oblong-spatulate, obtuse,
or sometimes retuse, tapering
below into a rather long petiole, 4-9 inches long;
calyx lobes membranous at tip, I'm hip,

                    corolla violet-purple

a deeper shade of
blue, the closer
I git   to   limonium commune californication

∠+╱

Eastern window, so
sun on my eye brings
me upright in bed, 7 AM
or so   .   I go

to the phone when it rings
petals of fire =
ize the positions .

> "Salt marshes and sea beaches
> along the coast, Los
> Angeles County to Humboldt County,
> July to December"
>
> Jepson sez.

Tho April only
by noon, let us see, what we
can bring to
blossom here this city by the Bay, or
once more, Saxifrage, flowers perfect,
perigynous, usually white, often red,

> never blue .

> "Seed with endosperm"

> Jepson sez.

Olé!
        an irregular movement of the light

                and all things

                move beneath it and

                are changed .

[1969/1975]

**APR/69**

Muddiness

    of the Columbia River in spring :
on takeoff . a springoff south .

        One wonders when it began

        what it looks like there in time

        We know our sources.

        I know what I have drawn from you this time

Can see the mountains below
still under snow
The Pacific to my far right
    fades into fogs   .

Have seen you as woman longer than
you, yourself have, wonder now at the tenderness
as we walk about the grass at yr/ wedding reception, smoking
grass upon the grass, yr/ hips moving gently, that
        between them all men prize
        blind their eyes—

Keep the Sierras out the window to my left, the
Pacific to my right, the plane comes down, San

Francisco . How

keep any of it down, it all keeps rising .


Matt Helm is a dirty old man who can't get it up

—white flesh—

he needs all that whisper around him

Speak to Dino about it, he knows.


Eldridge is Soul   .   Eldridge study

karate, man, the true prez

photographed on the cover of his

book on love,

Soul On Ice,

sing that twice,

holding cala lilies

for the tomb, man, of all that

Whiteness .


I read his book on the transcontinental Pan Am mutherfucking

plane, man, &

weep at the beauty of it

soul, right there, the tears go down

for all the hopeless love I've spent in my life

I'm a baby   .   I write pomes   .   I say

"Look at me, see what I can do?"

    I feed me on it  .  And weep

        the beauty of all our loves

          across mid America

            looking down, man,

all those clouds,

those white clouds  .  all that white

shit down there .

What you don't see

unless you see

through .

        (Over New Jersey,

      you can see the real estate from the air)

Cape May:

The American coastline cuts away to the left .

The left wing of the plane dips

      the turn  .  North, now .

                [1975]


## PLANS AND CHIPS

The three
trees on the corner square


      stand up
      & call to you

The two
lights on the doorway across the street

                  5 A.M.
                  shine in & are
                  my eyes

Birds outside
cheer up, how
can I say—sing?

        See? Carlos T.
        chirrups in his crib, quiet
                after long screaming

I'm going to
die, I'm afraid   .  O-
kay, I'm afraid, I
shall hold you in Front Royal, Ashville,
Nashville, Memphis, Springfield, Alamosa,
        Aspen even, Rawlings, Boise, Portland,
                other towns to the South .

Our asses, our mouths.

                            [1969/1975]

## A DIFFERENT POEM

Stay with me
sway with me
going up that road
looking back

        the green on either side
        trees, the green between
        the sounds

mad houses
mad streets
mad loves
mad mice or roaches
madmen

      spurting love
      streaming songs
      petting kittens
      stroking seashells

Sunshine, I
long for any moment of peace, a cat
quiet paws below the trajectory
          of seagulls crying
            garbage dumps
            for breakfast

some dry cereal
some coffee, hell, what is it
      any of us need — touch?
      that's not much
Love is no groove, love and simply catch
a path of talk
a patch of green either side, walk
      down it, swaying   (sway with me)
      in the drunken dawn, I
        feed you, I
        need you,
    how can I tell why

stay near you ever out of great fullness

        solitude,
        both our minds?

      Flesh come home, I
      seed you, it
flies like a gull
soars like a sound
runs like a dog or horse, runs
away, swift stalking like a cat
under cars, between buildings, down
    slope among the grasses   .

Did the animal die?
Is it lost & hungry somewhere?
Did it run away?   What
            did it find  .   I mean
            it's both our asses, I
            can ask, can't I?

[1969/1975]


**JOURNAL : JUNE, 1969**


Tangle of sheets in the backroom;

tableau with no sheet in the front :


    G. & E. heavy in the backroom
                        snarl of whites


    Joan in the front, a 5-week-old Carlos
    hangs from her front by suction  .   all sleep  .
                        I hang
out the window 5:30 A.M., 7th Street dawn.


                The sealpoint Siamese kitten got
itself locked out in the hall last night, wanted
        into the closet, probably  .   By
this morning everyone in the house
        must have heard him screaming .


The stairway in the ruins wanders up to a

windswept third floor, the stone steps

    worn to a  ⌣⌣  in the middle .

An aluminum handrail ruins the take & makes

the perspective, 700-odd-years later where

                once was a wall  .   Peire Vidal

    had fallen heavily against it, his way back

from that lovely bitch in the kitchen to his honored room

above, carrying his britches, to sleep alone in his shirt

sodden with wine to dream of that noble bitch in Marseille,

Barrals' wife, his own true love, the kiss he'd snatched

that morning, her lord out riding, not giving a damn except

for Vidal's weird conversation & the master singer's voice

& that the port run well, it did, but his priggish wife

took care of that, raising such a stink that he had to

(sternly) suggest to Vidal a prolonged absence, so

where did the fool go?

>to her brothers in the hills back of

>>Marseille, Guillem and Uc Les Baux  .  The lady'd been

born in that castle, Alazais de Rocamartina, against the rock

wall, the light falls against

>>Vidal falls heavily against it, damn the wine, light

>>but catches up to you, stands a moment, what was it

>>Uc had said? en Richart . . . another crusade . . . that's

>>the ticket, Coeur de Lion would keep his throat damp

>>with the light Rhône wines, by damn, over the sea it

>>would be, overseas, forget the stolen kiss, forget . . .

>>>another few steps, falls again


The stone stays

>the shadow moves

The songs stay, too, mostly unread, unsung, tho the language persists

in the village of Les Baux, those hills

stay, the stairway

                    where the feet have worn it .


Family   .   2 black cats & token whitey

        gather in the window,

                    look at the street .
The Gaucelm Faidit Uzerchemobile at the curb, the
family upstairs, double-park their Dodge, put the
trunk together for the Jersey beaches, pic-nic, getting
                    an early start
                    6 A.M.
        The father fat & bald and somewhat
        nervous, (beats his wife when necessary,
        smokes too much); the boy, the youngest,
also much too fat at   12   a golden
crown of curls, alert, piggish eyes
sees the family of cats first, watching them, speaks:
            "Hey, look!" The daughter
                    where the waters run
                a 16-yr-old, shapely mass
of eyeglasses, tooth-braces, & shyness (her
best years were between 12 and 14), that
second bloom yet to come, asks up:
        "Did you find the cat in the hall?"


            I nod, smile, hold
            up the kitten who yells.
Her mother I've had fantasies about for years,
one of the best figures of any married woman in the block
a body that takes the beatings, grows the kids up, is
too busy packing last-minute things to
even notice, does not look
            up. I nod to the father, mark the obvious:
                "You're getting an early start."
        He smiles and answers, then remembers
I do not speak Ukranian, puts it in English.

"It is be a good long day."

The cats check the *gorriones* out, sparrows
of the ledge above, the gutters below   .
                                    CHIP   .
                    repeatedly .

Joan stretches her hand & presses
against the wall
her feet search the bunched blanket, bottom of the bed,
        like small animals
        turns on her side, good legs curled .
                Carlos   CHIPS   & dozes again

The long greeen Dodge eases out of the street, I note
that one of the priests
from the orthodox church
across the street
        has been using a stretch of sidewalk in front of the church,
                turning always, it's a tether, two ends, friends,
                        the door of the nunnery one side,

the fire hydrant at the other, this side
of the identical-size & color house, serves as a rectory,

                        uses it

                as tho it were

        a graveled meditation walk

                to read his breviary, glances up

as a young nun comes down the church

steps, having set the altar for morning mass

        She

        does the steps more quickly, looks away down

        the street toward Second Avenue   .

A young matron with a broad ass and tight skirt,

                short skirt & green, goes up

                the steps from the street, 6:15

                confession?

I wonder, as the priest folds up his book, hikes
his cassock up with one hand, also
climbs the steps,
              goes in by a side door. She
                        is the organist, maybe?
                        Ends that scene  .


In slacks, Sara Penn crosses the street .
The cupulo rises green and exotic
        above the bell tower .
        the hour, 7:15


               ∠ .* ╱ 28 . VI . 69


None of the radio stations   /   in southern Pennsylvania
play programs of marches this Independence Day morning .
                        I miss my Sousa.

        My 'Fairest of the Fair'   however
        regales our Carlos, breast, bottle & dish.

                A full morning .

I wonder if all the Men's in the picnic areas
along 81 South paint the inside walls
        of their shithouses black. It's very depressing
just to start with   .   the roughcut slabs of pine
creosoted & browned on the outside, on the insides
are black, the sloppy brushstrokes showing
against the grain   .


        So you sit on the luxurious chemical toilets surrounded
                by blackness—not so cheerful .


I think I'll request the Pennsylvania Park Service
to paint the inside of their restrooms bright
        yellow, so you can see the friendly flies &
                spiders, that disappear against
                        creosote black   .   A

relief to look up to the inside of the
unpainted roof & see a wasp beginning
her nest,   some spider webs  .

      Sí, señor, HOW TO SEE IS
         MY PLEASURE, the

      black flies buzz my ass, my
      head, I cannot see them  .

        / ctb /

[1975]


## AUGUST 1969 : SOFTNESS

Scrambled in the dark dug of dawn

is warm against the cheek, is

a wet, salty sweetness to the

multiplication table of

mouth .

    Eiaeia-eh
    Eiaeia-eh
    Eia-eia-ng

Find the soft spot where the silence is   /is

    a rocking indeed .

    / /

"Wal, thet's a funny lookin jug

has a hole in it

shaped like a diamond on a playin card .

Think you cn drink outn that?"

Just north of the bar at Arroyo Hondo, N. M., make a right on a dirt road.
As you continue, the road curves gently to the right, pass the store and the
church, a fence begins on one side, the road continues . you do not . Make
a left thru that fence, but then take all the choices to your right . up till you
arrive at the top of the mesa . The map is a brown paper bag drawn back at
the bar. There are two six-packs of beer in it . Hardly
a fountain
but anyway
a blessing
on a hot day .

Three tepees, a trailer that fits on the bed of a pickup truck without the truck,
a small commonhouse : field to the left full of vegetables, field to the right
an adobe garden, corn growing therein : the main house is going up at the far
edge of the field to the right . the clay, under your feet, man, is what makes
the adobe . Six people, stripped or partly stripped, are stripping logs,
Douglas fir, already cut to size. Max with his mouth half-full of teeth, smiles
broadly when he sees the beer and me (one pack I'd dropped off at the small
house before we'd started across the mesa to where the people and Max were
working), hard body mahogany, lined face, a soft smile . The beer is
divided up among the work crew . Two girls bum me for cigarette, a
pleasure to light them up in the strong wind, bending toward my cupped
hands, the firm hang of tits brown in the wind bringing rain. One chub, a
loose miniskirt only, bent over the logs (the legs) with a sharp hatchet, brown
nates trimmed with a beautiful and enormous bush. She works. Max says
he's not writing these days, who needs to, just look at those mountains, I do
as we lift the beers, she straightens up and wipes sweat . the storm coming in
fast over the near peaks, great, hanging streamers of cloud, the rain itself .

Max talking of these girls moving the adobe chunks, loading a truck, how
many hours? We are all back stripping bark now. Twenty-four or -five people
live there for the summer . The Reality Construction Company, Box 701,
Arroyo Hondo, it is Max's second commune —New Buffalo was the first—
40-odd people over there including his girlfriend, now with someone else,
Max has their kid with him.

This mesa group ought to wear, the usual attrition, down to 9-10 people who might winter it out, the rest disappearing back to college or the cities in the fall .

The commune people, the chicanos, and the Indians against the Anglos? Cd shape up to that, especially with all the Texan crewcuts buying up land, New Mexico, even southern Colorado. Max and those few on the mesa, the winter a real isolation from supplies —that high, October thru March— the interior strength they'll all need to survive that mesa winter? . given the house gets done. It will, you'll see. A soft man too. That flatness with

the wind

laying drifts up against the wall, that

      mountain in his eye .

# THEY ARE NOT THE SAME

The panes

of six of the 13 windows in this wheelhouse

are fogged

      just breath & body heat

      this cool morning

            as the berth lies facing north

            sun rises to the starboard side

The gentle motion side to side

keeps just your shoulders & ass moving

gently, cheek to cheek, just to remind you

            water under you .  The same

      roll

triggers Dennis Kelly

to lust for

roar of the twin motors

yachtsman's cap to top his shaggy head, his belly

next the wooden wheel

a handgrasp to wooden pins

connects the shaft .  a power transmission

a good sea-stride from the gentle motion of the cheeks

above the harbor swell .   it is not the same


The gull stands on the piling hits my eye between

the locker shacks on the pier painted a dull identical

tan, consecutively numbered, they are not the same, not

by content or location of door, nor by width of board, nor

how the corner joints are laid & nailed or finished .


Another gull stood on that same pile yesterday, preening,

turning his head about to survey the prospects

water reflects

sun, wavering seaweeds of light against the underpinning timbers

of the pier another sameness always changing,   never quite

identical .  the same timelessness .  it is not the same

gull

"Can you tell one gull from another? They all look the

gull to me." They are not the same . They / all

are beautiful, they are not the same, there

              is difference even in their voices, one

trajectory of dive, level off or swooping patterns cut thru

flight in air, are no two the same gull, feet tucked up .


We sleep while we are waking

o, the easy swell

rocks us,

cheek-to-cheek, on timbers of the dock, on the hull of

the boat two berths away, on

ceiling of this cabin where we move

           softly, love, the flicker

      of the net of light and water

     where we live

changes . ripple glint in the tide turn .

it is not the same .

                    Berkeley Marina  .  Aug. 21


          Cold day  & bright sun

wind holding the flags straight out

               flap/flap

sound of lines & rigging clicking
against the masts all round us, cwy-
et insistence to ear as reinforcement
to eye   .   bell buoy beyond
in the bay
bounds &
bongs

Joan 'does' her exercises on the center deck
in bathing suit   in sun, the
handsome legs rising   .   moving an arc   .   falling
alternately
cool/warm
body
bikini for figleaf
goosepimples
smile.


Thus the   3   graces & the   4   dignities

thus the rules of Ch'an are

maintained

between us


| GRACE OF WORD | standing |
| | |
| OF DEED, | sitting |
| | |
| GRACE OF THOUGHT | walking |
| | & lying down |


This boat that has no name but a numbered berth rolls

gently   .   we

look upon one another

& our eyes are at peace .

[July-Aug. 1969/1971]

JOURNAL : JULY 21/22. 1969


Those boys comin' back fr/the moon
  Armstrong, Aldrin & company, & I
    make my own countdown : score
be
tween
dusk & midnite, I
missed one rabbit & got one, I think,
     rear wheels, one small bird, &
also about dusk
   (the small ones do a dance in front of the
       windshield in pairs)
  a young hawk crossed
  right to left &
  cut back


   hit the upper right side
   the VW truck's window
     W H A P
      & bounced off.
I bet he got a sore belly.
I never before met me a silly hawk
& that was surely just showoff stuff, that
cutting back.
   No point in counting the bugs.


  The small bird I prayed to, he
  protected me later that night.
  I couldn't pray to the rabbit, only
   apologize.

Springfield (Mo.) to near to Boise City (Keyes)

OKLA

HOMA


500 miles in a day

then Raton, Cimarron, Eagle Nest

Joan drove those mountains    , Raton to

Taos on 65 .  111 north to Tres Piedras &

285 straight up

into those hills (2 rainstorms, in the

distance lightning) & at La Jara, 14

miles south of our mark, our Car-

los starts

HOWLING   . we . stop . feed,

walk him around a bit

the driveway where are tanks and sheds, a fertilizer co-op, the

final quiet, then

6 miles in toward the San Juan range on Colorado 370, Bobby's

letter sd/ that's 15 kilometers, right?, then another mile

& a "dirty, yellow/brown house"

got that, there's

no   one   there.


Check the window

(I peer thru, see books, it's

the house alright) door's open

inside a cat with a half-moustache

talks back   .   what then?

2   empty bottles of Beam, the water's hot

what?

we're home

they're not

Another cat arrives later   .

We   3

fall asleep.

The cats probably also

                Those other boys too

                comin' in,

                back from the moon.

[1970]

## JOURNAL : AUG '69 : LAKE TAHOE

Douglas pines

about the lake

        I have passed many summers without you .

the wind thru them  . enormous

comes on the earth beneath them

cones, the stumpy phallus, the fat mind

We are barely in California

        6   miles in, I know, the

        tow truck told me so .

We wait

for days.

             I see

your steamy tits rising in the summer night, the

laugh and crag of yr/ face fuzzy

          against the mountain moon-

                    light .

Hip-hip        hip-hip

          & Cali-for-ni-yay

                    Cones fall .        a dog barks

                                        yip-yip .

                                        [July 1969/1975]


## BIRD POEM? WORD POEM

Under the leaves of the plane tree

under the leaves of the marronier,

a sparrow is born in Paris, he

will die in Paris .

                    Why not?


Chestnut shells crowd the walks in fall

He does not, he flutters down to check

what?

                    He will die in Paris . Go .

                    Gorrión   .   Moineau .

                                        [1969/1971]

# THE GHOST OF EN RAIMBAUT VISITS LES BAUX

> Raimbaut de Vaqueiras, son of a poor knight
> of Provençe, was reported to be the lover of
> madompna Biatrix, daughter of the marquis
> Boniface of Montferrat. He was joglar, trobador,
> & warrior, and flourished in the courts of
> Provençe and Italy around the middle and late
> parts of the 12th C. Guillem des Baux, prince
> of Orange, was one of his first patrons.

My lady Biatrix, Bel Cavalier,

you walked these high stone walls

with this poor sonofa

      mad knight


hand in hand

and laughed .

"That stairway there," you pointed, "brown-eyes."


      The top of all beauty

      and a sword of price .


We bested one another in that joust,

you giving more than you could have promised .

And the stories went out and around .


Roses grew by the walls

      thorns there, too :

the marquis your father's visit too short for us .

The walls now are full of rooks

the ruins of this high place

where hawks nested .

                    We have walked the valleys al-so.

                    Montferrat later, but

                    first Les Baux .

                                    [1969/1971]

## SEPTEMBER JOURNAL

My friend, Byrd, looks
at a moon just past first
quarter, late July, says:
    "Hey!
You bin stepped on!"    half
    quoting a poem of his .

        In September,
        I bring him back great

chunks of wood from
Idaho  .   bandsaw-split
Douglas pine  .  He
& Lee are not here, are
somehow in Tennessee  .  I
can't see why, but anyway

          like the flocks of birds resting
          on trees fringing this yard, their
          way south, our way east, we
stay a few days   .  Wind is
cold afternoons, there
          is hard rain  .

Between where Interstate 70 ends
          temporarily, all the
          traffic is back to East 40, (2 lanes, be
careful passing)
Teotopolis and Altamont, those towns, Shum-
way, Montrose, Effingham, to Terre Haute

Rest area just off 70, the johns
are in the gas station at a corner across the highway
likewise a farmyard full of pigs  .   but don't
mention animals : a Penn Central engine roars past hauling
the whole 27 cars of the Barnum & Bailey Circus, plus
          one green caboose .

          Hang loose, Ed. It's been a good year
          Our sons, Carlos & Kid born
     3 months apart .
Barnum & Bailey goes thru

The tender little end-of-summer grasses
move green & ragged in a southern
Illinois wind, will be
under snow soon .

The flies are sluggish on the
fallen leaves .
Warm weather's gone .

[1969/1975]

JOURNAL : DECEMBER 11, 1969

Rain        rain, the

        whole damn day,

Hatteras to Montauk

Cape Ann to Pasco Bay.


        At Kennebunk now

it still comes down

the thurgling sound in the drains

an extension of the coast to the outer edges of

no beach, that snow leak down

offn trees    .    upper

reaches of the Connecticut River

some other

4 A.M., different winter

different year .

[1975]

## MAYAKOVSKY

His father was a forest ranger
in the forests, in the mountains,
 the Transcaucasus
   (hello Snyder! hello Kerouac!)

Came to Moscow, age 13,
tall / had a lot of hair
   (hello Allen! hello Charles!) used

the word 'I' a lot in his poems
   (*In Full Voice*, top of whose lungs?)

At 37, time was approaching.
April 14, 1930  10:15 A.M.
Snow still on the ground
in Lubiansky Way
   (hello Stalin! hello Hemingway!)

"Across sierras of time"
  and
"Never get caught showing
good sense"
   ("The incident, as they say,
   is closed.")

        [1969/1971]

**TEN YEARS**

e i g h t   o f   ' e m   t o g e t h e r,   I

s t i l l   d o n ' t   u n d e r s t a n d .


I never made you, you

made me constantly, always, all ways .


               I learned to differentiate .  We

fucked, screwed, made love, made hate

your puritanical sense of order, my compulsive mess, compulsive-

ness, we made the days of the week

an instant hell   .   Such a

| Suchday | | Musty | (loons |
|---|---|---|---|
| Tunesday | | Chooseday | marty's |
| Wrensday | | Westerly | miracles |
| Fursday | into: | Gurusday | judy's |
| Frosty | | Frugday | some titty |
| Saddlebag & | | Grabado an' | sam |
| Domingo | | deFranch . | und der Mensch) |

                             awright,
                            start numbers
                   fun ein zum danzig :
bun, dewey, tree, floor, fife, sick, shaven, ate, snarl & ben   .   OR

anal, douche, free, fear, sink, sex, sever, ache, enuf, tease,
ounce, dice, freezing, forcing, fencing, disease, dessert (or summonsing),
deceit (or aching), Nanking (or this nerve). . . bent .

        (Variant: banked, swan-sick, granite, Vermont, or dainty)

        Gloria walks down the rock-strewn path, bag in hand, jacket

under the other, why shouldn't I? Three trees in the picture. Tree breeze.

No pitcher, a fo-to-

griff-in

    which she walks, talks, laughs, it's  .

        the same summer . 1967  .

                      [1970/1971]


## JOURNAL : MARCH/70


Syracuse a stopoff
en route to Buffalo, Saint
           Patrick's Day  .   Winter
           still on the land . We
           land        .  smoothly.

Roads wind black against snowfields
      Lakes still frozen  .   large
freeforms of white below  .   March
17th . ice still holding .

400   cops on the Buffalo campus . two
were fired on yesterday, 2:30 in the morning,
.22 caliber thought sufficient, or
            what we had?  .   I
take it I am part of the fourth week of chaos
& intermittent violence. Still holding .

           The ice is .
        You can't go to Cuba yet
          but illegally, but
you *can* get to China if the chinks will give you a visa .

And Agnew, after addressing a private luncheon, yet, of
the Association of Radio and Television News Anal-
ysts, remarked:
"I'm talked out."
I'll believe it when I read the seismographic reports.

How do you say "¡Venceremos!" in Chinese?

I travel also
to Buffalo .

[1970]

## AGAINST THE SILENCE OF STAIRCASES

Scrap .

whatwe bindoin' all week . Blow

all of it up . out .

down? what
do those steps mean, worn as they are by
centuries of walking up and down
them, literal *u*'s in the center of them . I
ask you, what does my 2nd wife's ass, (fo / to)
pinned to the wall of my workroom, great
generous curves either cheek, rosebush
of hair centering the photograph, the white shirt,
arm fallen over in speechless relaxation,

mean to you? Means to me

sleep  .  curling against it  .  seen

       much too often  .  Now

the  S U N  shines outside, first today, the rain and

grey gone from the streets  .

       Man rides a bicycle

up Hall Place, a drunk crosses on 6th St. totters east, the

S T O P  sign lays its white lettering up against

permanent red  .  We

can never go away  .

       Don't never

       go away  .  Not

       even in yr/ head .

                         [1970/1975]

## JOURNAL: MAY 1970

       These equations work out

       no work today . I don't believe it .

    Octavio Paz leans back against the fire escape across

    the street and waves  .  I don't believe it .

    Hollo is as Hollo does  .  I don't believe it .

I'm in one helluva doubtful mood this morning .

Peevish, pernicious . A spoonful is

as much as a spoon holds . June holds .  Moonholes

where cd we find the tropics if not west of here?

somewhere  .  let's get hot soon as we cross the border .


Have you seen something comparable?

My friend, I have not .

Ellen, Joan, Eunice, Rosemary, Frances, Barbara, and a

young actress who shit in a bag hung from her waist, which

encompasses that year  .  There's the kid to show for it, sits

middle of the floor, a milkcarton pendant from his right hand .

The 4th of May. His first

birthday this month . now the empty egg carton's on the floor .

What next? Bottle of vodka knocked over  .  He dances south, he

crawls east  .  he

bedaubs himself  .  Tell me some more .


Okay.

crawl                    yawl
sprawl                   mewl
brawl                    owl
drawl                    bowl
caterwaul                                        anything else?
prowl                    bowl
growl
bowel(?)                                 bowels or Bolles

lives two doors away .

We never could find Memphis . Out

Atlanta!  out Nephritite!  Athens

Ohio  .  Montgomery used to be a friend of mine. Aetna .

Gretna, Virginia  .  Gloria

still coming down that mountain trail, 11,000 ft. or so,

in shorts .

[1975]


## POEM FOR THE MANUFACTURERS

—Think I'll buy me a rifle.
           —You gonna hunt hawks?


—Nah, they're gone . I
think I'll hunt the manufacturers of pesticides.
Handsome game, they'd make
great awful stuffed heads to mount
on the walls of my new den .

[1970/1971]


## FROM HALL PLACE TO THE TANGIER MEDINA

The drunken boat
the drunken boat
bobbles & turns over
           amid the cunt of the waters
                dumps .


One bloated drunken man
helps another drunken man
           to his feet

on this street
It won't work . the one
walks backward and leans against the fender of Jerry's car.
The other lies back gently, his head against the building
that houses the Pollution Control Center and goes to sleep .
O, tender is the afternoon
on the Bowery, the
odor of verbena, the
smell of sandalwood,
whiff of musk far off  .  a different
city and a different sky
where the wretched are as wretched and it still won't work .

[1970/1970]


## THE DISCONTINUITIES


Why is it the Roman law sez:
Kümmel, you
are guilty!
"England became
Catholic, y'know, after—after the—"
YOU ARE GUILTY!


How keep the summer going?
and the pipe?
and Snowmass?


Take the road to the left. . .
another left to the monastery .
Little as you can live .
fife & guitar.

     —What was that?

"One of my ancestors commanded

the British Navy."

      O, I believe—Thomson, O'Brian, Kenney, the

ships of the Armada used to smash on the Irish shore, they

paid 5 shillings a head .

skull counts .

                [1970/1971]


**PHOTOSYNTHESIS I.**


Surrender the grass! Let

all those things grow we have

   so cut back

   all these years .

The crackling of ice in the glass as it

   melts   .   Our kilts but

   cover our asses   .   Tears

   upon the words

ask only other roundness to

encompass with our belly buttons in

a likely juxtaposition .


       Let the old hat roll . Charles

       holds a pipe between his big

easy fists, scarf hangs unevenly in the sun, ankles

crossed, knees wide   .   The glass of pastis

Julio holds to his mouth reflects light

vertically up his nose, the back of his head

      faces southwest  .  We are apt to

       look upon the stairway as tho the steps were

known . 700 years agone ,  Allen's glasses gleam . Gary

holds a hollow knuckle ball between the fingers of his left

hand   .  Ez's eye fixes the machine from under his neat

Alpine hat, the clean raincoat  .  fierce & friendly to

the moustache bristle, beard-jut, but the eye questions

the other end of this gondola, where do the steps lead?

The oarsman ferries him across to

ward a death with windows, romanesque windows flank the

oarsman's ass with balconies  .  The oarsman's headless .

Seated beside her man in the *traghetto*, Olga,

gloved and umbrellaed, speaks sensibly

       of the appointment  .  It is

the Grand Canale after all, and not the Styx .

I take pix

     that auger in, or down upon, or up

     the steps  .  That cold spring

       was plenty hot enuf,

an old anger evaporated . Her hand cups, touches the

flowers from underneath .

The unexpected kindness of the waters, all

of it fated, the

beauty of the old . of the young .

All of it sung .

VII. 70

[1971]

**WINDSOUND**

Stand of beech & elm, pin/oak, cherry,

hickory, ash,

screens my eye from sky

moves the pattern, wind

does  .  grey

sky, green grass   .   The wetlands

stretch below the bank   .   I let the

screen move

the focus flatten

against the grey  .   At

the top of my middle vision, a

bird flies over  .   Birds' sound

sharp in the flatness.

Windsound .

[1970/1971]

## MINE SUMP

The shrieking call of foolish owls pretending

to be wise  .  Our ears

pretend the wind  . pre-

fix the balls we hope to save  .  We howl

& hear our

own tears  .  fall down

& end the lies  .  smoke cigarettes & talk, hide

our fear from others . The

anecdote  not given as replacement,

not forgiven .  A polite

ness  .

Be rude rather, speak

truth outright  .  & all the while

rap rapidly  .  Overheard, his hand

over her generous breasts, cunt-form in sand .

Scratchy  .  guess

the rest, the birds

their mannered cries above the surfsound

wind that moves dune grasses .


I started this poem with owlsound .

Every word

moves it further away .

[1970/1971]

## AGAPE

I had already gotten back in my pants,
            coffeed, juiced, & caught
the Lex Local one stop to Bleecker,
transferred at Broadway-Lafayette
            to the D Brooklyn-bound,
past Grand St. and out across Manhattan Bridge, the river
            flashing yellow & silver under
early morning sun, great spreading wakes of barges up-
            river from Wall (St.) Eye and down
to where, off Newark, that green
bitch stands waving at you

            I discovered, checking my fly,
            I had not yet zipped up   .

Everyone smiles. That kind of morning   .   I thank
god my undershorts are bright yellow   .
            Here comes DeKalb!

                                    [1970/1971]


## OCTOBER JOURNAL : 1970

                        6 A.M.
                        and it's still dark
                        on a fall morning

                            in October,
                                you goober, you
                        keep coming back like the Kelly
                        in November, I sed you

                            NO-VEMB-ER

                        Sunrise is 7:18

The seven moons I can see from this window are

streetlights on campus

The black road is white

              under their light  .  Drops of

              yesterday's rain on the fallen leaves

shine like there are spiders under those leaves, wasps and bees

                       as well . hide there .

                       They hibernate?

                       O bears!


On warm days, bees, wasps, hover over clots of leaves seeking entrance,

or move among the needles

        on branches high in the spruce outside the

            upstairs bedroom window

find, however impossibly, some way in

between the window and screen,

           clenched on the sill  .  die there .


Winter move (ing)   in

My hand creaks

I put the milk back in the icebox

They die there clenched on the sill .


Joan and the boy still sleep away upstairs

Hemlock out the window moves in the light wind

Smoke a cigarette in the dawn-dark  .

    talk to myself .

        unheard . unseen .

    I look out the window at seven moons

                    (till night is gone

                    till dawn come )

        \* \* \* \* \* \* \* \* \*

1/5 gal. Virgin Island rum, Old Boston
1 qt. straight bourbon whiskey, Mattlingly & Moore (Lawrenceburg, Indiana)
1/5 gal. tequila, product of Mexico, the Matador Distilling Co, Hartford, Conn.
             and Menlo Park, California
½ qt. left of John Begg Blue Cap scotch, fr/ the Royal Lochnager Distillery,
             Balmoral (they ship it from Glasgow, Scotland, U.K.)
enuf Terry Brandy (Fernando A. de Terry, est. 1883) fr/ Puerto de
             Santa Maria (coñac de Xerez)
and 2 fingers left of Pernod

           The contents of my liquor cabinet   10   days before
        you arrive. Vodka's in the refrigerator along with
        sangria and sweet vermouth de Torino. The California
        wines are down and cooling. Be welcome.

        \* \* \* \* \* \* \* \* \*

Throw this one on your coordinates:

    28 west out of Kingston across
    the Catskill Forest Preserve to             Margaretville

    30 skinnying SW along (and across) the Pepacton Reservoir, a
    dammed sector of the Delaware River (eastern branch)
    down past Shinhopple and Harvard, connecting with Rte. 17
             at Eastbranch

    17 west, just before Binghamton catch Interstate 81 north.

The first exit that will jolt you says McGRAW-CORTLAND.

Don't let it tempt you; take the 2nd one, it say

just  CORTLAND .  end of the ramp  STOP sign:

turn left, under the highway to the first light  (2-3

gas stations & a Holiday Inn)  :  turn right

down Clinton into town.

Two more lights will stop you at Main St. (where Clinton ends his upriver

run—but sail on, captain, my brother) right on: the street

changes name to Groton Avenue. Second light on Groton, hard

by a hamburger stand called Hardee's, steep left up the hill

on Graham two long blocks

(the college will lie on yr/ right
dorms to your left)
to

Prospect & a STOP sign.

Pause carefully, edge, noting especially

the hill coming up fr/ yr/ left

(no STOP sign there), then:

a slate-grey shingled corner house, facing Calvert (extension of Graham)
Cape-Cod roof;
then an awkward, more modern contrivance, aqua & white with a carport,
very slow:
the white-porched #60 is where we is, the driveways a foot apart. With
luck you'll see the VW wain therein, dark green, shaming the maples.

The leaves will be on the ground, brother, and the branches bare, but

the welcome warm.

\* \* \* \* \* \* \* \* \* \* \* \* \* \* \* \* \* \* \*

Alternate route: Kingston, thruway to Catskill; 23 west skimming north end of the forest preserve, to Oneonta: left couple miles on 7, right, back onto 23 to 26 at North Pitcher; 26 to below Cincinnatus, 41 toward McGraw and Polkville. At Polkville take 11 into Cortland. At Main St. half-right into Tompkins, one block, I think to Prospect, right on Prospect, around up the hill; the second intersection is the one where you have the right of way (or that you have to look out for if following Plan One). A churchly building on the left downhill side, then count the three houses. Or, first white one. Where there's a will there're two ways at least. Usually. Maybe. You take train, huh?

[1975]

THE NEW YORK QUARTERLY / TRANSLATION

1. In your view, what is a translator?

A man who brings it *all* back home.
In short, a madman.

2. What special qualifications must a translator have?

He must be willing (& able) to let another man's life enter his own deeply enough to become some permanent part of his original author. He should be patient, persistent, slightly schizoid, a hard critic, a brilliant editor, and have an independent income. . . .

3. Is there any rule regarding the choice of subject matter for a translator? Should the translator stay away from any given original? Is it important that the translator be temperamentally close to the original, or the author of the original?

Stay away from third-rate work and outright shit. There's nothing to be gained but money and not much of that. If you don't love what you read in the original, or admire some major part of it, forget it. We are all hundreds, maybe thousands of people, potentially or in fact. Affinities help. Theoretically possible for a man who hates himself, say, to make a fine translation of someone whose work he *hates*. Do not think I have ever seen such a translation. Incompetence or beaky egotism are something else.

4.  Should a translator ever "improve" on the original? If so, under what circumstances?

First of all, it's hardly ever possible. One is lucky to be able to make an equivalent value. Most "improvements" prove to be distortions of one variety or another. If the distortion permits a more perfect Englished version consistent with the diction and style of the translation, then perhaps, yes. Here we get into matters of taste. Geniuses ought not to translate, unless they be truly mad.

5.  To what extent may a translator introduce variations which his own language permits, but the original language does not?

To a reasonable extent, if the distortion of meaning be not too great. Equivalencies are different in different tongues and different generations. Who's expected to read the final job?

6.  How far should a translator attempt to "modernize" an antiquarian piece?

Try first to find a diction, a modern diction which will translate as many values as possible of the original. I've seen Latin poetry translated into hip language that works very well for given pieces. Carried too far, of course, over a whole body of work, it'd be a stunt. Some stunts, however, are brilliantly executed. It evens out.

7.  What is the best way for a translator to approach the problem of multiple associations of word choice? Multiple meanings? (polysemia)

If the double-meaning or an equivalent is impossible in English, he chooses whichever single meaning seems most genial to his English text, or strongest to his understanding. Overtones are constantly being lost. Let him approach polysemia crosseyed, coin in hand.

8.  Must unit and line length be preserved under all circumstances?

No. You're talking about poetry here. If the original is interesting for its meaning, translate the meaning. If the meaning is irrelevant by comparison with the musical values of the piece, translate, as best possible, what Pound calls "the *cantabile* values." But choose, so you know WHAT it is you're doing.

9. What is the difference between free and strict, literal translation? between free translation and outright adaptation?

Very often readability. Strict translation usually makes for stiff English, or forced and un-english rhythms. Outright adaptation is perfectly valid if it makes a good, modern poem. Occasionally, an adaptation will translate the spirit of the original to better use than any other method: at other times, it will falsify the original beyond measure. Much depends upon the translator (also upon the reader).

10. What frauds have been foisted on the public recently? (And not so recently?)

Yo no sé.

11. Do you experience psychological impediments in translation? (Blocks, slips, unconscious mistakes?)

Starting a project is always difficult; it means rearranging one's whole time to make some continuity (of time and thought) fit. Done slowly enuf, moving into the author's head should present no problems, if one is ready for it. The process might make a few problems in one's life, however. That's part of the dues.

12. Why do you translate at all? How does it relate to your work? What long and short range effects does it have? What defects?

Complicated. I'm interested in the original for whatever reason. I'm interested in the language and the processes of language. Pace and time. Take that earlier answer: *yo no sé.* It's different in pace and overtone from *no sé* or I dunno, or *weis nicht,* or *sais rien,* or *non so.* Next question: usually my work will relate to it. It fills time when my own head is not working at poems regularly. There's an interaction. The long range effect is some kind of enrichment of human understanding. Short range? Everything from giggles to rage to a sense of words whose weight and meaning have changed, are changing. The sea of language. Defects? Sometimes I can no longer think English. Not sure that's a defect, tho it must be remedied before the job is delivered. Alternately: it gives me something else to do, so I don't have to write poems. But that's true also of my 17-month-old son who has a half-translatable language of his own, but IS no language, nor work of artlessness.... Suppose I liked horses better, or fencing, or were entomophogous?

13. At the end of his interview in NYQ issue #2, Paul
Blackburn commented:

> I do enjoy translating, getting into other
> people's heads.

Thass right . . .

> This is one motivation for translation. Are there
> others?

There must be . . .

Thank you for your time.

Quite all right. Thank you.

*Marina Roscher*

Marina Roscher
for NYQ

[1970/1975]

## JOURNALS : NOV/DEC . 1970 : HIBERNATION

> "He stuffed bear in a cave all winter.
> Now we know."

The darkness wins
here . We miss those early birds, the worms
are silent as always under the slow turf . the
spruce and hemlock move their branches against the window .

Our sense of strangeness
        displacement
               uneasiness       is soothed
(by the way) by the way
our bodies curl into each other  .  the early light
wenches thru, that freshness, then

                the busy sound of the pot flushing, the
                child waking up, cheerful for a change .
                the branches moan a bit in the cold wind.
                Day's begun.

              The darkness wins
here  .  a car on the street outside
soon disappears, the sound of birds
              loud at dusk, subsides . We live
in this near-winter dark, live near each
other in the darkness, the boy's pre-sleep
whimper-and-moan from the next room grows also
into silence as he goes
down into sleep  .  We
warm one another finally  .  The next sound you hear
will be the radiator .

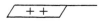

What the hours are,

lines on top of the mountain in November, a

word I 'ad never noticed but in sembral terms, I

    quote an ancient allibone, an

    alley of bones now turned into

                     a

semblance  .  My friend Bolles stays tight with young clits, and

              thinks he'll commit suicide by

hanging a show of his drawings on the reinforced steel

plates of a freighter headed for England,

        see what survives a 14-day trip  .  An

other friend has an earache which her friend will soften by

being close enuf to be by  .  But the

        question, what is the question? It is

        another wipeshed now  .  The child sleeps,


Young wife, my love, climbs sleepily to the floor and sits in my lap, I ex-

plore hell, only the certainties may wed death, let all that go, I want to

K N O W when I'll be there again, when

you will .

        zelda, granite moth, mary jane  .  the other

        chances were 50%  .  chances

are  .

        The anchor swings like a camel-quirt these days,

        the best stays, ma belle, not

        mirabelle, nor kitsch, no kirsch,

what we eliminate,

not picayunes or gauloises, but

where the N sits at the  $n$  of nite, not

out of sight  .  profane  .  prefound  .  commit, climb

into it altogether, o candle, o end of,


framboise, the eau de vie of  ..  How that mountaintop

looks like the plane of    .    the spotted trees, the lake we all saw from

some angle the

pilots differed, no matter, we

kept the difference    /    even

we did not know the difference

kept the anger & the love

equal    .    there's a sequel?    no, there

is no sequel    .    Read the trib tomorrow morning, there's

no sequel    .    wimmins lib

has take she all, Mr. Hall .

Donald,

keep your prick up    .    it won't last .

(Witches passed)

The magic stays    .    the boat leaves    .    arrives S'thhampton .

Cramped in the lifeboat, still she twitch her ass, an

equal

movement, left to right    .    Whatsit

doing?

that hand around my right tit?

The hand is steady    .    Are you ready?    Present

passports, please.

/11/25/

"Take it easy, but take it."

Sittin by the farmhouse,
                    waitin for my friend to come

dog
barks in the distance
boats on the bay as well, it's
a long time, David,
we ain't had no right to some
other girl, some other time of our own, hell,
I don't know what you think of when I think of struggle, but
bit off more than he could   .   it was apple-blossom time in old
hat and walkin down to the farmhouse by the bay, he stood
                    for a time, listenin to dogs bark


I think of mountainsides, slickery mud between the rocks
and tree-holds under light rain, my ass full of mud in full camera,
                    mist across the eyelashes .
I think of driving   72   hours to find
they've already left   .   Fieldful of snow, 7 feet deep
you gotta walk thru .


                    What'll we do before lunch?

Brush the sweat off our arms, eyebrows, forehead, nose itches .

How we do not walk or climb or wait, but stand   :   scan   "take it

easy, but take it"

any way you can .
                    (for Tobe & David : 28.XI.70)

/ +++ /


5.XII.70 :   morning conversation


I sit in the kitchen
        from the first light
            on, look at the light snow
drifted to the edge of garage roof, snuggled
            into the leaf drift

Carlos eats

the coffee heats

sky lightens to yellow

pale sunlight on

the white walls of white houses


He talks

wanting a refill on the applejuice


Red

coffeegrinder sits

full of

new-ground coffee


The coffeepot coming to boil

talks to me .


Mint grows higher .
cigarette smokes itself in the ashtray .
Carlos lifts the cereal bowl to finish the milk

He talks to me    .    His own words .


(the news at 5° below: for Ron & Michelle)


Wind out of the West at
10 mph, and snow

drifts down across this hill
slowly and fine   .   Branches
with a ragged leaf or two   move
lightly in the wind outside the window
wisps of white blow from drifted and plowed
piles   .   Blue
is a color I remember
yesterday from further south   .   The sun
is California Dreamin'   .   This is the news .


Mouth pressed to another mouth
the sprit of semen, a massive unload-
ing of selves and seed .   Food
for our tongues, o very nice indeed .


Fish lie quiet beneath the frozen streams
Ragged leaves move in the wind while
we smile at one another in the dark .
move near sleep .

(after hearing sonia sanchez down at corey)

All that sweet, warm

blackness going down

what do be more dream

than real, sometime, it

bein this grey boy talkin, after

all that hard, sweet

blackness solfening up his heart, seems I

trudge uphill thru the snowfall

thru the trees and lights and havto

spend the next two hours shovelin

sidewalk and driveway clear

of all this white shit .

                              " . . . temperature's rising

                                 it isn't surprising,

                               she certainly can . . . "

The roofs are high

and the gutters deep .

           The sound of

water falling

               feeds

               our sleep . we are bound

to wrap the sky around us, while

we try to become that tree

                    our bodies

              wave around

while the rain falls and the gutters run full and

the seed leaps .

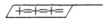

                    18.XII.70  :  wings

Rain water this thaw, snow

water  .  water drops

on the needles of spruce  .  the wind

blows in from west southwest  .  Water

drips from icicles along the gutters, gutters

loosing a piss-stream of water that the wind

controls, wavers the stream.　　The birds dream
　　　　　　　　　　　　　　too soon of seeds.

　　　　　The top of the hemlock

cracked under the snowload last storm,

tender branches flutter and scratch the west window.

A pattern of sounds and wind　.

　　　　　　　　What's the matter?

Driveway's clear　.　why worry, friend?

Words come or do not come　.　The thaw persists

in all our minds　.　A single crow far off

talks to himself .

　　　　　CAW . CAW /

　　　　　be well, crow .

　　　　　Find yr brothers

　　　　　someplace south of here .

　　　　　　　　　　　　　　[1971]


## THE BARRICADES TOMORROW : THE GUNS TODAY

　　　O god, it 'as all grey fistfuls
　　　of hair in't　.　Look you about
　　　yarely lads, advance upon 'em

carrying red   S T O P   signs to protect yr vitals


That might just psych 'em out, grey flannel-headed
CIA & FBI, the green uniform of the green National
Guardsmen, safe in their nests, State Police grey or
blue of any big town's Finest .
Marksmen, when they have a black or puerto rican
back to shoot at .
                      So true-blue also
                  to collect their due from pushers,
      bars, et al., we fall
ten down aslant .

                                                    [1970/1971]




We cannot agree

ever, quite, about

              the cats .

I cannot keep them by me, that close

sense, as I keep you and Carlos T., the anger

demand, needs, flow from you all, the love is

there, unequal always, never indifferent. Tangle

all this household in your mind, the kinds

of loving care we all give one another, all

              are necessary .

And our two figures are

        set forth from Paris south,

are set forth from Les Baux west and

still return   .   Past that

there are no more resurrections

      planned .


A week from now I put the garbage out again.

A week from now I give finals to my freshmen.

A week from now the kittens will be gone.

A week from now is payday — Joan,

you keep me sane   .   please


          6 . I . 71

             [1975]


## THESE FOOLISH THINGS

Shadow net

a net of

treebranch

shadows cover the

roof of my garage

Sunshine, Superman, after

a morning of heavy snow . We

go out into the day, it's

crisp, say, at

10° above .


Love, no paseo yet, no

promenade in old San Juan, even

the muddy or dusty streets of Boquerón escape us this year .

"Up in the air, it's a bird, it's a plane . . ."


Sunshine on the garage roof and the net

work, treebranch net

a firkin of butter to cover what's left

of the economy .

Better to think of the bills to be paid

or of getting laid three times a day . hair, clothes, life

in disarray .

Remind me.

[1971/1975]

# E.P. IN VENICE : REMEMBERING APRIL 1968, AND I SMILE

*Eagle is old man* .

We sit for a bit & smoke, look

out at the snow .


Old eagle never scream anymore, he

                keep his silence . Say

two words now and then   .   Go

to the restaurant next door

or the café three blocks away

                on the *canale* . sit

look out over the lagoon .   Old


eagle never smoke . never talk, never

drink but maybe a half-glass of wine with meals .

Hardly touched his soup.   Remembering this,

we sit for a bit & smoke, looking out, steal

glances at bare tree shapes, shadows .


Look out at the snow.

It's near noon .

It's January   .

[1971/1975]

**FEBRUARY JOURNAL : 1971**

Sun reaches in thru the window

strikes the kitchen wall

takes a key—click .

Clouds open and the sun hits the icebox.


       fick-fick, fick-fick,

       fick-fick, fock-fick,

       fick-fock, fick-fick, fock—

the sound of boots on snow)

              new inches overnight

              trackless white  .   under the black

              net of branches  .   yellow sun

casts a pale branchnet across the path fick-fick, fock, fick . . .


A five-minute walk in this

              barely-moving air,

my left hand inside the mitten  .   cold

and my left ear .

              Light gusts from the south.

           * * * * * * * *


the  "smoothrunning cold tides"  of rain keep coming all day .

By late afternoon the temperature drops two degrees an hour

until

driveway cleared of slush as best can, I wonder, will I be

able to back the car out tomorrow afternoon?

how turn?

how turn her from

        an idea?

Don't mind keeping the house neat

otherwise .

Do the dishes, feed the cat, sleep

in one bed, always

sleep in one bed . otherwise the walls, other-

wise the man can separate the compost out, the

biodegradable from the dreck that

must be put out wednesdays for

the city to collect .

Build the house.

Keep it warm .

\* \* \* \* \* \* \* \* \* \* \*

[1975]

Snow falls and drifts

lightly beyond the window

wanders

in the light wind

(she

    said I wrote "out-of-the-window" poems:

    it is true .)


Tape recorder and tape-deck that

fuck when so programmed, sit

erect facing me, push their

nipples out at me, try

to get me to caress their metal tits, to

flip their little switches

on   .   And the snow wanders out of the window .  I


see there are stones on the desk, blank

tapes, cartridges, head and guide lubricant

for the double-head, the triple-head, kleenex

to wipe the whole mess up . my shirt is frayed


I have a date in Adelaide, Melbourne, Pago-Pago

14 hours from now, change

planes in San Francisco or the city of Los Angeles

for Honolulu this side of .

I cross

the International Date Line solely

    to keep the date .

                    Feb. 1971

                         [1975]

The wind blowth

snow fallth

branches whip in the wind

    down, rise, forth and back,

        drifts groweth summat


It's going to take us two days at least to

shovel out of this one, off to Buf-fa-lo, o

March, after all, Spring

cometh .

                    4. III. 71


    students walking backwards

down the hill west

against the wind  .  two cars

headed the other way, east across Prospect, also

crawling in reverse.

                    [1975]


**17.IV.71**


My shoes .

I have just taken them off,

            my shoes.

Stare out the darkened window, damn, 've

forgotten the cigarettes in the car, empty

pack in my hand, crumple it, drop it in . 2 points

Have to put my shoes back on   .   they

look at me reproachfully from the floor


       laces loose . their

       tongues slack.

so scruffed already they are .

& had just relaxed

-----------------------------------------------------------


Cities & towns I have to give up this year

on account of my cancer:   Amster-

dam, Paris, Apt, Saignon and Aix,

(Toulouse I'll never loose), Perpignan and Dax,

Barcelona and south

           (or the other way,

              Catania . I warn ya)

The hell, I read a review of a reading in January.

They loved me in Shippensburg, Pennsylvania.

-----------------------------------------------------------


Top of the 8th, after

four fouled off Gentry, still

2 and 2, a plastic bag

blows over home plate, Dave

Cash of the Pirates steps

out of the box, steps

    back in, after speeding the plastic

        on its way

        with his bat, fouls

        two more off, then 3 & 2, then

infield bounce to the shortstop, out at first.

----------------------------------------------------------------


"Anything you want?"

    she asks, heading out the door, leading

    downstairs, get the bicycle out of the cellar .

—No, nothing, thanks. The slacks are brown, she is

carrying anything I want downstairs to take it for

a ride on the bicycle .

----------------------------------------------------------------

[1975]


## JOURNAL: APRIL 19 : THE SOUTHERN TIER


I

look out the window in upstate New York, see

the Mediterranean stretching out below me

down the rocky hillside at Faro, three

years, two months, fourteen days earlier .

8:25 A.M.

Rosemary gone back to sleep, pink & white . I

stand at the livingroom window drinking coffee, open

the doors to the balcony . Warmth beginning, tho

I wrap my hands about the cup, count

fishing boats in the sunglare, moving shoreward now

slowly, or

sitting there motionless on the flat sea .

a fat blue arm stretches out from the coast, ripples

where wind and currents show

muscle below the blue skin of sea

stretched out below me  .

                The coffee's

cold toward the end of the cup . I go

back to the kitchen for more hot . put

orange in bathrobe pocket, reach for knife, return

to the balcony with the fresh cup where the flat blue sea

fills my eye in the sunglare . stretches out below me.


The Southern Tier:   the maple outside the window

warms in the early sun  .  red buds at the ends of branches

commence their slow bursting  .  Green soon

                Joan moves

       her legs against mine in the hall, goes down to

start my egg  .  Carlos thumps the lower stairs  .  We move.

All our farewells al-

ready prepared inside us  .  aaaall our

deaths we carry inside us, double-yolked, the

fragile toughness of the shell  .  it makes

sustenance possible, makes love    possible

as the red buds break against the sunlight

possible green, as legs move against legs

possible softnesses  .    The soft-boiled

egg is ready now .

Now we eat.

19 . IV . 71

[1975]

## ALONG THE SAN ANDREAS FAULT

for Mark McCloskey

Low, mostly naked hills

dying scrub and rock

Juncture of Golden State and San Diego freeways

end of that american dream   .   Ghosts of

old insurance salesmen walk the ramps  .  Dairy

Queen and

taco stands in

valley flatlands

intersecting freeways insanely

landscaped by chickens in

constantly revolving baskets

The neon donuts blink  .  Other

side of the mountains / yr in the desert  .  Here

you really know it  .  Barry

Goldwater, Jr. is Congressman

These are his people .

[1971/1975]


**JOURNAL : 20 . V . 71**


When I had

finished the book

I could not remember your name, had

to turn, re

turn to the first page

to find who had written these poems .


Fire on the mountain, light

crossing a bridge between

the twin peaks of death and

the blind eye

of God, your father  .  Burt,

never

the boat on the sea, never

the horse in the mountain .

    Blood in the dirt, Burt, Federico

    is dead,

& no one knew who he was .

        *el barco sobre el mar*

        *y el caballo en la montaña* .

y una aguja de luz en el centro

de tu cabeza, hombre   .

              [1975]

**THE JOURNALS: MAY, 1971**     **The Blue Mounds Entries**

M A R Y  L A I R D

is not afeard

Walter Hamady

keeps her happy

morning, afternoon, and

"Always merry and bright" is

not a girlscout motto, Mary,

    right?

    Rain  again-

    st the

    windows

drums

down

on the roof,

hard in Walter's

garden

    the syndrome is

    /was/  talk

Were met

watering can in one hand  (we had

interrupted that work upon the garden

at 6 P.M.—what proved

unnecessary finally)    so .


The talk was helpful, tho,

as was the eating & drinking

    Ed brought the roast & rice

    and talked

    tenderly to my wife about carpets

    one eye warming to the task

    of making two new eyes see

    the colors, the pattern, the wear

that hung that rug on the kitchen wall :

the care of the owners to place it there

(light from the kitchen windows

colors move .


But now past midnite :          rain on the roof

thunder in the air               lightning in the sky

the cat throwing up in the kitchen .

Everyone else asleep but me &

the barfing cat

Lightning scatters the trees

they run

about the sides of this valley between flashes

the cat comes to my left foot, stands, paws on my knees & purrs

crosseyed & clean  .  I mean

rain on the roof, they call it

patter?   Lightning leaps across

We wonder at the thunder, the

cat and I  .  Cows

on the hillside, huddle under the storm  .  Caught out

they / we

are all asleep & warm .

The talk helped  .  the rain

comes  .  the trees dance.

ALL  US  FLOWERS
(living for the moment)


L I ̲K E   I T   L O T S  .


I drank some wine tonite .


"Schools closed when they drove the cattle
past—a thousand heads lowing and bellowing...
Cattle after cattle went by until at last a wagon
with an old bearded man, sober-faced and
silent. He is too rich and full of thought to
have a good time like the others."

—Lehtinen's *History of Jaffrey, New Hampshire*

Goodby old cattle baron, goodby

old baron and drovers . We

shall not look upon your like again, goodby

old sweethearts and pals  .  I want you two

to have these two

pieces of stone . Keep

them as yr/own

to remember this moment.


Try it on, try it on  .  We have a future in carpets .

---

PD county trunk

La maize pousse
et les choufleurs

The farmer, he

kneel behind his cultivator

joust the motor .                    Irregular patches

looking like islands

of old snow, dot

the upper meadows

lie along the ridges to the west . oho, the glacier

driving thereover .

---

Carl is not coming to the reading . he has papers to correct

Marcia is not coming to the reading . she has a new baby

Joan is not coming to the reading . Carlos T. wants to

play with the new baby & won't sleep

Walter is not coming to the reading because he thinks Carl will be there

besides, Diane arrived today for a visit, and she

was at the reading in Milwaukee yesterday

Gerth is not coming to the reading because he's behind time as usual

and thinks that 9 o'clock is too late .

It's my reading . I take Marcia's mother to the reading .

A pleasant surprise, Mary and Ed are at the reading .

I forgot to get batteries for my cassette recorder today

no one else records it .

I read until 10:30   .   It's a good reading.

---

# THE FARM

Goats in the oats

stoats are in the shoats


the karma's in the barn


the house is in the valley
      past the bridge
             (narrow bridge)

bitchin' in the kitchen
drinkin' coffee & cognac
at   4   in the morning

The girl is in the bed
      with her own head

The poet's downstairs
      with his two ears
         & cold hands . We

do what we can . This
cognac isn't bad .
It's Martell .

                    The moon is down, the
                    light'll be up soon

                    o hell,
                    The sin is in the not doing.
                    The farmer's in the dell.

                    Nothing is well.

## LA LISIÈRE

How we move
about the wealth
of friendships :
too often at the edge of it

How rare, the move to center
where we live

Selvage, that word,
each of us stands shyly
at the edge of woods

fearing the valley
chary of the sun
waiting .

Carl's eyes at parting, turning away, not
wanting to let go  .  We

all go the way we go

all the way   .   we

go, each his own

way   .   we all go

away   .   we go.

---

The tide runs high, the

evening star explodes .


What          is the sign

we mean to live by, we

mean, to live by  .   (?)

---

seething anger
silent cunt . cat
got her tongue . she
*is*   very young.

        It's 3:15 in the Midwest now
        Time for poets to be in bed
            not up and scribbling.
        I'm down .
        The coffee heats
        I'm downstairs
        I'm shot down  .  shit up
Shut up & keep dreaming
drink the coffee
drink the cognac
We all sleep sometimes, we
all come back

sometimes .

---

                1st   we win
                2nd is place
                3rd we show

        1st Person,
        very singular
        First is place
        where  .  what
        we show is secondary

    First we show
    Second we win  (or lose)
    Third is place
        (second
        person

Cooze we lose
when we show, win
or place
    (is person .

Which is, if we win,
what we win

Place  I S   person
                  where
if we are lucky
we can show where,
         win or place .

D R A W !
                         (smile,
         when you say that, friend.)

All three women are
stacked .

                     So are the cards.
                              W H A C K !

---

**LIKENON**


L i k e
i n
         o n   t h e   s t o n e


L i e ,   k i n

         o n   t h e   s t o n e


L i c h e n   o n   t h e   s t o n e

---

**envoi in mid-June / WALTER GOES TO THE GARDEN & GETS A HARDO**

                   "A t e   a   w h o l e   r o w   o f   r a d i s h
                   T h e y   w e r e   c r i s p . "

                                        —Mary Hamady

Your teeth & Walter's

crunching down into

those bowlsful of radishes

    red & white & firm

rhymes with lettuce  .  swiss chard  .  spinach  .

green onions  .  yum.

               Mary, please,

               forget the nightshade soup &

               the jimsonweed salad, huh?

                      17 . VI . 71

                      [1975]


**JOURNAL: 31 . V . 71**               **late weather**

Crabapple blossoms white,

        tight to the branches, dwarf

trees in front of the building  .  mid-quad  .  Mist

in the morning

sun in the afternoon

million flowers .

        May 31st, & the evening weather report

     showed a sparkling of

snow into the Sierras on

the California side, Lake Tahoe  .  O

blossoms here

in Cortland now, the

tulips near gone by, but

Nevada City

caught it  .  s n o w !

Gary got it this time.

---

## WHAT'S UNTIED ON WHITSUNTIDE?

The last nite before June, I lean

over the hot air register

to warm my hands

Ate 1/8 of a banana

threw it up.

I count the Pentecost

I throw it up.

I plan.

[1975]

## NEW DIRECTIONS 23.

Between   5   sonnets by Bill Bronk

and   6   poems by Carl Rakosi,

I take 3 or 4 sips of my milkshake (coffee)

from the Friendly Ice Cream Corp.

Wilbraham, Mass.

from a straw

and my son wakes up from his nap, comes

to climb in my lap.

kicks the book from the table

onto the floor   .   what more

can I say? It's one

                    way to begin a long summer. haha.

                                        31 . V . 71

                                        [1975]


JOURNAL: JUNE, 1971                              110 in the shade

Sitting in the tub
waiting for the ache in
my shoulders to go away
                    ˙
                        nerves shlow down, the
                        muscles relax .

The tax is refunded in full   .   I feel
the skinnyness of arms, the bony chest
cavity, front & back, as I soap up .

It's something else for the fingertips to remember
I haven't had a body like this since I was   15 .
What is it the ribs remember, the clavicles, the
          wingbones so unfleshed?
                    To recognize the differences
in the quality of flesh tho, something else   .

          [+ +]


a doomed man planting tomatoes
backyard of a house he lives in
belongs to somebody else   . kneeling
on the earth
his hands move earth
feeling earth   .
                [+ +]


                                        [1975]

JOURNAL: JUNE 1971


T H E   2   A. M.
of a summer night in Cortland, this street
                    high on the hill is
virtually (virtuously?) soundless, it
                    has the virtue of near
                    silence  .  The far
sound of a truck, mile away on the interstate,
a bird or two waking up (hence thee, fear), two
faucets that run (do not drip to the nearest), the
                    sound of my fat pen
                    writing this down .

The bath room faucets sound like the overrun
                    of a fountain in Granada .
                    The birds go back to sleep.
The truck climbs away north toward Homer, Preble,
Tully, Syracuse  .  just the sound of fountain, no breeze.

How say goodnite to you all, dear friends?
Easy.
Goodnite!        The bed
awaits my head,
waits on the
sound of this pen
stopping now .

                                        12 . VI . 71

                                        [1975]


JOURNAL : JUNE 1971


The spruce outside the bedroom

        window is full of wasps and

                bees again this year  .  The

birdfeeder's nailed further down the other side the tree

        high enuf for birds, low enuf for me to fill it

                from the ground  .  Yesterday,

Joan saw two cardinals close up  .  A pair

:bright red of the male, reddish buff of the

    lady  . stayed around calling all

        morning . made her day .

                13 . VI . 71


Picked up the wire fencing today at the lumberyard

150 feet of it (having paced out the back) and

14 stakes, got

it home & realized I had no maul to

drive them with . . . nor the strength nor weight

these days  .  To make an oversized

playpen of the backyard

anyway puts my head in the tree  .

Where are the bees? The yard dies, the

tulips go by, what fun!

I write letters these days to everyone .

                14 . VI . 71

                      [1975]


    SAILBOAT

reflected in the lake .. The

rectangles of iron, so

composed, the waves are so

hang there rusting

lightly at the seams   .  below

the door to the garden opens

on a field   . there

   is the green in evidence,

   the tree   .   hello!

   these many years back,

   Robert Creeley!

          15.VI.71

            [1975]


## JOURNAL: JUNE 1971

How it turns

in again, the pain

   across my shoulders these mornings .


   Possession of the mind

   a fragile thing / when the pain

   goes,

then's the time to use it  .  what's left of it .


Men with shovels directed a stream

of sizable pebbles into the excavations

about young new-planted mountain ash trees

set mid-quad in the concrete

from a dump truck   .

I brought back home

a single rhododendron bloom that had fallen  .

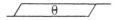

Outside the cellar door, I spoke to a bee, he
danced before me, crotch to face, he checked me out, he
            buzzed, I talked, he sat
                in my beard for a moment   . We
                    talked.  I wanted to go inside   . I told him
                        so   . I did   .

16.VI.71

---

12:30 A.M.
June 17th

Way over to work tonite
I followed the walks assiduously, feet
        clicking the concrete
        dried from the morning's rain.

After writing poems for an hour or some
thing like that, the way back I angled across
lawns
        walks
            gravel
                never
                    mind the ache in the shoulder, in the
right leg, so it's damp, it's
the shortest way home .

9:20 A.M.

CORN
8 in. to a foot high in some fields

Flocks of blackbirds cross the roads and land  . talk .

black . talk . back

The cows are merely silent and further away. Queer.
One red-winged blackbird, his orange trim,
crosses the windshield, flirts his tail  .  Good

M O R N I N G ,   dear
milkmen!

/ 0- /

9:45

Allison likes the music boxes
Allison likes the pink telephone
and the white telephone  .
Carlos T.
develops a sense of property .

Livingroom loud with both their angry tears .

/ -0- /

10:05

Robins on the lawn

always facing away   .   attentive.

/ -0- /

12:30    S U N S H I N E   S U P E R M A N

I.     Buttercups .

gardners & tools along the walks.

another robin, Donovan.

II.   Walking the power mower along

     the slope   single-handed .

         phys-ed major .

possible title: W H E R E   P B   S U C K S   /   T H E R E   S U C K  I

[1975]

**JOURNAL: JUNE 1971**

TOP floor, then

when I look out, I look

out into the tree

outside .

       (This is not a
       plea for the economy)
          but

It's nice to think

(Carlos running & laughing downstairs

    Joan joking with him)

there is nothing we need .

"KITTY KAT!   PAPPI!"

    my son suggests,

    pounding at my door,

    lightly, tho .

"Where's your truck?"

        It

is not an alternative.


And the cat's in the

    laundryroom

        having supper .

            17/VI/71

               [1975]


## JOURNAL: JUNE 1971

Three hawks over the northern Catskills

North Pitcher, Norwich, past Oneonta

    23 across the state .

Honey at Hunter on 23A .

across the river, the Kelly,

    nearly awake, smiles .

           18.VI.71

It's   2   minutes before midnite . I

am about to read   2   poems, no

3 poems of Bobby Byrd's

see where the magic comes in.

It does.

It is human and inhuman


It are the birds on the dump.

They fight   .   the feathers

fall.   The feathers are

dark & bright .

That's all.

20. VI. 71

[1975]


**JOURNAL : JUNE 1971**


S H A D O W   of a large bird
                                    floats
down the sunny half of the road
                    runs west to east   .   We

here, under the shade of trees, south
                    side of the street
wait for the lizard to come,
for the cat to arrive at the roof window
                    calling for entrance .

We are hungry animals prowling this road.

I wonder,  I S   I T   A L L   L O V E ?

We lie here in the shadow of the afternoon
        shadow of the bedclothes   slipped up .

Love & hunger      .      the bird

        the lizard, the cat,

                ourselves  .   Treecrown shadows

move over this half of the street, over
driveway and gutter.   down.

                        leaf shadow.

                22 . VI . 71

                        [1975]


**REDEFINITIONS**

Take off another man's style

in a poem about flying  .   takeoff of the plane .

Mid-flight, the hostesses

take off their clothes & sit in the passengers' laps .

        Call the poem:   TAKEOFF.

                        22.VI.71

                        [1975]

## ALPHABET SONG

Before men

were gods, animals

were themselves, no

sense of immortality we

can speak of.   How

        live with one another

        somehow, never

        was no problem .  The


god wears a jackal's head, the

lion the head of a woman, the

gorgons were the man's protectors on

        a long journey   .  We

carry the   W O R D   with us.

Come now, read:   there's

        a new world comin'


        25 . VI . 71

        [1975]

JOURNAL: 26. VI. 71     THE NEWS


"TO THE REAR, HARCH! —to the

   right front, harch!"

                   (hup, 2—)

The blossoms

in the jar, the

petals on the roses are

beginning to fall to the table   . The

wild flowers have sense enuf to close up tight

                        for the night .

     "GET THAT FORMATION TIGHT, CLOSE IT UP!"

We do .


The girls spread out on the sand

          in the sun, half-

thinking, half-

listening to the remarks, half

             asleep   . Why move at all?

                   The sun.

keeps us talking

       L O V E   &   D E A T H

     P L A N T S   N O W   R E A D Y

Petunias, pansies, snaps, alyssum, early cabbage,
sweet spanish onions, LARGE selection of geraniums,
all colors, and perennials. Urns filled . . .

Urns filled with specifically precious, precious

What is it, Tim, we can fulfill

       after specifically precious Death, we
       speak to. Will I talk to you then, fill
       yr/ ears with words   .   I want to

       [Do not want that. Let
          each man's words be his own.]

                        It

               smiles at me

from underneath the table   .   That

green and yellow

ball .

Or what severances are offered?

what the doctors predict, what

the gods prescribe?

              How can we

offer it all, Paul? how

ignore the earth movers . will

take it all down?

You ask a lot of questions tonite. Enuf of that .

                   The cats

move quietly about the house, lie

down where it is most comfortable

to lie  .  As

the goat bucks his leash, it snaps

tight, the

two-year length of that rope, tonite, love,

so buck I .

Figure that last year.   I want

to set it  .  year-after-next

        hopefully without pain


      N O T H I N G   I   C A N ' T   S T A N D !


      I   d o n ' t   b e l i e v e   t h a t   e i t h e r  .

Let

the mountain be set

the house there forever

a final summer

gazing at the sun.

      Mediterranean .

             [1975]


sundaysundaysundaysundaysunday

s u n

d a y

a quiet along the empty walks

single bird speaks to blue sky to

elm heavy with summer

E M P T Y   A N D   A L I V E

E M P T Y   A N D   A L I V E

E M P T Y   A N D   A L I V E

        The simple act of drinking a cup of coffee

        The simple act of pulling up one's trousers

buckling the belt . having shit, washed hands and face,

go to work . empty and alive . heavy with summer .  light

with the promise of death . bright books in the bookcase,

window open, the day comes in, o fade the carcinoma, lay

down the two dollars, all those others rolling dice, but

it's my body, I'll bet on that  . o, it floats thru the blood

with the greatest of ease . the pain goes and comes again . the

cat hunts in the grass, the gull swings over the sea, the blood

sings a very old tune .  Take it

easy, it's sunday, no?

All day.

                      27 . VI . 71

                        [1975]

JOURNAL: JUNE 1971

If the chairs are comfortable, why
    not sit in them?

I hunch on the top rail of a fence in
    the sun  .  whitewashed.

Six ducklings squeak, follow one an-
    other, a straggling line down
    past the adjacent building into the weeds .

They're panicked by trucks oiling &
graveling & rolling out
the yard of this garage.   Andre
with folded arms, impassively
twitches his moustache in the doorway, checks
the line of gravel-dump.

One duckling's gotten trapped
in the growth of weeds alongside the building hiding.
    I free it .

Another's got covered with burdocks : overweight,
it falls on its back & can't get up  .  I
clear enough burrs off its head and neck
so it can rise : it runs. Tough. It's
bound to get caught again.
Where's the mother?

_____

Two bulbs replaced in the back, and
the left tail lens the mechanic broke by stepping on it.
The Gaucelm Faidit Uzerchemobile has been in-
spected, the State of New York, 1972.

30 . VI . 71

[1975]

## REDUCTIO AD SUBURBIUM

Plymouth (Mass.)

variety of mailboxes,

    Glad ys avenue, Grand

        Haven (Mich.), bearing

a likely number

        (1640)

—You can

see the backs of their Bermuda shorts

when they turn on the lawn sprinklers,
                      Susan says .

                5.  VII.  71

                            [1975]

## DOWN ALONG M–45

THE PARTICI-

        (pants are abt to descend)

pants are about to descend

July the 5th, this

Year of Our Nixon, 1971, upon

        Tom Jefferson

(within the infrastructure of

Grand Valley (Mich.) State College)

for a festival of poesy!

Goodbye, minions of Dave Lorenz!

Hello, poets!

PB
Unofficial Greeter

[1975]

## JULY 15

Over the river soundlessly

a fish jumps  .   Late sun

along the Maumee—or the Sandusky—

assuming it's the Sandusky River flows thru

Sandusky into Lake Erie at that point—

at 8 A.M., cool morning, two

ducks, a pair, no, a brace of ducks,

wing it, their long necks stretched up

over the river soundlessly.

(A fish jumps).

---

Interstate 81 North   .   late sun, 8:30 P.M., on the

Pennsylvania hills   .

Crossing state line, the rest area

has but one vehicle in it. I

miss the Uzerchemobile!

Big lovely clouds to the north after sundown .

Great purple fish pursued by great violet dog

in a pink sea  . Mediterra-nean. San

dusky is far, o far.
 +
Last light in the sky

drops spatter the windshield

Thunderstorm greets us home .

---

JULY 17.

Lines of sunlight across the base of the skull

    Windows shining  . Trees move .

      Mysterious skull bumps.

      Roll tenderly against the wood.

---

JULY 18

Barn smell, old wood, hayloft .

Out over the cut fields, a fat

goldfinch, black-&-yellow

    moves heavily   .
                Only larks flit.

---

JULY 23.


Hermes
in dark glasses
Mercury in shades

at the cafeteria table with
three other shades (Tom, Al, Sonia)
    sits, dis-
cussin the news
from De-troit, Californ-ya,
    many other fine places .

Wednesday lunch: I think it was Armand
came worriedly over, asked me:
    "Is David here?"        (David's day
                            to read with me
                            and Gregory &
                            Donald Hall)
"Right over that table there."

From a far country,
David Henderson has
come unto Michigan,
Hermes in shades, to
    give us the word, BURN.

                    (signed) Paul Blackburn

                                        [1975]



JOURNAL: JULY 1971


Branches bend

in the wind, leaves

wave thru the window at me,

            and whistle .



I'm very popular today.

Gloria, Carlos T., and Joan

are down at Steve and Nancy's


Male cat comes in thru the window

    to talk to me. The

room is filled with evening light

3 hours yet to sundown. Hey!

       it's summer!

            20 . VII . 71

---

evening fantasy:

Traveling ahead again
in my head again
which cannot know that I'm dead again .
Beshit, fathered, and Magillicuddy
      am I?

People to talk with in those streets
      delight me
Spicer, I am not afraid :
Olson as a gigantic cherub
      garbed in nightgown, thinking;
Steve Jonas rolling happily for once in angeldust;
Kerouac writing the true novel of the Golden Eternity
on a ribbonless typewriter, without paper, never revising

Some /time/    finally to talk with Dr. Williams,
tho it seems I stammer,
he don't

            "if you like it, we
              like it too,
              we clued it with you"

    and I, beyond all likelihood, get to that grove before Ezra,
walk about, saying:
           "I must prepare, I must
           prepare."

            22.VII.71

Young, dying yellow birch on Owego St.
   half-block from the IGA .

fat black ants tool along beside me
or troll across the sidewalks . I am careful

Because I think maybe words are coming, I sit
on a stump in the sun in front of number 28,
staring at pink and white hollyhocks under its front windows,
an ambivalent paleness of hollyhock .
I always thought they were a
            somewhat gross plant,
               those scratchy leaves .

The running samaritan this noon-hour, I've
delivered a bottle of freshmade orange juice iced, &
a suppository   25 mg. Adult .
insert one as directed for vomiting . and am
on my way
to the IGA
for cigs and a cold 6-pak of Coca Cola for Howard
to help celebrate
his first post-celebration-of-being-21 day .

Beware friends and well-meaning bar owners bearing gifts
that resemble three fingers high of excellent bourbon in a whiskey sour glass,
beware even the double shot . uh, *stark!*

On the way back to Tomkins St,
the ants accompany me in the hot sun. Don't
they know that sidewalks are terrible places to cruise,
for ants anyway?

And we always treated hollyhocks like
second class citizens, poor relations, bums, we
kept them out by the garage in back .
Those delicate blooms. The awkward stems. The hairy leaves.

23 . VII . 71

[1975]

"Sorry to keep you waiting, sir—"

    —That's all right

        All the time in the world—

            (pleased voice of the operator)

                "Thank you!"


That hour of night   .   It

must be so for all of us .


                23 . VII . 71

---

Mist rising along the ridges of hills

mist rising from the surfaces of ponds

        Homer, Preble, Dante's

hell or English countryside . Fast, we

go over hills & roads, across

the city of Syracuse to the airplane

takes us West .

        = = = =

We manage the flight to Chicago okay

—Joan's flying student standby—even

manage to sit together, with a member of

the Board of Trustees for Roberts Wesleyan

sitting window seat, who,

taking Joanie for student, asks about

student/professor relationships.

      Some nerve, I'd say. At

O'Hare I find out Paul Carroll's middle

initial, that he now lives on North Mohawk,

is D., and from Inara that his office number

University of Illinois, is 633-2285.


      Then disaster:

only the military standbys make it on.

I wave out window sadly, in case she's there behind

      the rain-stained glass  . I'm in, she's out

or: She's in, I'm out here, but *we're* not

      out of O'Hare  .  We seem

to be twelfth in line for takeoff, & taxi

      a lot, slowly . The captain

even turns off the NO SMOKING sign

      I have a cigarette . I have a second.

      20 minutes after departure time

Joan and I are both on the ground, still,

except we're turning a corner toward another runway

& Joan is checking out the next two sets of possibilities

we know the direct at 3:55 arrives Boise at 6:20.

      + + + +

10:36 the sign goes on, I don't get to

      finish the 2nd cigarette, and

      at 10:36½ we're air

      borne, bound in separate

      elements, bound by seatbelt in air

      or grounded in the snackbar, o we've

      been there before.   I think

      I'll drink, and read, then sleep.

Try to ripoff the airlines, will we? They'll show us.

      Five minutes before 11, we cross the Mississippi.

          \* \* \* \* \*

Iowa, Nebraska, small white clouds far below (we're

            some 26,000 ft. Then over

Rock Spring, Wyoming, the Continental Divide

              coming up. Groundspeed

              520 mph


What a gas, maybe

Louie Armstrong & I

die, back to back,

cheek to cheek, maybe the same year.   "O,

I CAN'T GIVE YOU

ANYTHING BUT LOVE,

Bay-aybee"

1926, Okeh a label then

black with gold print, was

one of my folks' favorite tunes, that year

that I was born . It is all still true

& Louie's gone down &

I, o momma, goin down that same road.

Damn fast .

+ + + +

Salt Lake City's hot .

cragged & scorched, the mountains

to the east .

The desert begins, the

desert's hard   .   I buy

4 postcards of the desert

(after checking for Joan's alternates

with a desk clerk at United

I climb back on the plane slowly, this heat. She may

arrive Boise

4:50 or

6:20)


Salt flats and brackish water

as I take off

in the heat.

+ + + +

Take a shit at 5:15

A.M., Cortland, N.Y.


Fly about 2,000 miles and in

Boise, Idaho, some

literal 12 hrs., 35 minutes later,

    take another shit.


Bigod, I must have been full of shit.

+ + + +

[1975]

# Index of Titles

The following abbreviations have been used to indicate earlier collections in which the poems in this volume have appeared:

BMT      *Brooklyn-Manhattan Transit* (New York: Totem, 1960)

C      *The Cities* (New York: Grove Press, 1967)

DF      *The Dissolving Fabric* (Palma de Mallorca: Divers Press, 1955)

ESYM      *Early Selected Y Mas* (Los Angeles: Black Sparrow, 1972)

G      *Gin: Four Journal Pieces* (Mt. Horeb, Wisc.: Perishable Press, 1970)

IOOATP      *In . On . Or About the Premises* (London/New York: Cape Goliard/ Grossman, 1968)

J      *The Journals*, ed. Robert Kelly (Santa Barbara: Black Sparrow, 1975)

N      *The Nets* (New York: Trobar, 1961)

OJ      omitted journals\*

RP      *The Reardon Poems* (Madison: Perishable Press, 1967)

SS      *Sing-Song [Caterpillar #4]* (New York: December 1966)

SSH      *Sixteen Sloppy Haiku & a Lyric for Robert Reardon* (Cleveland: 400 Rabbit Press, 1966)

TD      *Three Dreams and an Old Poem* (Buffalo: Univ. Press at Buffalo, 1970)

TNP      *Two New Poems* (Madison: Perishable Press, 1969)

Broadsides, books consisting of only one poem, and posthumous books not authorized by Blackburn are omitted from this list. Information about the order of poems in the earlier volumes and publication data on the uncollected poems may be found in *The Authorized Edition of The Collected Poems of Paul Blackburn* by Edith Jarolim (University Microfilms, 1984).

---

\*Based on a study of Blackburn's canon and of the black-binder manuscript of the book, a re-editing of the posthumously published *The Journals* would add seven poems to the Black Sparrow volume. These pieces, with the exception of "A Very Great Treasure," were published in 1984 by Perishable Press under the title *The Omitted Journals*.

Although the arrangement of the poems chronologically by date of composition precludes preserving the arrangements of earlier collections, for readers familiar with the publication history of Blackburn's work, one bit of additional datum on *The Cities* is provided in the index. In 1964 Blackburn first began to circulate, under the title *The Recognitions*, the manuscript of what became *The Cities*. When Grove Press accepted this manuscript for publication two years later, it was with the stipulation that it be cut. Blackburn removed forty poems from the 122-poem book, but also added fourteen, thereby reducing the volume by less than one-fourth. Those poems originally intended by Blackburn for *The Recognitions/Cities* are marked here with an asterisk. It may be observed that a number of them ended up in *In . On . Or About the Premises*; of all the poems cut, there are only seven that Blackburn never placed for publication elsewhere.